W0245770

Lecture Notes in Economics
and Mathematical Systems

434

Springer
Berlin
Heidelberg
New York
Barcelona
Budapest
Hong Kong
London
Milan
Paris
Santa Clara
Singapore
Tokyo

Mark W. J. Blok

Dynamic Models of the Firm

Determining Optimal Investment,
Financing and Production Policies
by Computer

 Springer

Author

Dr. Mark W. J. Blok
System and Control Technology Group
Eindhoven University of Technology
P.O. Box 513
NL-5600 MB Eindhoven
The Netherlands

and
A. T. Kearney
P.O. Box 22926
NL-1100 DK Amsterdam
The Netherlands

Cataloging-in-Publication Data applied for

Die Deutsche Bibliothek - CIP-Einheitsaufnahme

Blok, Mark W. J.:
Dynamic models of the firm : determining optimal investment,
financing and production policies by computer / Mark W. J.
Blok. - Berlin ; Heidelberg ; New York ; London ; Paris ;
Tokyo ; Hong Kong ; Barcelona ; Budapest : Springer, 1996
 (Lecture notes in economics and mathematical systems ; 434)

NE: GT

ISBN-13: 978-3-540-60802-8   e-ISBN-13: 978-3-642-48401-8
DOI: 10.1007/978-3-642-48401-8

Typesetting: Camera ready by author
SPIN: 10516207   42/3142-543210 - Printed on acid-free paper

Contents

Chapter 1

Introduction

The research described in this book contributes to the scientific field of optimal control theory applied to dynamic models of the firm. In 1963, Jorgenson first wrote about the use of optimal control theory in order to analyze the *dynamic* investment behaviour of a hypothetical firm. A decade later, reports appeared of work on more realistic models of the firm carried out by, amongst others, Lesourne [1973] and Bensoussan *et al.* [1974].

In The Netherlands, P.A. Verheyen, Professor of Management Science at Tilburg University, further instigated studies in this field which led to several publications, for example: Van Loon [1983], Van Schijndel [1988], Kort [1989], Van Hilten [1991] and Van Hilten *et al.* [1993]. Their investigations are characterized by an analytical approach to optimization problems (The Maximum Principle of Pontryagin combined with the path coupling procedure of Van Loon). Inherent to this approach, a good economic interpretation of solutions is obtained; however, analytical solving becomes practically unfeasible when simulation models become more complex, e.g. by stronger non-linearity, explicitly time-dependent functions and larger numbers of state variables, control variables and subsidiary conditions. For example, the path coupling procedure is complicated for optimization problems where discontinuities in the costate variables occur.

At Eindhoven University of Technology, P.M.E.M. van der Grinten, Corporate Vice President Planning & Development of a large chemical company and Associate Professor of System and Control Engineering, for many years, has been supervising research in the field of applied control theory to long-term planning problems, and that resulted in the development of more complicated models of the firm which, in essence, are similar to those mentioned earlier: Van der Grinten [1979, 1984], Faessen [1986], Van de Putten [1988], Van de Schoor [1989], Kocken [1990], Hardy [1991], Naus [1992], Van den Bersselaar [1992]. Another important difference is the way that they tackle solving the problems, namely, numerically with the aid of a powerful computer and special programs for optimizing non-linear functions with a finite number of variables under non-linear subsidiary conditions. Though having an influence on the processor time required, greater complexity of the model does not introduce any fundamental problems.

The numerical approach to dynamic optimization problems has long been encountered in technology; for example, when determining optimal flight trajectories in aeronautics (Machielsen [1987]). Within the System and Control Technology Group at Eindhoven University of Technology, numerical dynamic optimization of non-stationary processes has often been used successfully, amongst others, to evaluate models for producing ammonia and methanol, as well as for cracking ethane, naphta and gas oil (Meiring [1981], De Grefte [1984]). Other areas of application have included the optimal control of thermal energy systems (Blok [1988], Van Delft [1989]).

Given the complexity of the models of the firm studied in this book, numerical methodology is used also to find optimal control strategies under different circumstances.

In Chapter 2, a short account is given of analytically solving time-continuous optimal control problems with pure state constraints, and of how they can be tackled numerically after discretization. Additionally, a general economic interpretation of adjoint variables is discussed in relation to both continuous and discrete problems.

Chapter 3 presents the model of the firm which forms a starting point for the models of the firm in the succeeding chapters. Essentially, that model (called 'the basic model' hereafter) can be traced back to Lesourne [1973] and later it served a similar purpose as the core of most models developed by Van Loon [1983], Van Schijndel [1988], Kort [1989] and Van Hilten [1991]. Unlike the studies reported in literature, here, attention will be paid to relatively short planning periods in which a stationary state cannot be reached.

In Chapter 4, a model with start-up costs is discussed. The reasoning behind it being that in real-life, after an expansion of capital assets, often it is impossible to fully utilize these immediately, as a result of unavoidable start-up problems: a certain amount of time must transpire before normal utilization can be reached. This is simulated by replacing the static relationship between the production rate and the stock of capital assets needed in the basic model with a semi-dynamic one. As a consequence of doing so, the change in the operating income resulting from an extra investment will show an inverse response: firstly negative and later positive. The great influence that this has on an optimal control strategy is also discussed.

Chapter 5 builds on the earlier work of Van Hilten [1991]. The first model studied there is a natural development of the basic model assuming that a business cycle can be simulated by an explicitly time-dependent price function. As Van Hilten stated, depending on the parameter values used, discontinuities (jumps) in the costate variables occur with an optimal dynamic strategy. For the sake of economic interpretation of these jumps, analytical expressions for the costate variables are presented. The second model is an extension of the first by a variable for capacity utilization. It is possible for the firm to underutilize its capital assets and to dispense with labour. The third model discussed is the first one extended with a cash balance, so the firm has an opportunity to retain a reserve of money. Up to now maintaining a cash balance does not appear in literature on deterministic dynamic models of the firm. The last model treated in this chapter is expanded to include an inventory of finished goods.

Finally in Chapter 6, a model of the firm is presented that has been essentially expanded in two places from the basic model in the third chapter. The first expansion concerns the production function of the model which forms a relationship between the production rate and the minimum quantity of production factors required; it describes the achievement of increasing returns to scale ('economies of scale'). The second expansion concerns the price function, which shows the yield per unit of goods sold as a function of the sales rate and time; it attributes increasing returns to experience ('experience curve'). Both expansions emphasize the dynamic nature of product-market combinations.

Chapter 2

Mathematical Background to Dynamic Optimization

2.1 Introduction

This chapter starts with a brief description of solving time-continuous optimal control problems with pure state constraints analytically (Section 2.2). For a more detailed treatment of this type of problem, refer to Feichtinger & Hartl [1986]. Subsequently, discretization of time-continuous problems is explained so that numerically solving with the aid of a computer and specific programs for optimizing non-linear functions of a finite number of variables under non-linear subsidiary conditions will be possible (Section 2.3). Then Section 2.4 gives a general economic interpretation of adjoint variables as shadow prices, both for continuous and discrete time problems. The last section deals with the procedure followed with the various models of the firm in this book.

2.2 Analytical approach to the optimization problem

2.2.1 Problem formulation

The optimal control problems studied in this book can be formulated generally as follows:

$$\max_{\boldsymbol{u}(t)} \int_0^z \mathrm{e}^{-it} F\big(\boldsymbol{u}(t)\big)\,\mathrm{d}t + \mathrm{e}^{-iz} S\big(\boldsymbol{x}(z)\big) \qquad (2.1\mathrm{a})$$

$$\dot{\boldsymbol{x}}(t) = \boldsymbol{f}\big(t, \boldsymbol{x}(t), \boldsymbol{u}(t)\big), \quad \boldsymbol{x}(0) = \boldsymbol{x}_0 \qquad (2.1\mathrm{b})$$

$$\boldsymbol{g}\big(\boldsymbol{x}(t), \boldsymbol{u}(t)\big) \geq \boldsymbol{0} \qquad (2.1\mathrm{c})$$

$$\boldsymbol{h}\big(\boldsymbol{x}(t)\big) \geq \boldsymbol{0} \qquad (2.1\mathrm{d})$$

with:

$x(t) \in \mathbb{R}^n,$

$u(t) \in \mathbb{R}^m,$

$F : \mathbb{R}^m \rightarrow \mathbb{R},$

$S : \mathbb{R}^n \rightarrow \mathbb{R},$

$f : \mathbb{R} \times \mathbb{R}^n \times \mathbb{R}^m \rightarrow \mathbb{R}^n,$

$g : \mathbb{R}^n \times \mathbb{R}^m \rightarrow \mathbb{R}^p$

$h : \mathbb{R}^n \rightarrow \mathbb{R}^q$

It is assumed that the functions F, S, f and g are all continuously differentiable in their arguments, and that the function h is twice-continuously differentiable. Furthermore, the state constraint (2.1d) is assumed to be of the first order, which is to say that in the first total derivative of h with respect to time:

$$k\big(x(t), u(t), t\big) = \frac{\partial h}{\partial x}\big(x(t)\big) f\big(x(t), u(t), t\big) \tag{2.2}$$

the control variable $u(t)$ appears explicitly.

If f is not explicitly dependent on t, the problem becomes one of autonomous optimal control.

A couple $\big(x(t), u(t)\big)$ for $t \in [0, z]$ is called a *feasible* solution for the optimal control problem (2.1), if $u(t)$ is piecewise continuous in $[0, z]$ and conditions (2.1b) to (2.1d) are satisfied.

The *weak constraint qualification* reads as follows:

$$\left(\ \frac{\partial g}{\partial u}\big(x(t), u(t)\big) \quad G\big(x(t), u(t)\big) \ \right) \text{ has full row rank } p. \tag{2.3}$$

where: $G(x, u)$ forms a $p \times p$ diagonal matrix with $G_{i,i}(x, u) = g_i(x, u)$ $(i = 1, 2, \cdots, p)$. Thus, the weak constraint qualification says that the gradients $\partial g_i / \partial u$ for all the active constraints $g_i \geq 0$ $(i = 1, 2, \ldots, p)$ must be linearly independent.

As an extension of (2.3) the *strong constraint qualification* is defined as:

$$\left(\begin{array}{ccc} \frac{\partial g}{\partial u}\big(x(t), u(t)\big) & G\big(x(t), u(t)\big) & 0 \\[2mm] \frac{\partial k}{\partial u}\big(x(t), u(t), t\big) & 0 & H\big(x(t)\big) \end{array} \right) \begin{array}{l} \text{has full} \\ \text{row rank } p + q, \end{array} \tag{2.4}$$

where: $H(x)$ is a $q \times q$ diagonal matrix with $H_{i,i}(x) = h_i(x)$ $(i = 1, 2, \cdots, q)$.

An instant of time $\tau \in [0, z]$ is called:

a *contact point* when $h_i\big(x(\tau)\big) = 0$, $h_i\big(x(\tau-\epsilon)\big) > 0$ and $h_i\big(x(\tau+\epsilon)\big) > 0$;

an *entry point* when $h_i\big(x(\tau - \epsilon)\big) > 0$ and $h_i\big(x(\tau + \epsilon)\big) = 0$;

an *exit point* when $h_i\big(x(\tau - \epsilon)\big) = 0$ and $h_i\big(x(\tau + \epsilon)\big) > 0$.

for at least one $i = 1, 2, \ldots, q$ and each sufficiently small $\epsilon > 0$. These three points are collectively known as *coupling points*.

The optimal control problem (2.1) can be tackled with the direct adjoining approach, in which case the state constraint (2.1d) is provided with a multiplier and adjoined *directly* to the Hamiltonian. Consequently, the Hamiltonian and Lagrangian can be defined as[1]:

$$\mathcal{H}(\boldsymbol{x}, \boldsymbol{u}, \lambda_0, \boldsymbol{\lambda}, t) = \lambda_0 F(\boldsymbol{u}) + \boldsymbol{\lambda}^{\mathrm{T}} \boldsymbol{f}(\boldsymbol{x}, \boldsymbol{u}, t) \tag{2.5}$$

$$\mathcal{L}(\boldsymbol{x}, \boldsymbol{u}, \lambda_0, \boldsymbol{\lambda}, \boldsymbol{\mu}, \boldsymbol{\nu}, t) = \mathcal{H}(\boldsymbol{x}, \boldsymbol{u}, \lambda_0, \boldsymbol{\lambda}, t) + \boldsymbol{\mu}^{\mathrm{T}} g(\boldsymbol{x}, \boldsymbol{u}) + \boldsymbol{\nu}^{\mathrm{T}} h(\boldsymbol{x}) \tag{2.6}$$

as well as the control range:

$$\Omega(\boldsymbol{x}) = \{ \boldsymbol{u} \in \mathbb{R}^m \, | \, g(\boldsymbol{x}, \boldsymbol{u}) \geq 0 \} \tag{2.7}$$

Theorem 2.1 (necessary conditions for optimality)
Let $\big(\boldsymbol{x}^*(t), \boldsymbol{u}^*(t)\big)$ be an optimal couple of the control problem (2.1) and let the constraint qualification (2.3) be satisfied for all $t \in [0, z]$, $\boldsymbol{x} = \boldsymbol{x}^*(t)$, $\boldsymbol{u} \in \Omega\big(\boldsymbol{x}^*(t), t\big)$, then a constant $\lambda_0 \geq 0$, piecewise continuously differentiable adjoint functions $\boldsymbol{\lambda}(t) \in \mathbb{R}^n$, piecewise continuous multiplier functions $\boldsymbol{\mu}(t) \in \mathbb{R}^p$ and $\boldsymbol{\nu}(t) \in \mathbb{R}^q$, constant multipliers $\boldsymbol{\gamma} \in \mathbb{R}^q$, as well as for each instant of time $\tau_j \in (0, z)$ where $\boldsymbol{\lambda}(t)$ is discontinuous, jump-size parameters $\boldsymbol{\eta}(\tau_j) \in \mathbb{R}^q$, with $(\lambda_0, \boldsymbol{\lambda}, \boldsymbol{\mu}, \boldsymbol{\nu}, \boldsymbol{\gamma}, \boldsymbol{\eta}(\tau_1), \boldsymbol{\eta}(\tau_2), \ldots) \neq \mathbf{0}$ for all t, exist, so that the following equations hold for all instants exept for the discontinuity points of $\boldsymbol{u}$ and the coupling points:

$$\mathcal{H}(\boldsymbol{x}^*(t), \boldsymbol{u}^*(t), \lambda_0, \boldsymbol{\lambda}(t), t) = \max_{\boldsymbol{u} \in \Omega(\boldsymbol{x}^*(t), t)} \mathcal{H}(\boldsymbol{x}^*(t), \boldsymbol{u}, \lambda_0, \boldsymbol{\lambda}(t), t) \tag{2.8}$$

$$\dot{\boldsymbol{\lambda}}(t)^{\mathrm{T}} - i\boldsymbol{\lambda}(t)^{\mathrm{T}} = -\frac{\partial \mathcal{L}}{\partial \boldsymbol{x}}\big(\boldsymbol{x}^*(t), \boldsymbol{u}^*(t), \lambda_0, \boldsymbol{\lambda}(t), \boldsymbol{\mu}(t), \boldsymbol{\nu}(t), t\big) \tag{2.9}$$

$$\frac{\partial \mathcal{L}}{\partial \boldsymbol{u}}\big(\boldsymbol{x}^*(t), \boldsymbol{u}^*(t), \lambda_0, \boldsymbol{\lambda}(t), \boldsymbol{\mu}(t), \boldsymbol{\nu}(t), t\big) = \mathbf{0} \tag{2.10}$$

$$\boldsymbol{\mu}(t) \geq \mathbf{0}, \quad \boldsymbol{\mu}(t)^{\mathrm{T}} g\big(\boldsymbol{x}^*(t), \boldsymbol{u}^*(t)\big) = 0 \tag{2.11}$$

$$\boldsymbol{\nu}(t) \geq \mathbf{0}, \quad \boldsymbol{\nu}(t)^{\mathrm{T}} h\big(\boldsymbol{x}^*(t)\big) = 0 \tag{2.12}$$

---

[1] Here, Hamiltonian and Lagrangian are defined in current-value notation. Multiplying the left- and right-hand sides of (2.5) and (2.6) with e^{-it} leads to the definitions of Hamiltonian and Lagrangian in present-value notation:

$$\tilde{\mathcal{H}}(\boldsymbol{x}, \boldsymbol{u}, \lambda_0, \tilde{\boldsymbol{\lambda}}, t) = \lambda_0 \mathrm{e}^{-it} F(\boldsymbol{u}) + \tilde{\boldsymbol{\lambda}}^{\mathrm{T}} \boldsymbol{f}(\boldsymbol{x}, \boldsymbol{u}, t)$$

$$\tilde{\mathcal{L}}(\boldsymbol{x}, \boldsymbol{u}, \lambda_0, \tilde{\boldsymbol{\lambda}}, \tilde{\boldsymbol{\mu}}, \tilde{\boldsymbol{\nu}}, t) = \tilde{\mathcal{H}}(\boldsymbol{x}, \boldsymbol{u}, \lambda_0, \tilde{\boldsymbol{\lambda}}, t) + \tilde{\boldsymbol{\mu}}^{\mathrm{T}} g(\boldsymbol{x}, \boldsymbol{u}) + \tilde{\boldsymbol{\nu}}^{\mathrm{T}} h(\boldsymbol{x})$$

where: $\tilde{\mathcal{H}} = \mathcal{H}\mathrm{e}^{-it}$, $\tilde{\mathcal{L}} = \mathcal{L}\mathrm{e}^{-it}$, $\tilde{\boldsymbol{\lambda}} = \boldsymbol{\lambda}\mathrm{e}^{-it}$, $\tilde{\boldsymbol{\mu}} = \boldsymbol{\mu}\mathrm{e}^{-it}$ and $\tilde{\boldsymbol{\nu}} = \boldsymbol{\nu}\mathrm{e}^{-it}$.

$$\lambda(z)^{\mathrm{T}} = \lambda_0 \frac{\partial S}{\partial x}\big(x^*(z)\big) + \gamma^{\mathrm{T}}\frac{\partial h}{\partial x}\big(x^*(z)\big) \tag{2.13}$$

$$\gamma \geq 0, \quad \gamma^{\mathrm{T}} h\big((x^*(z)\big) = 0 \tag{2.14}$$

At instants τ where (2.1d) is active[2], discontinuities (jumps) appear in the following form:

$$\lambda(\tau^-)^{\mathrm{T}} = \lambda(\tau^+)^{\mathrm{T}} + \eta(\tau)^{\mathrm{T}}\frac{\partial h}{\partial x}\big(x^*(\tau)\big) \tag{2.15}$$

$$\eta(\tau) \geq 0, \quad \eta(\tau)^{\mathrm{T}} h\big(x^*(\tau)\big) = 0 \tag{2.16}$$

with $\lambda(\tau^-) = \lim_{t\uparrow\tau}\lambda(t)$ and $\lambda(\tau^+) = \lim_{t\downarrow\tau}\lambda(t)$

Theorem 2.2
The jump-size parameter disappears: $\eta(\tau) = 0$, and the costate variable λ is continuous therefore, either:
a) the control variable u is continuous and the strong constraint qualification (2.4) is satisfied; or:
b) the entry or exit of the state constraint occurs in a non-tangential way.

Observation 2.1 For *normal* problems in which $\lambda_0 \neq 0$, λ_0 can be made unity without affecting generality. For eliminating the abnormal case $\lambda_0 = 0$, for each control problem it has to be proved that the supposition $\lambda_0 = 0$ will lead to exclusion. So, $\lambda_0 \neq 0$ can often be deduced from the non-triviality condition $(\lambda_0, \lambda, \mu, \nu, \gamma, \eta(\tau_1), \eta(\tau_2), \ldots) \neq 0$, such as when (2.1d) is not active at $t = z$ ($\gamma = 0$). Without proof, it is proposed from now onwards that all optimal contol problems be normal.

Observation 2.2 Generally speaking, condition (2.8) is not needed when determining the potential optimal solutions.

Observation 2.3 Under the assumption that $\mathcal{H}(x, u, \lambda_0, \lambda, t)$ is concave in (x, u); $S(x)$ is concave in x; $g(x, u)$ is quasi-concave in (x, u), and $h(x)$ is quasi-concave in x, the necessary conditions of Theorem 2.1 in case $\lambda_0 = 1$ are also *sufficient* for optimality of a feasible solution of the optimal control problem.

Observation 2.4 The transversality condition (2.13) must be read as follows:

$$\lambda(z^+)^{\mathrm{T}} = \lambda_0 \frac{\partial S}{\partial x}\big(x^*(z)\big), \quad \lambda(z^-)^{\mathrm{T}} = \lambda_0 \frac{\partial S}{\partial x}\big(x^*(z)\big) + \gamma^{\mathrm{T}}\frac{\partial h}{\partial x}\big(x^*(z)\big)$$

From this observation it appears that γ can be seen as a jump-size parameter. So generally, λ is continuous in z only if $\gamma = 0$.

---

[2]In the most practical examples, λ will only jump at coupling points; however jumps at other points cannot generally be excluded. In this book, jumps will occur only at coupling points.

2.2.2 Solving through path coupling

The path coupling procedure is an iterative procedure developed by Van Loon [1983] in order to find an optimal strategy $u^*(t)$ for the whole planning period $[0, z]$.

Identifying the paths. The optimal development of control and state variables over a period of time can be seen as a string of phases (*paths*), which are seperated from each other by differences in the set of active constraints. So, a path is identified by means of the multipliers μ_i $(i = 1, \ldots, p)$ and ν_j $(j = 1, \ldots, q)$ in a given period: a multiplier has a positive value if the corresponding constraint is active, or it is zero if the related constraint is passive. In principle, this means that 2^{p+q} different paths can be distinguished. The points of time $\tau_1, \tau_2, \ldots$ $(0 < \tau_1 < \tau_2 < \ldots < z)$ where the active set changes (coupling points), as well as the start and end point of the planning period, do not necessarily have to form part of a path.

Determining the feasible paths. The next step in the path coupling procedure is the exclusion of paths that do not conform with the assumptions of the model and/or the necessary conditions for optimality. Likewise, paths for which the number of positive Lagrange multipliers exceeds m (the dimension of the control variable) can be excluded beforehand when the required constraint qualifications are satisfied. In a situation where a certain expression has both an upper and lower boundary that should never coincide, the paths with both adjoint variables positive may be excluded. For other paths, testing to the necessary conditions for optimality has to point out if they can be excluded beforehand. Additionally, further conditions may be derived that have to be satisfied before a path is feasible.

Solving the synthesis problem: coupling of the feasible paths into an optimal strategy. This process commences with determining the potential final paths. They will be the paths which obey the transversality conditions (2.13) and (2.14). In principle this requires checking 2^q different combinations of $\gamma_i > 0$ or $\gamma_i = 0$ $(i = 1, \ldots, q)$.

Then, the synthesis problem can be solved recursively backwards by examining for each potential final path which paths could serve as predecessor. The criterium for doing so is the continuity of the state variables at the coupling points, which implicitly assumes boundaries on the control variables at each instant of time. If the state constraint (2.1d) is not active, continuity of the costate variable will also be a criterium. In other cases Theorem 2.2 will have to be used in order to see if continuity of the costate variable is a criterium or not. Discontinuities in the costate variable will complicate the synthesis problem considerably.

For each combination of paths obtained this way, again all potential predecessor paths which can be coupled in a feasible way are determined. The reverse recursion will end as soon as it is impossible to find a predecessor for any string of paths. The string with the greatest value of the objective function that complies with the initial conditions $x(0) = x_0$, implies an optimal solution for problem (2.1).

Symbolically, an optimal string of paths is denoted by placing the numbers of the paths that form part of it, in the correct sequence separated by:

'–'   when ν_i is limited and continous at a coupling point $(i = 1, \ldots, q)$;

'o'   when all Lagrange multipliers at the coupling point are limited and at least one is discontinuous;

'⋆'   when at least one Lagrange multiplier at the coupling point is unlimited (and therefore, it is discontinuous).

2.3   Numerical approach to the optimization problem

In the numerical approach, a solution of the optimal control problem is no longer searched for in a space of piecewise continuous functions which are defined at a finite interval of time. Instead, a time discrete estimate of this solution has to be found in a finite dimensional vector space, which will be more precise as the discretization becomes finer and actual will be optimal for the original problem in the hypothetical case where the discretization step at limit equals zero. The dynamic optimization problem will become altered to a finite dimensional (static) optimization problem. For solving such problems, numerical methods exist which are suitable for programming on a computer. In this research, a routine from the NAG Library was used for solving problems of the following general form:

$$\min_{x \in \mathbf{R}^n} F(\mathbf{x}) \tag{2.17}$$

$$\text{under the subsidiary conditions: } l \le \left\{ \begin{array}{c} \mathbf{x} \\ \mathbf{A_L x} \\ \mathbf{c(x)} \end{array} \right\} \le \mathbf{u} \tag{2.18}$$

where $F(\mathbf{x})$ is a non-linear objective function, $\mathbf{A_L}$ is a $n_L \times n$ matrix of constants, and $\mathbf{c(x)}$ is a n_N-element vector of non-linear constraints. The objective function and the non-linear constraints are assumed to be at least twice-continuously differentiable. The routine is based on the so-called SQP-algorithm (Sequential Quadratic Programming algorithm) and it delivers the value of $\mathbf{x}$ in the optimum as well as the adjoint variables that belong to the subsidiary conditions. Hereby it can be seen that the upper and lower bounds will be specified for all variables and subsidiary conditions. An equality constraint will be obtained from $l_i = u_i$. In case fixed bounds are not available, the relevant values of l and u should be equated to a special value which becomes treated as ∞ or $-\infty$. Furthermore, it becomes clear that a maximization problem can be solved in the same way with this routine by minimizing the opposite objective function.

In the following subsection, the discretization method employed is explained briefly. Afterwards, the original continous time optimization problem is formulated into two discrete time versions which, in principle when solved, will give identical results. However, big differences in computing time may arise due to the different numbers of variables and (non-)linear constraints.

2.3.1 Discretization

The interval $[0, z]$ is devided into N sub-intervals of the same size with length equal to:

$$\Delta t = \frac{z}{N} \tag{2.19}$$

The limits of these sub-intervals give $N+1$ equidistant instants of time t_k ($k = 0, \ldots, N$) where the various quantities are evaluated. The independent variable t_k is replaced by the independent variable k by means of the relationship:

$$t_k = k\Delta t \tag{2.20}$$

The following notational convention is used:

$$x_k = x(k\Delta t) \qquad\qquad (k = 0, \ldots, N) \tag{2.21}$$

$$u_k = u(k\Delta t) \qquad\qquad (k = 0, \ldots, N-1) \tag{2.22}$$

$$f_k(x_k, u_k) = f\big(x(k\Delta t), u(k\Delta t), k\Delta t\big) \qquad (k = 0, \ldots, N-1) \tag{2.23}$$

The differential equation (system equation) is exchanged for a a suitable difference equation, via a first order Taylor development of x:

$$x\big((k+1)\Delta t\big) = x(k\Delta t) + \Delta t \frac{\mathrm{d}x}{\mathrm{d}t}(k\Delta t) \tag{2.24}$$

$$= x(k\Delta t) + \Delta t f\big(x(k\Delta t), u(k\Delta t), k\Delta t\big) \tag{2.25}$$

in other words:

$$x_{k+1} = x_k + \Delta t f_k(x_k, u_k) \tag{2.26}$$

It will be self-evident that the integral from the continuous objective function has to be replaced by the Riemann sum:

$$\int_0^z e^{-it} F\big(u(t)\big)\, \mathrm{d}t \quad \longrightarrow \quad \sum_{k=0}^{N-1} (1+i\Delta t)^{-(k+1)} F(u_k) \Delta t \tag{2.27}$$

Here continuous discounting is consistently replaced by a periodic. Furthermore, $F(u_k)$ is discounted with $(1 + i\Delta t)^{-(k+1)}$ instead of with $(1 + i\Delta t)^{-k}$, which might be more obvious from a mathematical point of view. The underlying reason is that in this way discretization artefacts can be avoided at the end of the planning period for specific models of the firm in the following chapters.

2.3.2   Method 1

A discretized version of the continuous time problem (2.1) can be formulated as follows:

$$\max_{\{x_{k+1}, u_k\}} \sum_{k=0}^{N-1} (1 + i\Delta t)^{-(k+1)} F(u_k)\, \Delta t \; + \; (1 + i\Delta t)^{-N} S(x_N) \qquad (2.28a)$$

$$x_{k+1} - x_k = \Delta t f_k(x_k, u_k), \quad x_0 \text{ given} \qquad (2.28b)$$

$$g(x_k, u_k) \geq 0 \qquad (2.28c)$$

$$h(x_{k+1}) \geq 0 \qquad (2.28d)$$

where: $k = 0, \ldots, N - 1$[3]. That is an optimization problem in $(n + m)N$ variables with nN equality constraints and $(p + q)N$ inequality constraints.

Under the assumption that a given constraint qualification, which is not discribed explicitly here, is satisfied, the necessary conditions for optimality can be deployed for the discretized problem with the aid of the Kuhn-Tucker Theorem. For this purpose form the Lagrangian:

$$\hat{\mathcal{L}}(x_1, \ldots, x_N, u_0, \ldots, u_{N-1}, \hat{\lambda}_1, \ldots, \hat{\lambda}_N, \hat{\mu}_0, \ldots, \hat{\mu}_{N-1}, \hat{\nu}_1, \ldots, \hat{\nu}_N) =$$

$$\sum_{k=0}^{N-1} (1 + i\Delta t)^{-(k+1)} F(u_k)\Delta t \; + \; (1 + i\Delta t)^{-N} S(x_N) -$$

$$\sum_{k=0}^{N-1} \hat{\lambda}_{k+1}^{\mathrm{T}} \big(x_{k+1} - x_k - \Delta t f_k(x_k, u_k) \big) +$$

$$\sum_{k=0}^{N-1} \hat{\mu}_k^{\mathrm{T}} g(x_k, u_k) + \sum_{k=0}^{N-1} \hat{\nu}_{k+1}^{\mathrm{T}} h(x_{k+1}). \qquad (2.29)$$

Theorem 2.3 (Necessary conditions for optimality)
Let $(x_1^*, \ldots, x_N^*, u_0^*, \ldots, u_{N-1}^*)$ be an optimal solution to the discrete optimization problem, in which the constraint qualification is satisfied. Then vectors

---

[3]Because x_0 is fixed, constraint $h(x_0) \geq 0$ is redundant.

$\hat{\lambda}_1,\ldots,\hat{\lambda}_N$, $\hat{\mu}_0,\ldots,\hat{\mu}_{N-1}$ and $\hat{\nu}_1,\ldots,\hat{\nu}_N$ can be determined unambiguously, so that the following equations hold for $k = 0,\ldots,N-1$:

$$\frac{\partial \hat{\mathcal{L}}}{\partial x_{k+1}}(x_1^*,\ldots,u_{N-1}^*,\hat{\lambda}_1,\ldots,\hat{\nu}_N) = 0 \tag{2.30}$$

$$\frac{\partial \hat{\mathcal{L}}}{\partial u_k}(x_1^*,\ldots,u_{N-1}^*,\hat{\lambda}_1,\ldots,\hat{\nu}_N) = 0 \tag{2.31}$$

$$\hat{\mu}_k \geq 0, \quad \hat{\mu}_k^{\mathrm{T}} g(x_k^*,u_k^*) = 0 \tag{2.32}$$

$$\hat{\nu}_{k+1} \geq 0, \quad \hat{\nu}_{k+1}^{\mathrm{T}} h(x_{k+1}^*) = 0 \tag{2.33}$$

Working out (2.30) and (2.31) produces:

$$\hat{\lambda}_{k+1}^{\mathrm{T}} + \Delta t \hat{\lambda}_{k+1}^{\mathrm{T}} \frac{\partial f_k}{\partial x}(x_k^*,u_k^*) - \hat{\lambda}_k^{\mathrm{T}} + \hat{\mu}_k^{\mathrm{T}} \frac{\partial g}{\partial x}(x_k^*,u_k^*) +$$

$$\hat{\nu}_k^{\mathrm{T}} \frac{\partial h}{\partial x}(x_k^*) = 0 \qquad (k = 1,\ldots,N-1) \tag{2.34}$$

$$(1+i\Delta t)^{-N}\frac{\partial S}{\partial x}(x_N^*) - \hat{\lambda}_N^{\mathrm{T}} + \hat{\nu}_N^{\mathrm{T}}\frac{\partial h}{\partial x}(x_N^*) = 0 \tag{2.35}$$

$$(1+i\Delta t)^{-(k+1)}\frac{\partial F}{\partial u}(u_k^*)\Delta t + \Delta t \hat{\lambda}_{k+1}^{\mathrm{T}}\frac{\partial f_k}{\partial u}(x_k^*,u_k^*) +$$

$$\hat{\mu}_k^{\mathrm{T}}\frac{\partial g}{\partial u}(x_k^*,u_k^*) = 0 \qquad (k = 0,\ldots,N-1) \tag{2.36}$$

In order to get a better impression of the analogy with the continuous time problem, the adjoint variables are defined as follows:

$$\lambda_{k+1} = (1+i\Delta t)^{k+1}\hat{\lambda}_{k+1} \qquad (k = 0,\ldots,N-1) \tag{2.37}$$

$$\mu_k = (1+i\Delta t)^{k+1}\hat{\mu}_k/\Delta t \qquad (k = 0,\ldots,N-1) \tag{2.38}$$

$$\nu_0 = 0 \tag{2.39}$$

$$\nu_k = (1+i\Delta t)^{k+1}\hat{\nu}_k/\Delta t \qquad (k = 1,\ldots,N-1) \tag{2.40}$$

$$\gamma = (1+i\Delta t)^N \hat{\nu}_N \tag{2.41}$$

Additionally, the Hamilton functions $\mathcal{H}_k : \mathbb{R}^n \times \mathbb{R}^m \times \mathbb{R}^n \to \mathbb{R}$ will be formed by:

$$\mathcal{H}_k(x,u,\lambda) = F(u) + \lambda^{\mathrm{T}} f_k(x,u) \tag{2.42}$$

and the Langrange functions $\mathcal{L}_k : \mathbb{R}^n \times \mathbb{R}^m \times \mathbb{R}^n \times \mathbb{R}^p \times \mathbb{R}^q \to \mathbb{R}$ by:

$$\mathcal{L}_k(x,u,\lambda,\mu,\nu) = \mathcal{H}_k(x,u,\lambda) + \mu^{\mathrm{T}} g(x,u) + \nu^{\mathrm{T}} h(x) \tag{2.43}$$

where: $k = 0, \ldots, N - 1$. Furthermore, λ_0 is defined as:

$$\lambda_0 = \left(\lambda_1 + \Delta t \frac{\partial \mathcal{L}_1}{\partial x}(x_0, u_0, \lambda_1, \mu_0, \nu_0)\right) / (1 + i \Delta t) \qquad (2.44)$$

Now, the Kuhn-Tucker conditions (2.30) to (2.33) can be re-written as:

$$\frac{\lambda_{k+1}^{\mathrm{T}} - \lambda_k^{\mathrm{T}}}{\Delta t} - i \lambda_k^{\mathrm{T}} = -\frac{\partial \mathcal{L}_k}{\partial x}(x_k^*, u_k^*, \lambda_{k+1}, \mu_k, \nu_k) \qquad (2.45)$$

$$\frac{\partial \mathcal{L}_k}{\partial u}(x_k^*, u_k^*, \lambda_{k+1}, \mu_k, \nu_k) = 0 \qquad (2.46)$$

$$\mu_k \geq 0, \quad \mu_k^{\mathrm{T}} g(x_k^*, u_k^*) = 0 \qquad (2.47)$$

$$\nu_k \geq 0, \quad \nu_k^{\mathrm{T}} h(x_k^*) = 0 \qquad (2.48)$$

$$\lambda_N^{\mathrm{T}} = \frac{\partial S}{\partial x}(x_N^*) + \gamma^{\mathrm{T}} \frac{\partial h}{\partial x}(x_N^*) \qquad (2.49)$$

$$\gamma \geq 0, \quad \gamma^{\mathrm{T}} h(x_N^*) = 0 \qquad (2.50)$$

where: $k = 0, \ldots, N - 1$. The above system of equations is a time discretized version of the system (2.9) to (2.14) for $\lambda_0 = 1$ and it becomes clear that the equations (2.15) and (2.16) now cancel out.

According to the method described in this subsection, the NAG routine directly gives the values of x_{k+1}^* and u_k^* with the related values of $\hat{\lambda}_{k+1}$, $\hat{\mu}_k$ and $\hat{\nu}_{k+1}$ ($k = 0, \ldots, N-1$). Using the definitions (2.37) to (2.41), the discrete equivalents of the continuous adjoint variables from Section 2.2 can be obtained.

2.3.3   Method 2

An alternative discretized version of the optimization problem (2.1) can be written in the following manner:

$$\max_{\{u_k\}} \sum_{k=0}^{N-1} (1 + i \Delta t)^{-(k+1)} F(u_k) \Delta t + (1 + i \Delta t)^{-N} S(x_N) \qquad (2.51a)$$

$$g(x_k, u_k) \geq 0 \qquad (2.51b)$$

$$h(x_{k+1}) \geq 0 \qquad (2.51c)$$

in which:

$$x_{k+1}(u_0, \ldots, u_k) = x_0 + \Delta t f_0(x_0, u_0) + \sum_{j=1}^{k} \Delta t f_j\big(x_j(u_0, \ldots, u_{j-1}), u_j\big)$$

$$(2.52)$$

where: x_0 is known and $k = 0, \ldots, N-1$. This is an optimization problem with mN variables and $(p+q)N$ inequality constraints.

Once again, the Kuhn-Tucker Theorem can be used for the derivation of the necessary conditions. For this purpose form the Lagrangian:

$$\hat{\mathcal{L}}(u_0, \ldots, u_{N-1}, \hat{\mu}_0, \ldots, \hat{\mu}_{N-1}, \hat{\nu}_1, \ldots, \hat{\nu}_N) =$$

$$\sum_{k=0}^{N-1} (1 + i\Delta t)^{-(k+1)} F(u_k)\Delta t \; + \; (1 + i\Delta t)^{-N} S(x_N) \; +$$

$$\sum_{k=0}^{N-1} \hat{\mu}_k^{\mathrm{T}} g(x_k, u_k) + \sum_{k=0}^{N-1} \hat{\nu}_{k+1}^{\mathrm{T}} h(x_{k+1}). \tag{2.53}$$

Theorem 2.4 (Necessary conditions for optimality)
Let $(u_0^*, \ldots, u_{N-1}^*)$ be an optimal solution to the discrete optimization problem, in which the constraint qualification is satisfied. Then vectors $\hat{\mu}_0, \ldots, \hat{\mu}_{N-1}$ and $\hat{\nu}_1, \ldots, \hat{\nu}_N$ can be determined unambiguously, so that the following equations hold for $k = 0, \ldots, N-1$:

$$\frac{\partial \hat{\mathcal{L}}}{\partial u_k}(u_0^*, \ldots, u_{N-1}^*, \hat{\mu}_0, \ldots, \hat{\nu}_N) = 0 \tag{2.54}$$

$$\hat{\mu}_k \geq 0, \quad \hat{\mu}_k^{\mathrm{T}} g(x_k^*, u_k^*) = 0 \tag{2.55}$$

$$\hat{\nu}_{k+1} \geq 0, \quad \hat{\nu}_{k+1}^{\mathrm{T}} h(x_{k+1}^*) = 0 \tag{2.56}$$

Partial differentiation of the Langrangiaan with respect to the control variables requires meticulous application of the Chain Rule and it will eventually lead to somewhat complicated expressions. This can be easily seen, since u_k not only influences x_{k+1} but also the future state variables via this state variable.

Following the method just described, the routine from the NAG Library that is employed here directly gives the values of u_k^* with the related values of $\hat{\mu}_k$ and $\hat{\nu}_{k+1}$ $(k = 0, \ldots, N-1)$. On the basis of equation (2.52), it follows that x_{k+1}^* $(k = 0, \ldots, N-1)$ can be calculated. Via the definitions (2.38) to (2.41), the discrete equivalents of the continuous adjoint variables from Section 2.2 can be obtained. Moreover, λ_{k+1} $(k = 0, \ldots, N-1)$ can be calculated from the stationarity condition (2.46).

2.4   Economic interpretation of the adjoint variables

For the time discretized optimization problem, the well-known 'shadow price' interpretation holds for the adjoint variables:

$\hat{\lambda}_{k+1}^{\mathrm{T}}\partial x$ is the change in the maximum attainable value of the objective function when the equation $x_{k+1} - x_k = \Delta t f_k(x_k, u_k)$ is replaced by $x_{k+1} - x_k = \Delta t f_k(x_k, u_k) + \partial x$, with $\partial x \in \mathbb{R}^n$ infinitesimal.

$\hat{\mu}_k^{\mathrm{T}}\partial g$ is the increase in the maximum attainable value of the objective function when the inequality constraint $g(x_k, u_k) \geq 0$ is replaced by $g(x_k, u_k) \geq -\partial g$ with $\partial g \in \mathbb{R}^p$ infinitesimal.

$\hat{\nu}_k^{\mathrm{T}}\partial h$ is the increase in the maximum attainable value of the objective function when the inequality constraint $h(x_k) \geq 0$ is replaced by $h(x_k) \geq -\partial h$ with $\partial h \in \mathbb{R}^q$ infinitesimal.

For the time continuous problem in general, only a simple economic interpretation of the costate variable can be given:

$\lambda(t)^{\mathrm{T}}\partial x$ is the discounted change to t in the maximum attainable value of the objective function when x is increased by ∂x on t.

Van Hilten [1991] proved that $\nu_i(\tau)$ can be interpreted as the rate at which the maximum attainable value of the objective function would grow, when the pure state constraint $h_i(x(t)) \geq 0$ at an instant τ is removed momentarily, and as the rate at which the maximum attainable value of the objective function would reduce when the pure state constraint is violated momentarily.

For μ_i, a simple economic interpretation is usually possible when it is related to an upper or lower bound of the control variable.

2.5   General procedure

For the models of the firm in this book, the necessary (and sufficient) conditions for optimality are always derived. The first two steps of the path coupling procedure - identifying the paths and determining the feasible paths - are performed. A couple of paths may be further explained economically. Furthermore, the tranversality conditions are worked out so that it becomes explicitly clear which equations the potential final paths have to satisfy. Analytical solving of the synthesis problem i.e. the actual coupling of the paths is omitted completely. Optimal strings of paths are determined via analysis of the numerical results for equivalent time discretized models of the firm, obtained with the aid of a computer using Method 2 and a chosen set of parameters. In discussing the results most attention is paid to their economic implications.

Chapter 3

The Basic Model

3.1 Introduction

In this chapter, the model of the firm that serves as the starting point of the research work reported in this book will be treated briefly. Essentially, this basic model can be traced back to Lesourne [1973]; later, it was also used as the foundation of most models by, amongst others, Van Loon [1983], Van Schijndel [1988], Kort [1989] and Van Hilten [1991]. Contrary to the research described in literature, here, attention will be paid to relatively short planning periods.

In the second section, the model equations and the assumptions made will be presented and explained. Adjoint variables will be introduced in Section 3.3 and the feasible paths as well as an economic interpretation of some paths in particular will be given. The numerical results of a case study are discussed in Section 3.4 before closing the chapter with a summary and the conclusions.

3.2 The model and its assumptions

The model of the firm that serves as the starting point of this research is:

$$\max_{I(t),D(t)} \left\{ J = \int_0^z e^{-it} D(t)\,\mathrm{d}t + e^{-iz} X(z) \right\} \tag{3.1a}$$

$$\dot{K}(t) = I(t) - aK(t), \quad K(0) = K_0 > 0 \tag{3.1b}$$

$$\dot{X}(t) = (1-f)\left\{ S\big(Q(t)\big) - wL(t) - aK(t) - rY(t) \right\} - D(t),$$

$$X(0) = X_0 > 0 \tag{3.1c}$$

$$Q(t) = k^{-1}K(t) \tag{3.1d}$$

$$L(t) = lQ(t) \tag{3.1e}$$

$$K(t) = X(t) + Y(t) \qquad\qquad\qquad\qquad\qquad (3.1\text{f})$$

$$Y(t) \geq 0 \qquad\qquad\qquad\qquad\qquad\qquad (3.1\text{g})$$

$$Y(t) \leq bX(t) \qquad\qquad\qquad\qquad\qquad\qquad (3.1\text{h})$$

$$I(t) \geq 0 \qquad\qquad\qquad\qquad\qquad\qquad\quad (3.1\text{i})$$

$$D(t) \geq 0 \qquad\qquad\qquad\qquad\qquad\qquad\quad (3.1\text{j})$$

Equation (3.1a) represents the objective function of the firm: the firm aims to maximize the discounted value of future dividends plus the discounted value of its equity at the end of a planning period. The resources available for doing so - the control variables - are the investments I and the dividends D.

When at a certain instant of time the firm's total investments exceed those needed for replacement, the capital assets will grow which in turn may lead to greater returns and dividends in future. Consequently, the decision problem of the firm is clearly a dynamic one. Equations (3.1b) and (3.1c) show the development with time of the capital assets and the book value of equity. K and X are the state variables. Together, they contain all the relevant information from the past: the only things that the firm should know at any instant of time t, in order to make an optimal plan for the future, are the values of $K(t)$ and $X(t)$. The initial values of K and X are given by K_0 en X_0. Equation (3.1b) shows that the capital assets are increased by investments and reduced by wastage (exponentially at rate a)[1]. Mathematically, the price of a capital asset is taken to be unity. According to (3.1c) the profit after taxation (profit is equivalent to the turnover minus labour costs, depreciation[2] and interest payments) will be used for paying out dividend and/or supplementing the stock of equity. The turnover $S(t, Q)$ is a strictly concave function of the production rate Q and moreover increasing on the relevant interval for Q, which means respectively that:

$$\frac{\partial^2 S}{\partial Q^2}(Q) < 0 \quad \text{and} \quad \frac{\partial S}{\partial Q}(Q) > 0 \qquad\qquad\qquad (3.2)$$

The concavity requirement of S clearly has a mathematical reason. As well-known, for a maximization problem concavity is required to assure that a solution exists (see also Chapter 2). The economic interpretation is decreasing marginal returns. The second inequality implies that the demand elasticity of price is less than unity. Moreover it holds that:

$$S\big(Q(t)\big) = Q(t)P\big(Q(t)\big) \qquad\qquad\qquad\qquad (3.3)$$

---

[1] This modelling of the wastage of capital assets is simple although it mostly implies a wastage rate that is too big in the initial stage; Bekker [1991] presents more appropiate simulation models for this.

[2] The firm writes off its assets exponentially at a rate equal to the 'rate of wastage'.

where: $P(Q(t))$ is the price per unit of goods sold. Equations (3.1d) and (3.1e) give the relationships between the production resources, capital and labour, and the production rate. This points to a Leontief technology with constant returns to scale. Equation (3.1f) is the balance sheet equation: the firm has two sources of funds, equity and debt. Equations (3.1g) and (3.1h) determine the upper and lower bounds of the amount of debt, whilst (3.1i) and (3.1j) determine the interval from which the decision variables must be chosen. Note that the inequality (3.1i) shows that investment is irreversible.

The term i in the objective function (3.1a) is the time preference rate of the shareholders and it can be seen as the minimum return that they expect, or as the cost of equity. The boundary case, where the cost of equity is the same as the cost of debt, is excluded for mathematical reasons:

$$i \neq (1 - f)r \tag{3.4}$$

When: $i < (1 - f)r$, then, the cost of equity is less than the cost of debt. This may occur, for example, if the capital market operates imperfectly and it becomes difficult for the firm to get 'cheap' loans, or if the owner-manager of the firm wishes to remain in business, although its profitability is low compared with the interest rate.

An interesting economic magnitude, with which a good insight into the way that this model operates can be obtained, is the so-called operating cash flow (after interest). Given the values of the variables K and Y at a certain instant of time t, the operating cash flow will be equal to the net profit plus the depreciation. After elimination of $Q(t)$ and $L(t)$, the expression becomes:

$$O_{ni}(K(t), Y(t)) = (1 - f)\{S(k^{-1}K(t)) - wlk^{-1}K(t) -$$

$$aK(t) - rY(t)\} + aK(t) \tag{3.5}$$

Given the definition of the operating cash flow and with the aid of the model equations above, the following identity can be derived easily:

$$O_{ni}(K(t), Y(t)) = I(t) + D(t) - \dot{Y}(t) \tag{3.6}$$

This identity can be seen as a permanent equality between the left- and right-hand sides of the 'Sources and Uses of Funds Statement'; it implies that the net cash flow, represented by the difference between sources and uses, is always zero. That cannot be otherwise, because the model of the firm contains no provision for a cash balance, which follows directly from the balance sheet equation (3.1f).

Thus, the problem which confronts the firm is how to use the operating cash flow in order to obtain the maximum value for the objective function (3.1a). The firm can choose from three activities:

• investing in capital assets,

- reducing/increasing debt,

- paying out dividend.

Actually, the firm has only two choices open to it (I and D); the third activity
is already determined by the identity (3.6).

3.3   Examination of the paths

3.3.1   Introducing the adjoint variables

It is shown in Appendix A that the optimization problem (3.1) satifies the
required constraint qualification; therefore, Theorem 2.1 can be applied for
deriving the necessary conditions. For this purpose, the Hamiltonian and Lagrangian are defined as follows ($\lambda_0 = 1$, see Observation 2.1):

$$\mathcal{H}(K, X, I, D, \lambda_1, \lambda_2) = D + \lambda_1 \left[I - aK \right] +$$

$$\lambda_2 \left[(1 - f) \left\{ S(k^{-1}K) - wlk^{-1}K - aK - r(K - X) \right\} - D \right] \qquad (3.7)$$

and:

$$\mathcal{L}(K, X, I, D, \lambda_1, \lambda_2, \mu_1, \mu_2, \nu_1, \nu_2) = \mathcal{H}(K, X, I, D, \lambda_1, \lambda_2) +$$

$$\mu_1 I + \mu_2 D + \nu_1 \left[K - X \right] + \nu_2 \left[(1 + b)X - K \right] \qquad (3.8)$$

respectively, where:

$\lambda_1(t)$: costate variable of capital assets

$\lambda_2(t)$: costate variable of equity

$\mu_1(t)$: Lagrange multiplier for lower bound of investment rate (3.1i)

$\mu_2(t)$: Lagrange multiplier for lower bound of dividend rate (3.1j)

$\nu_1(t)$: Lagrange multiplier for lower bound of debt (3.1g)

$\nu_2(t)$: Lagrange multiplier for upper bound of debt (3.1h)

$\lambda_i(t)$ and $\mu_i(t)$ ($i = 1, 2$) can be interpreted in simple economic terms as shadow
prices[3]:

- $\lambda_1(t)$ is the change in the maximum attainable value of the objective
  function discounted to t, when the firm has to acquire a single unit of
  capital assets at time t.

- $\lambda_2(t)$ is the change in the maximum attainable value of the objective
  function discounted to t, when the firm gets an extra single unit of equity
  available at time t.

---

[3]The economic interpretation of ν_i (i=1,2) for such continuous time problems is formally
somewhat more difficult (see Section 2.4 and Van Hilten [1991]).

Table 3.1 Identifying the paths using the multipliers μ_i and ν_i.

path	1	2	3	4	5	6	7	8	9	10	11	12
μ_1	+	0	+	0	+	0	+	0	+	0	+	0
μ_2	+	+	0	0	+	+	0	0	+	+	0	0
ν_1	+	+	+	+	0	0	0	0	0	0	0	0
ν_2	0	0	0	0	+	+	+	+	0	0	0	0

- $\mu_1(t)$ is the change in the maximum attainable value of the objective function discounted to t, when the firm may sell (at book value) a single unit capital assets at time t.

- $\mu_2(t)$ is the change in the maximum attainable value of the objective function discounted to t, when the firm may attract a single unit of equity externally - for example from a share issue - at time t.

The set of necessary conditions that results after applying Theorem 2.1 is given in Appendix A, where it is also shown that the necessary conditions are sufficient too.

3.3.2   Determining the feasible paths

Since the simulation model (3.1) contains four inequality constraints, in principle, sixteen (2^4) different paths can be distinguished. However, the four paths with positive values of ν_1 ànd ν_2 can be eliminated directly, because the upper and lower bounds of debt are never active at the same time[4], The remaining twelve paths are identified in Table 3.1 using the multipliers.

Paths 1 and 5 in Table 3.1 each contain three positive Lagrange multipliers which is more than the number of control variables ($=2$), therefore, these paths can be eliminated too (see Chapter 2). In Appendix A, it is shown that $i = (1-f)r$ is implied when testing paths 11 en 12 against the necessary conditions. As this boundary case, where the cost equity equals the cost of debt, has been excluded, paths 11 and 12 can be removed. In the same way it can be deduced that, respectively, paths 3 and 4, and 7 and 8, can only appear in an optimal string if: respectively, $i < (1-f)r$ and $i > (1-f)r$. Table 3.2 shows the eight paths that may appear in an optimal string and the conditions, if any, that must apply.

In Appendix A it is shown that *all* paths in Table 3.2 are potential final paths. There is a striking difference with studies reported in literature (Van

---

[4]Indeed, this event only occurs for $K(t) = X(t) = 0$ which is in contradiction with $K(t) \geq K_0 e^{-at} > 0$, $t \in [0, z]$.

Table 3.2 The eight paths which may appear in an optimal string for the basic model. The last column contains the conditions, if any, that must apply.

	μ_1	μ_2	ν_1	ν_2	
path 2	0	+	+	0	
path 3	+	0	+	0	only when $i < (1-f)r$
path 4	0	0	+	0	only when $i < (1-f)r$
path 6	0	+	0	+	
path 7	+	0	0	+	only when $i > (1-f)r$
path 8	0	0	0	+	only when $i > (1-f)r$
path 9	+	+	0	0	
path 10	0	+	0	0	

Loon [1983], Van Schijndel [1988], Kort [1989], Van Hilten [1991]) where only paths 4 and 8 are considered as potential final paths. The difference is explained by the assumption in these studies that z, the planning horizon, is sufficiently distant. After the next subsection, examples are treated in a case study where other paths appear as final one in an optimal string as well.

3.3.3   Economic interpretation of paths 4, 8 and 10

Along the paths 4, 8 and 10, it always holds that the marginal return on capital assets before taxation equals the marginal cost of capital assets before taxation:

$$\frac{\partial S}{\partial K}\left(t, k^{-1}K(t)\right) = wlk^{-1} + a + \begin{cases} c_4 & : \text{path 4} \\ c_8 & : \text{path 8} \\ c_{10} & : \text{path 10} \end{cases} \qquad (3.9)$$

where:

c_4, c_8, c_{10} : are the financing costs before taxation of a single extra unit of capital assets ('Cost of Capital', see Weston & Copeland [1989] for example).

The financing costs of a single extra unit of capital assets are not the same for all three paths, because the way that an extra unit is financed differs. On path 4 it is financed from equity entirely, so that:

$$c_4 = \frac{i}{1-f} \qquad (3.10)$$

On path 8 the firm has debt and equity at its disposal, up to the maximum permitted ratio of $b : 1$. Then, an extra unit of capital assets is financed from debt and equity in an equal ratio, so that the resulting financing costs will be:

$$c_8 = \frac{b}{b+1}r + \frac{1}{b+1}\cdot\frac{i}{1-f} \qquad (3.11)$$

Finally, on path 10, the firm possesses both debt and equity, however usually, in a changing ratio that is smaller than the maximum permitted. Exclusively debt is used for financing an extra unit of capital assets, resulting in the financing costs becoming:

$$c_{10} = r \qquad (3.12)$$

Directly from the marginal returns and costs being equal, the time-invariable sizes of the capital assets belonging to the three paths can be calculated; they are called K_4, K_8 and K_{10} respectively. Then, on paths 4 and 8, the time-invariable sizes of equity, X_4 and X_8 respectively, are also known.

On path 4, the firm's capital assets and equity have the most desirable size in the case of equity being cheaper than debt. For a sufficiently distant planning horizon, the solution of an optimal control problem will be characterized as one of reaching path 4 as soon as possible, given the subsidiary conditions and the initial values of the state variables; then maintaining that path to the end of the planning period. When the planning period is made shorter, so that path 4 cannot be attained in time, the optimal strategy will remain the same as that during an equivalent period with a more distant planning horizon.

Similar reasoning as that for path 4 above, also applies to path 8 in the case of debt being cheaper than equity. The other paths shown in Table 3.2, in principle, can be seen as interim stages 'by force' for attaining one of the two paths named earlier as soon as possible.

3.4 Case study

In this section, some numerical examples of the basic model are discussed from which it will become clear that next to paths 4 and 8 other paths can appear as the final one in an optimal string. This occurs when path 4 $(i < (1-f)r)$ or path 8 $(i > (1-f)r)$ cannot be attained, given the planning horizon, control restrictions and initial values of the state variables. In literature on analytical solutions to such problems using a path coupling procedure, it is implied that the planning periods are always long enough to attain paths 4 or 8 before the end of the planning period (Van Loon [1983], Van Schijndel [1988], Kort [1989], Van Hilten [1991]).

Both in the event of $i < (1-f)r$, as well $i > (1-f)r$, this study gives examples of a firm with a high and a low initial stock of capital assets with different values of the planning horizons. The following price function was chosen:

$$P(Q(t)) = \overline{P} \left(1 - \frac{Q(t)}{\overline{Q}} \right) \qquad (3.13)$$

The values of the parameters assumed in this case study were obtained from statistics for the chemical industry and can be explained as follows: the stock of capital assets decreases at a rate of ten percent per unit of time ($a = 0.1$) as a result of wastage. In the examples where the initial stock of capital assets is low, the firm is allowed to possess an amount of debt maximum twice the amount of equity, i.e. $b = 2$; at the outset, $Y_0 = bX_0 = 0.0024$ so that $K_0 = 0.0036$. In the examples where the initial stock of capital assets is high, the maximum debt-equity ratio is nine, i.e. $b = 9$; at the outset, $Y_0 = bX_0 = 0.162$ so that $K_0 = 0.18$. The firm has to pay forty percent of its gross profit to the taxman ($f = 0.4$). The interest rate on debt amounts to ten percent per unit of time ($r = 0.1$). For the time preference rate of the shareholder it was chosen: $i = 0.04$ in the case that equity is cheaper than debt, and $i = 0.08$ when the reverse is the case. With the size of capital assets fixed at a thousand units, the firm can (and will) produce sixteen units of goods per unit of time, i.e. $k = 1000/16 = 62.5$. The labour cost per unit of goods produced amounts to eighty monetary units ($wl = 80$); As the parameters of the price function, $\overline{P}$ and $\overline{Q}$ were taken to be 95.263 and 0.0625 respectively. The discretization stepsize always is $\Delta t = 0.25$.

3.4.1   The case of $i < (1 - f)r$

Low initial stock of capital assets.   Firstly, the situation is discussed when the planning horizon is sufficiently distant ($z = 50$). In Figure 3.1, the graphs for $I(t)$, $D(t)$, $K(t)$, $Y(t)$, $\mu_j(t)$ and $\nu_j(t)$ are depicted, where $j = 1, 2$. The optimal strategy can be included in a simple chronological decision rule beginning at time instant 0 and ending at z:

1. As long as $K < K_{10}$, invest all of the cash flow plus the maximum sum that can be borrowed.

2. At τ_1, K becomes equal to K_{10}; maintain K at this fixed level and pay off debt with the rest of the cash flow.

3. From τ_2, the instant when debt is completely paid off, provided that $K < K_4$, use all the cash flow for investments.

4. At τ_3 when path 4 is reached, maintain K at the fixed level K_4 and pay out the rest of the cash flow as dividend.

From the decision rule, it appears that the planning horizon z has no effect on the optimal strategy at any previous instant of time. Stated differently, the decision rule (including instants τ_i, $i = 1, 3$) stays the same whenever the planning horizon changes. For a smaller planning horizon, however, the possibility of z being reached already in prior stages of the decision rule, certainly exists.

Figures 3.2 to 3.4 display the graphs for $\mu_i(t)$ and $\nu_i(t)$ for three smaller planning horizons that show that not only path 4, but either paths 2, 6 or 10 can appear as the final one in an optimal string. In all these cases, it holds that $\mu_1(z^-) = 0$, $i = 1, 2$, so that the transversality condition (see Appendix A) is satisfied.

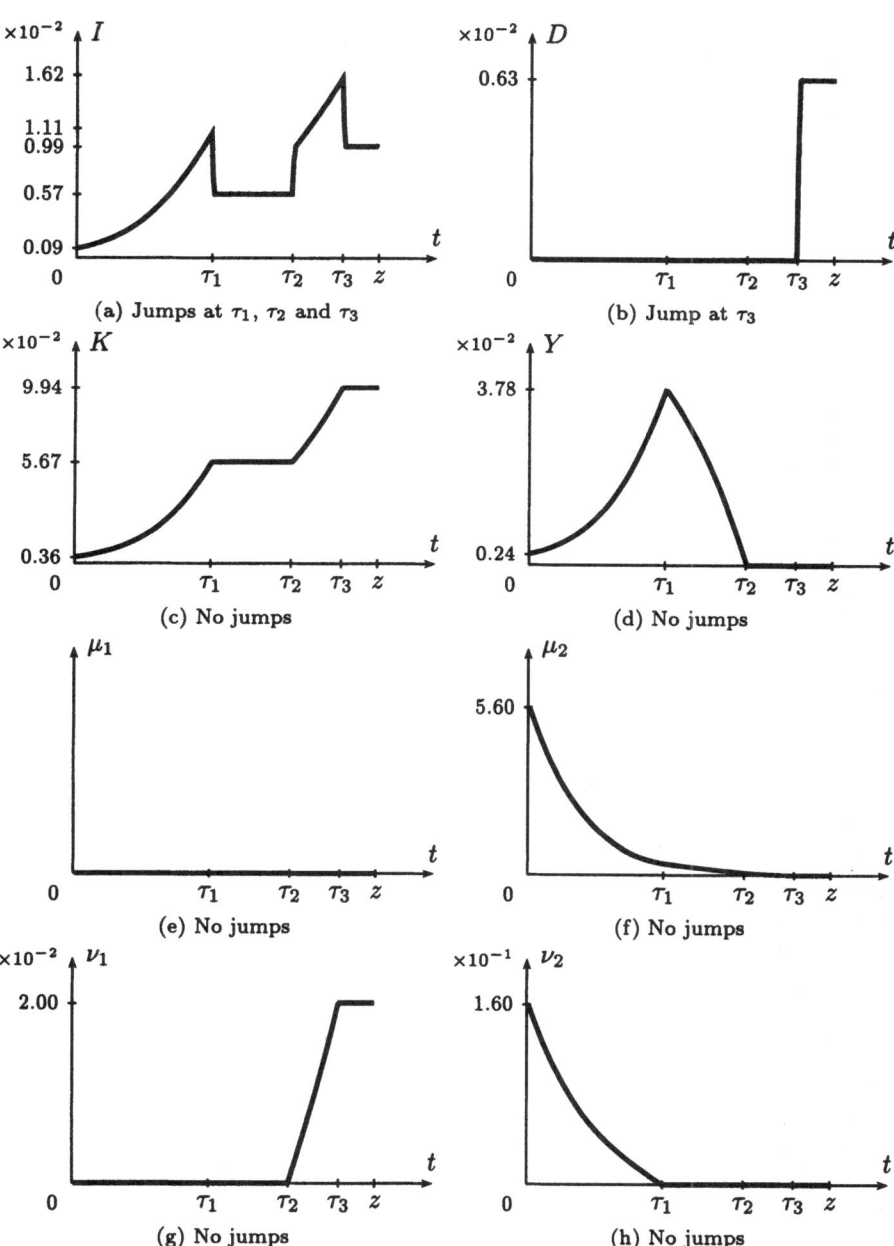

Figure 3.1 $i < (1-f)r$: low initial stock of capital assets with a sufficiently large z. Path 4 will be reached within the given planning period and it is the final path. Optimal string of paths: 6-10-2-4.

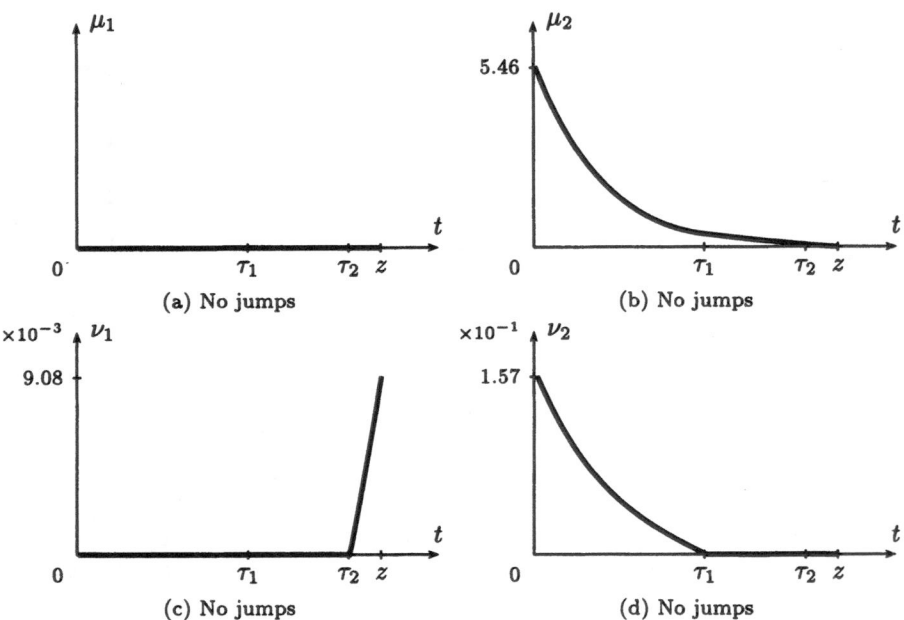

Figure 3.2 $i < (1-f)r$: low initial stock of capital assets where $\tau_2 < z < \tau_3$. The firm cannot reach path 4 before the planning horizon. Path 2 is the final path here. Optimal string of paths: 6-10-2.

High initial stock of capital assets. Once again, the situation of a sufficiently distant planning horizon is first discussed ($z = 50$). The graphs in Figure 3.5 include $I(t)$, $D(t)$, $K(t)$, $Y(t)$, $\mu_j(t)$ and $\nu_j(t)$, where $j = 1, 2$. Again the optimal strategy can be included in a simple chronological decision rule beginning at the instant of time 0 and ending at z.

1. As long as $K > K_{10}$ and $Y > 0$, use all the cash flow for paying off debt.

Now there are four possible alternatives. In the first alternative, i.e. the one displayed in Figure 3.5, K_{10} is reached at τ_1 before debt is paid off completely. Then, the next steps of the decision rule are steps 2, 3 and 4 of the decision rule for low initial stock of capital assets.

For the second alternative, at the precise instant τ_1 when debt is paid off completely it holds that: $K_{10} < K(\tau_1) < K_4$. Then, the next steps of the decision rule are steps 3 and 4 of the decision rule for low initial stock of capital assets.

For the third alternative, at the precise instant τ_1 when debt is paid off completely it holds that: $K(\tau_1) = K_4$. Then, the next step of the decision rule is step 4 of the decision rule for low initial stock of capital assets.

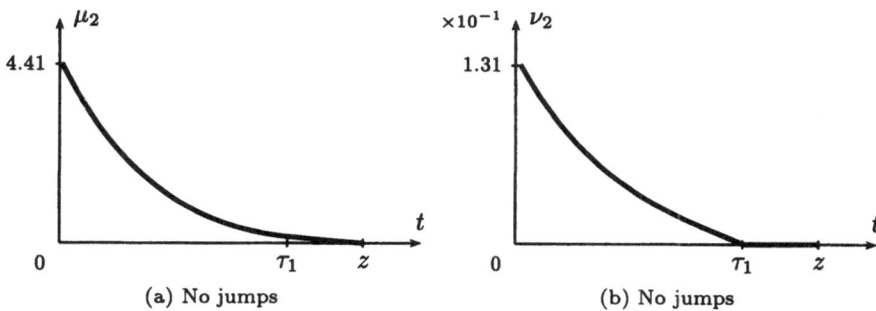

Figure 3.3 $i < (1-f)r$: low initial stock of capital assets where $\tau_1 < z < \tau_2$. Here, path 10 is the final path. Optimal string of paths: 6-10.

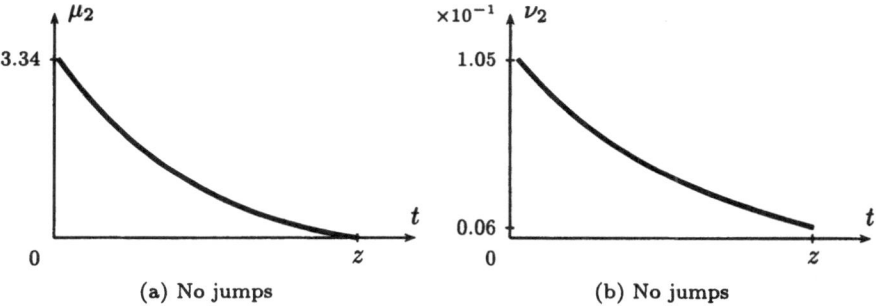

Figure 3.4 $i < (1-f)r$: low initial stock of capital assets where $0 < z < \tau_1$. Path 6 is the final path and it is the only path in the optimal string.

For the fourth alternative, at the precise instant τ_1 when debt is paid off completely it holds that: $K(\tau_1) > K_4$. Then the next steps of the decision rule are:

1. As long as $K > K_4$, use all the cash flow to pay out dividend.

2. When path 4 is reached, maintain $K = K_4$ and use the rest of the cash flow to pay out dividend.

Again from the decision rule, it appears that the planning horizon z has no effect on the optimal strategy at any previous instant of time.

Figure 3.6 displays the graphs for $\mu_1(t)$ and $\mu_2(t)$ when $0 < z < \tau_1$; they show that path 9 too can appear as the final one in an optimal string.

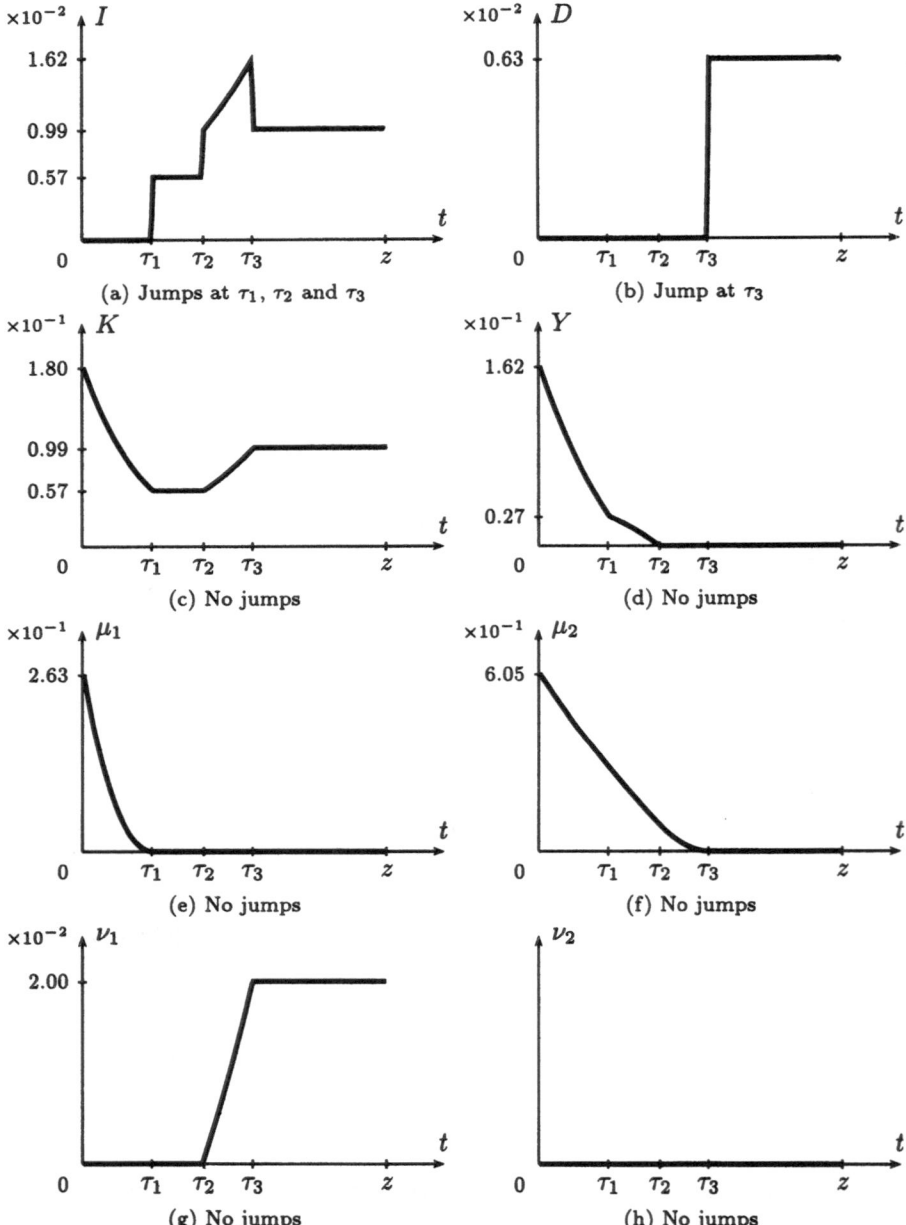

Figure 3.5 $i < (1 - f)r$: high initial stock of capital assets for a sufficiently large z. Path 4 will be reached within the planning period and it is the final path. Optimal string of paths: 9-10-2-4.

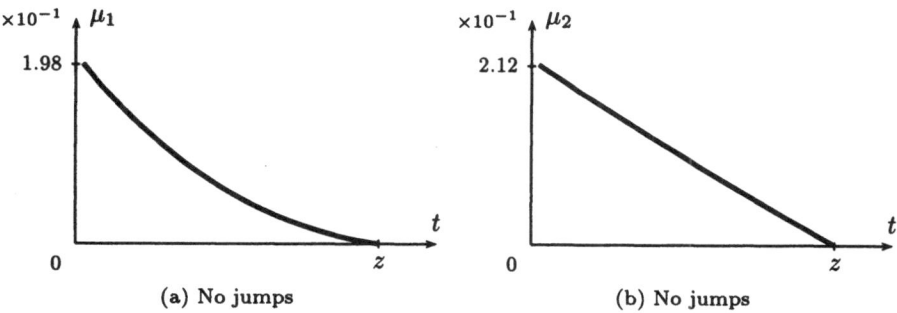

(a) No jumps   (b) No jumps

Figure 3.6 $i < (1 - f)r$: high initial stock of capital assets where $0 < z < \tau_1$. Path 9 is the final path and it is the only path in the optimal string.

3.4.2 The case of $i > (1 - f)r$

Low initial stock of capital assets. Initially, the situation is discussed where the planning horizon is sufficiently distant ($z = 50$). In Figure 3.7, the graphs for $I(t)$, $D(t)$, $K(t)$, $Y(t)$, $\mu_j(t)$ and $\nu_j(t)$ are shown, where $j = 1, 2$. The optimal strategy can be included in a simple chronological decision rule beginning at the instant of time 0 and ending at z:

1. As long as $K < K_8$, invest all the cash flow plus the maximum that can be borrowed.

2. At τ_1, path 8 is reached; maintain K at the fixed level K_8 and pay out the rest of the cash flow as dividend (while maintaining maximum debt).

High initial stock of capital assets. Once again the first situation examined has a sufficiently distant planning horizon ($z = 50$). Figure 3.8 displays the graphs for $I(t)$, $D(t)$, $K(t)$, $Y(t)$, $\mu_j(t)$ and $\nu_j(t)$, where $j = 1, 2$. Again, the optimal strategy can be included in a simple chronological decision rule beginning at the instant of time 0 and ending at z, which however only deviates in the first stage from the decision rule for low initial stock of capital assets:

1. As long as $K > K_8$, use a part of the cash flow in order to pay off debt, provided that the amount of debt remains at its upper bound, then pay out the remainder of the cash flow as dividend.

2. Identical to the decision rule for low initial stock of capital assets.

From the decision rule, yet again, it appears that the planning horizon z has no effect on the optimal strategy at any previous instant of time.

Figure 3.9 displays the graphs of $\mu_1(t)$ and $\nu_2(t)$ when $0 < z < \tau_1$; they show that path 7 too can appear as the final one in an optimal string.

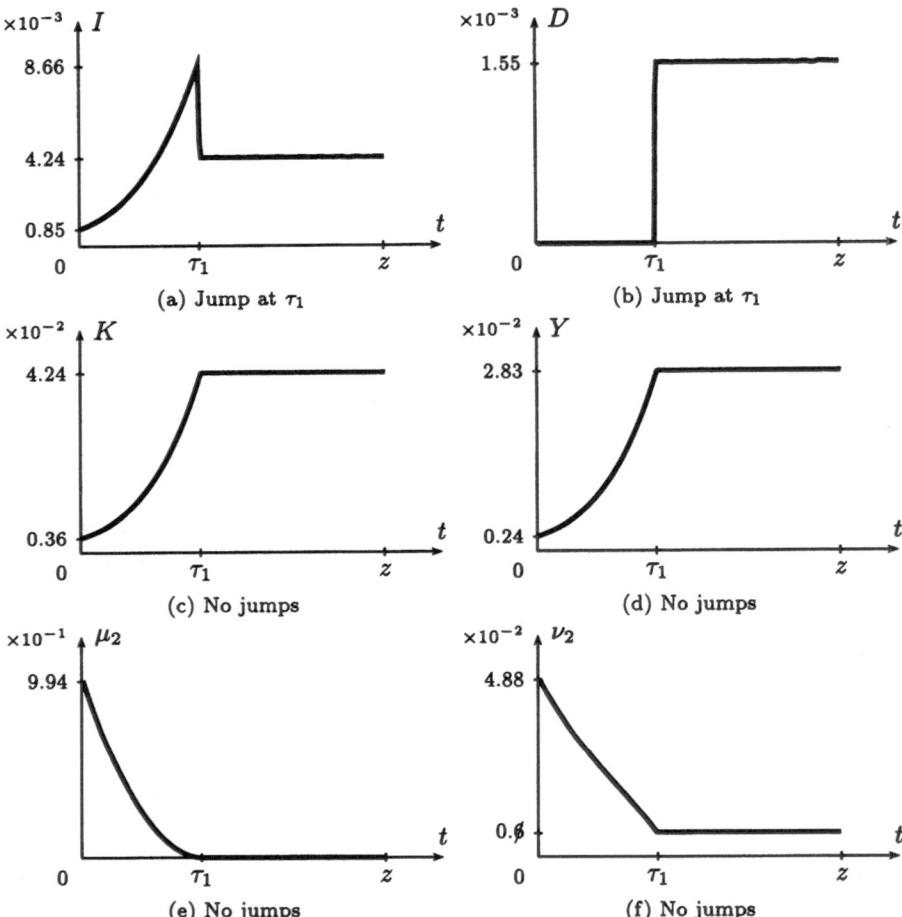

Figure 3.7 $i > (1 - f)r$: low initial stock of capital assets with a sufficiently large z. Path 8 is reached within the planning period and it is the final path. Optimal string of paths: 6-8.

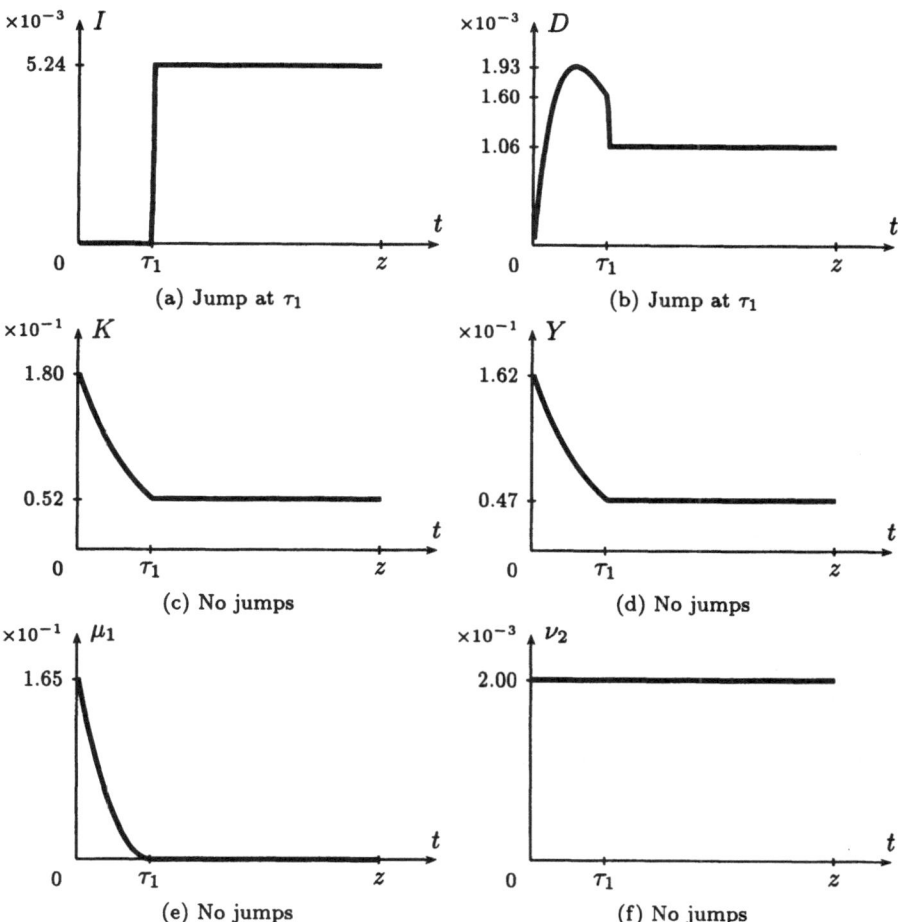

Figure 3.8 $i > (1 - f)r$: high initial stock of capital assets with a sufficiently large z. Path 8 is reached within the planning horizon and it is the final path. Optimal string of paths: 7-8.

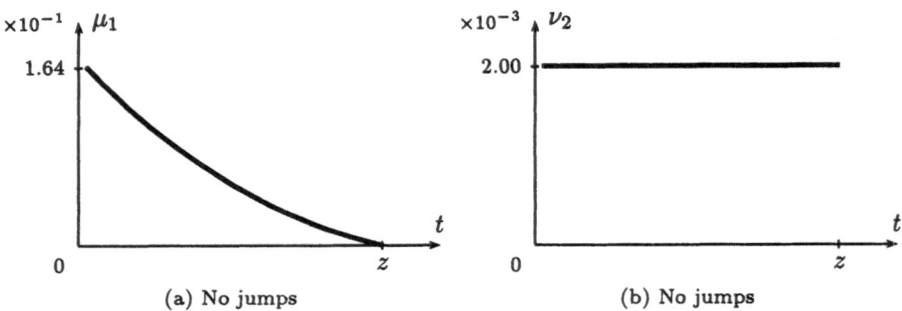

(a) No jumps   (b) No jumps

Figure 3.9 $i > (1 - f)r$: high initial stock of capital assets where $0 < z < \tau_1$. Path 7 is the final path and it is the only path in the optimal string.

3.5   Conclusions

The basic model that has been discussed in the literature many times, is characterized by the existence of a firm's most desirable time-invariable state where the marginal returns on capital assets equal the marginal costs (path 4 in the event that equity is cheaper than debt, and path 8 in the opposite case). This conditions directly fixes the size of the stock of capital assets and the amount of equity.

Generally, the optimal dynamic strategy can be included in a simple chronological decision rule and, given the initial state and subsidiary conditions, it comes down to attaining the optimal state as soon as possible and maintaining it subsequently, provided that the planning horizon is sufficiently distant, or to approximating it as closely as possible when it is not. In this procedure, the planning horizon has no effect on the policy required during the planning period.

Chapter 4

A Model with Start-up Costs

4.1 Introduction

In the model of the firm from the previous chapter, a static relationship between the production rate $Q(t)$ and the stock of capital assets $K(t)$ is suggested:

$$Q(t) = k^{-1}K(t) \qquad (4.1)$$

This means that the utilization rate defined as:

$$\frac{kQ(t)}{K(t)} \qquad (4.2)$$

is always 100%.

In practice, for example in the chemical industry, it appears however that expanding the capital assets will not give full utilization directly as a matter of course. After completion of a new factory, the rate of utilization will increase only gradually, due to inevitable start-up problems. A characteristic time to reach normal utilization is around three years; as a consequence, a situation will arise where cost comes before benefit: an increase in the stock of capital assets at the same time involves increased depreciation and usually increased interest payments too; the benefits in the form of a greater return is delayed. In other words: when investing a single monetary unit only once does the operating income show an inverse response, i.e. at first negative before changing to positive. In this chapter, a model of the firm is studied in which the previously mentioned start-up costs are interpreted. Section 2 gives the model equations; subsequently, the adjoint variables are defined and a table of feasible paths is presented which is followed by an explanation of the stationary paths in it (Section 3). Section 4 discusses a case study and the results are compared with those of the basic model in the previous chapter. Finally, Section 5 contains a summary and the conclusions.

4.2   The model and its assumptions

The situation described in the introduction can be modelled in principle by replacing the static relationship between production rate and stock of capital assets from the basic model (4.1) with a dynamic one:

$$\vartheta_Q \dot{Q}(t) + Q(t) = k^{-1} K(t), \quad Q(0) = Q_0 \geq 0 \tag{4.3}$$

where: ϑ_Q is the characteristic time to reach a normal utilization rate. This differential equations implies that $Q(t)$, in addition to $K(t)$ and $X(t)$, are the three state variables in the model. Therefore, the utilization rate is given by:

$$\frac{kQ(t)}{K(t)} = 1 - \frac{\vartheta_Q k \dot{Q}(t)}{K(t)} \tag{4.4}$$

so that it will become less than 100% as production grows.

Figure 4.1 shows, amongst others, the response of the utilization rate and the operating income as a function of time, for both the basic model and the model with start-up costs, when the investment rate is increased stepwise. Here the operating income is defined as:

$$B\big(K(t), Q(t)\big) = S\big(Q(t)\big) - wlQ(t) - aK(t) \tag{4.5}$$

The stepwise increased investment rate leads, in the first instance, to a decline of the operating income and only in the second instance, to a rise asymptotically to a positive final value.

A disadvantage of the model above is that with a declining production rate, the utilization rate will become more than 100% which is unrealistic. For an unchanged objective function towards the end of the planning period, the firm 'misuses' this opportunity by prematurely ceasing to invest and paying out extra dividend[1]. Consequently, this results in a direct decline of depreciation and possible interest payments, but only in a delayed decline of turnover.

Therefore, when modelling with start-up costs, it is better to replace equation (4.1) in the basic model with the following inequality constraints instead of replacing it with (4.3):

$$Q(t) \leq k^{-1} K(t) \tag{4.6}$$

$$\vartheta_Q \dot{Q}(t) + Q(t) \leq k^{-1} K(t) \tag{4.7}$$

where: with regard to the basic model, the production rate Q is introduced once again as the third state variable (along with the stock of capital assets K and equity X; $Q_0 \leq k^{-1} K_0$), and furthermore, the growth of the production rate $\dot{Q}$ becomes the third control variable (in addition to the investment rate I and the dividend rate D).

---

[1]This can be proved mathematically by deriving up the necessary conditions for this problem and investigating which paths satisfy the transversality conditions.

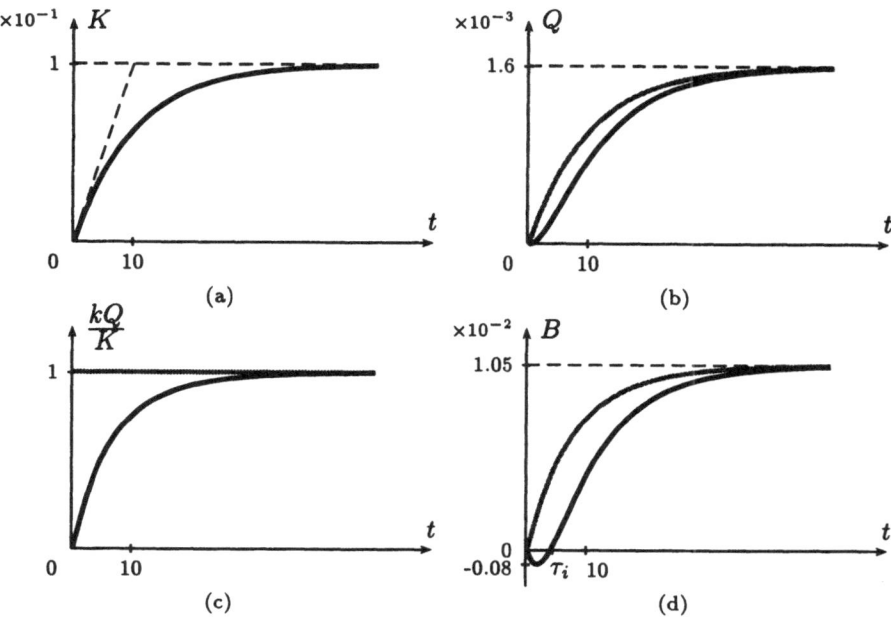

Figure 4.1 Response of (a) stock of capital assets, (b) production rate, (c) utilization rate and (d) operating income to a stepwise increase in the investment rate at $t = 0$, for both the basic model (grey line) and the model with start-up costs (black line). The parameters and turnover function used are: $\Delta I = 0.01$, $K(0) = Q(0) = 0$; $\vartheta_Q = 3$; $a = 0.1$; $k = 62.5$; $wl = 80$; $S(Q) = 95.263(1 - 0.016Q)Q$. The inversion time is found to be: $\tau_i \approx 3.43$.

Now in principle, the firm is free to choose a production rate lower than is technically possible. Knowing that this possibility is absent in the original model, here only control problems are considered for which an optimal string will consist of paths with at least one of the above two inequality constraints having a positive adjoint variable related[2]. Thus, although $\dot{Q}(t)$ is modelled as the third control variable, its value is fixed by:

$$\dot{Q}(t) = \begin{cases} k^{-1}\big(I(t) - aK(t)\big) & \text{if } Q(t) = k^{-1}K(t) \wedge \dot{K}(t) \le 0; \\ \vartheta_Q^{-1}\big(k^{-1}K(t) - Q(t)\big) & \text{if } Q(t) < k^{-1}K(t) \vee \dot{K}(t) > 0, \end{cases} \tag{4.8}$$

For the utilization rate, the following applies:

$$\frac{kQ(t)}{K(t)} = \min\left\{1, 1 - \frac{\vartheta_q k\dot{Q}(t)}{K(t)}\right\} \tag{4.9}$$

---

[2] A sufficient condition for this is: $S'(k^{-1}K_0) > wl$ which follows directly from the necessary conditions.

so that the utilization rate is less than 100% with an *increasing* production rate, and 100% in all other instances.

Complete formulation of the problem now becomes:

$$\max_{I(t),D(t),\dot{Q}(t)} \left\{ J = \int_0^z e^{-it} D(t)\,dt + e^{-iz} X(z) \right\} \tag{4.10a}$$

$$\dot{K}(t) = I(t) - aK(t), \quad K(0) = K_0 > 0 \tag{4.10b}$$

$$\dot{X}(t) = (1-f)\left\{ S(Q(t)) - wL(t) - aK(t) - rY(t) \right\} - D(t),$$

$$X(0) = X_0 > 0 \tag{4.10c}$$

$$Q(0) = Q_0 \le K_0/k \tag{4.10d}$$

$$L(t) = lQ(t) \tag{4.10e}$$

$$K(t) = X(t) + Y(t) \tag{4.10f}$$

$$Y(t) \ge 0 \tag{4.10g}$$

$$Y(t) \le bX(t) \tag{4.10h}$$

$$Q(t) \le k^{-1}K(t) \tag{4.10i}$$

$$\vartheta_q \dot{Q}(t) + Q(t) \le k^{-1}K(t) \tag{4.10j}$$

$$I(t) \ge 0 \tag{4.10k}$$

$$D(t) \ge 0 \tag{4.10l}$$

For the optimization problem with three pure state constraints (4.10g) to (4.10i) and three mixed constraints (4.10j) to (4.10l), the same assumptions hold as for the basic model in Chapter 3.

4.3   Examination of the paths

4.3.1   Introduction of the adjoint variables

It is shown in Appendix B that the optimization problem (4.10) satifies the required constraint qualification, so that Theorem 2.1 can be retained for deriving the necessary conditions. To this end, Hamiltonian and Lagrangian will be defined as:

$$\mathcal{H}(K, X, Q, I, D, \dot{Q}, \lambda_1, \lambda_2, \lambda_3) = D + \lambda_1 \left[I - aK \right] +$$

$$\lambda_2 \left[(1-f)\{ S(Q) - wlQ - aK - r(K-X)\} - D \right] + \lambda_3 \dot{Q} \tag{4.11}$$

and:

$$\mathcal{L}(K, X, Q, I, D, \dot{Q}, \lambda_1, \lambda_2, \lambda_3, \mu_1, \mu_2, \mu_3, \nu_1, \nu_2, \nu_3) =$$

$$\mathcal{H}(K, X, Q, I, D, \dot{Q}, \lambda_1, \lambda_2, \lambda_3) + \mu_1 I + \mu_2 D +$$

$$\mu_3 [k^{-1} K - Q - \vartheta_Q \dot{Q}] + \nu_1 [K - X] +$$

$$\nu_2 [(1 + b) X - K] + \nu_3 [k^{-1} K - Q] \qquad (4.12)$$

in which:

$\lambda_1(t)$: costate variable of capital assets

$\lambda_2(t)$: costate variable of equity

$\lambda_3(t)$: costate variable of production rate

$\mu_1(t)$: Lagrange multiplier for lower bound of investment rate (4.10k)

$\mu_2(t)$: Lagrange multiplier for lower bound of dividend rate (4.10l)

$\mu_3(t)$: Lagrange multiplier for upper bound of production rate (4.10j)

$\nu_1(t)$: Lagrange multiplier for lower bound of debt (4.10g)

$\nu_2(t)$: Lagrange multiplier for upper bound of debt (4.10h)

$\nu_3(t)$: Lagrange multiplier for upper bound of production rate (4.10i)

Economic interpretation of $\lambda_1(t)$ and $\lambda_2(t)$ have already been given in Chapter 3. For $\lambda_3(t)$, the following applies:

- $\lambda_3(t)$ is the discounted change to t in the maximum attainable value of the objective function, when at t the firm has to acquire k units of capital assets at book value with a production capacity equal to one.

The set of necessary conditions that result after applying Theorem 2.1 is given in Appendix B, where it is shown that they are sufficient as well.

When compared with the basic model presented in Chapter 2, two extra constraints arise, at least one of which has to be active. This means, in principle, that each path for the basic model will split into three paths for the model with start-up costs. The designation of the paths for the latter model comes about in the following way:

path xa if $\mu_3(t) = 0$, $\nu_3(t) > 0$, so that $Q(t) = k^{-1} K(t)$, $\dot{Q}(t) \leq 0$

path xb if $\mu_3(t) > 0$, $\nu_3(t) = 0$, so that $Q(t) \leq k^{-1} K(t)$, $\dot{Q}(t) \geq 0$

path xc if $\mu_3(t) > 0$, $\nu_3(t) > 0$, so that $Q(t) = k^{-1} K(t)$, $\dot{Q}(t) = 0$

Table 4.1 The fourteen paths which may appear in an optimal string for the model with start-up costs. The last column contains the conditions, if any, that must apply.

	μ_1	μ_2	μ_3	ν_1	ν_2	ν_3	
path 2b	0	+	+	+	0	0	
path 3a	+	0	0	+	0	+	only when $i < (1-f)r$
path 3b	+	0	+	+	0	0	only when $i < (1-f)r$
path 4a	0	0	0	+	0	+	only when $i < (1-f)r$
path 4c	0	0	+	+	0	+	only when $i < (1-f)r$
path 6b	0	+	+	0	+	0	
path 7a	+	0	0	0	+	+	only when $i > (1-f)r$
path 7b	+	0	+	0	+	0	only when $i > (1-f)r$
path 8a	0	0	0	0	+	+	only when $i > (1-f)r$
path 8c	0	0	+	0	+	+	only when $i > (1-f)r$
path 9a	+	+	0	0	0	+	
path 9b	+	+	+	0	0	0	
path 10a	0	+	0	0	0	+	
path 10c	0	+	+	0	0	+	

with $x = 1, \ldots, 12$ being the path numbers from Table 3.1. Of these thirtysix paths, six will drop out in advance, namely, the paths with $\mu_1(t)$, $\mu_3(t)$ and $\nu_3(t)$ positive ('path xc' with x uneven); for, a situation where $\mu_3(t)$ ànd $\nu_3(t)$ are both positive implies that $\dot{Q}(t) = \dot{K}(t) = 0$, so that $I(t) = aK(t) \geq 0$ and $\mu_1(t) = 0$.

In Appendix B, it is shown that sixteen of the remaining thirty paths can be eliminated immediately from taking part in any optimal string. Table 4.1 contains the fourteen paths which may be feasible for an optimal solution. In the next subsection some of the paths are examined further, afterwards, a case study is given.

4.3.2   Further examination of the stationary paths

Four paths imply that $\dot{K}(t) = \dot{X}(t) = \dot{Q}(t) = 0$ and they will be called stationary paths; e.g. paths 4c and 8c by definition, as well as paths 4a and 8a, because the optimization problem is autonomous. These four paths are explained below. For the related calculations, consult Appendix B.

Firstly, the situation of $i < (1-f)r$, i.e. relatively cheap equity, is considered. For a sufficiently distant planning horizon, the optimal dynamic strategy is recognized by a stationary final stage with financing entirely provided from equity and full utilization of the capital assets[3], that is to say: $K(t) = X(t) = kQ(t) = kQ(\tau)$ for $t \in [\tau, z]$, in which τ is the instant of time when the stationary final stage is reached. Developing the necessary conditions for paths 4a and 4c produces the following results. On path 4a the production rate equals:

$$Q(\tau) = (S')^{-1}\left(wl + \left(a + \frac{i}{1-f} \right) k \right) \tag{4.13}$$

On path 4c, these expressions will apply:

$$\mu_3(t) = (1-f)\left\{ S'(Q(\tau)) - wl - \left(a + \frac{i}{1-f} \right) k \right\} \frac{1 - e^{-i(z-t)}}{i\vartheta_Q} \tag{4.14}$$

$$\nu_3(t) = (1-f)\left(a + \frac{i}{1-f} \right) k - \mu_3(t) \tag{4.15}$$

So that $\mu_3(t) > 0$ stands for $t \in (\tau, z)$, the following must hold:

$$Q(\tau) < (S')^{-1}\left(wl + \left(a + \frac{i}{1-f} \right) k \right) \tag{4.16}$$

So that $\nu_3(t) > 0$ stands for $t \in (\tau, z)$, it is sufficient when $\lim_{t\downarrow\tau} \nu_3(t) \geq 0$, which implies:

$$Q(\tau) \geq (S')^{-1}\left(wl + \left(a + \frac{i}{1-f} \right)\left(1 + \frac{i\vartheta_Q}{1 - e^{-i(z-\tau)}} \right) k \right) \tag{4.17}$$

Thus, the production rate during a stationary final stage will lie in a closed interval with the righthand side of inequality (4.17) as the lower bound and the righthand side of equality (4.13) as the upper bound. The upper bound is independent of time, while, the lower bound increases as $z - \tau$ increases. In the limiting case where $z = \infty$ the following applies:

$$Q(\tau) \geq (S')^{-1}\left(wl + \left(a + \frac{i}{1-f} \right)(1 + i\vartheta_Q) k \right) \tag{4.18}$$

The ultimate size of the production rate during a stationary final stage will also be determined now by the width of the planning horizon and the initial values of the state variables. This is in contrast to the basic model in which the width of the horizon and the initial values of the state variables have no effect on the production rate during a stationary final stage.

In order to obtain a better economic insight into the upper and lower bounds of the production rate during a stationary final stage, they will be determined in different ways by deriving an expression for the marginal change in the

---

[3] Assuming that $S'(0) - wl - ak > \frac{i}{1-f}$.

objective function following a marginal increase or decrease in the production rate respectively.

Consider a firm that is entirely financed from equity at instant t and produces goods with an utilization rate of 100% ($K(t) = X(t) = kQ(t)$). Take J° as the value of the objective function when the production rate during the remaining period $(t, z]$ is maintained at the level it was at instant t; $J^\circ + \partial J_-$ as the value of the objective function in the event of the production rate decreasing instantaneously at instant t by an infinitesimal amount before being maintained as far as z at the new level; $J^\circ + \partial J_+$ as the value of the objective function in the event of the production rate increasing instantaneously at instant t by an infinitesimal amount before being maintained as far as z at the new level, with the annotation that financing is always entirely provided from equity. So that $Q(s) = Q(t) - \partial Q$ and $Q(s) = Q(t) + \partial Q$, successively, stand for $s \in (t, z]$, with $\partial Q > 0$, the following must hold:

$$K(s) = K(t) - k\partial Q \tag{4.19}$$

and

$$K(s) = K(t) + k\partial Q + k\vartheta_Q \partial Q \cdot \delta(s - t) \tag{4.20}$$

respectively, where $\delta(s - t)$ is the Dirac Impulse defined by:

$$\delta(s - t) = \lim_{\Delta t \downarrow 0} \Pi(s - t) \tag{4.21}$$

with:

$$\Pi(s - t) = \begin{cases} 0 & \text{if } s - t \leq 0 \\ \frac{1}{\Delta t} & \text{if } 0 < s - t < \Delta t \\ 0 & \text{if } s - t \geq \Delta t \end{cases} \tag{4.22}$$

For the case of a marginal decrease in the production rate, the following static relationship will be used:

$$Q(t) = k^{-1}K(t) \tag{4.23}$$

The marginal variation in the objective function discounted to t is now equivalent to:

$$e^{it}\partial J_- = \left(1 - e^{-i(z-t)}\right) k\partial Q +$$

$$- (1 - f)\left\{\frac{S'(Q(t)) - wl}{k} - a\right\}\left(\frac{1 - e^{-i(z-t)}}{i}\right) k\partial Q \tag{4.24}$$

The first term is the difference between the increase in dividend at t, because an amount $k\partial Q$ is released only once, and the decrease in equity at the end of the planning period. The second term is the integral of the discounted differential flow of dividend over the interval $(t, z]$.

For the case of a marginal increase in the production rate, the following dynamic relationship will be used:

$$\vartheta_Q \dot{Q}(t) = k^{-1} K(t) - Q(t) \tag{4.25}$$

The marginal variation in the objective function discounted to t then becomes:

$$e^{it} \partial J_+ = - \left(1 - e^{-i(z-t)} \right) k \partial Q +$$

$$+ (1 - f) \left\{ \frac{S'(Q(t)) - wl}{k} - a \right\} \left(\frac{1 - e^{-i(z-t)}}{i} \right) k \partial Q +$$

$$- \lim_{\Delta t \downarrow 0} \left\{ \left(1 - e^{-i\Delta t} \right) \frac{\vartheta_Q k \partial Q}{\Delta t} \right\} +$$

$$- \lim_{\Delta t \downarrow 0} \left\{ (1 - f) a \left(\frac{1 - e^{-i\Delta t}}{i} \right) \frac{\vartheta_Q k \partial Q}{\Delta t} \right\} \tag{4.26}$$

The first term is now the difference between the decrease in dividend at t, because an amount $k\partial Q$ must be invested, and the increase in equity at the end of the planning period. The second term is the integral of the discounted differential flow of dividend over the interval $(t, z]$, once again. The third and fourth terms follow from the last term in equation (4.20). In the third term, the argument of the limit-operator represents the financing costs ('interest payments') whenever during a period Δt, an amount $\vartheta_Q k \partial Q / \Delta t$ is borrowed from the shareholders, or better stated, is withheld from the dividend distributed to them (against the cost of equity, the discounting rate). In the fourth term the argument of the limit-operator represents the 'depreciation cost' of $\vartheta_Q k \partial Q / \Delta t$ capital assets during a period Δt. Since:

$$\lim_{\Delta t \downarrow 0} \left\{ \frac{1 - e^{-i\Delta t}}{\Delta t} \right\} = i \tag{4.27}$$

the marginal variation in the objective function (discounted to t) resulting from the marginal production increase, now becomes:

$$e^{it} \partial J_+ = - \left(1 - e^{-i(z-t)} \right) k \partial Q +$$

$$+ (1 - f) \left\{ \frac{S'(Q(t)) - wl}{k} - a \right\} \left(\frac{1 - e^{-i(z-t)}}{i} \right) k \partial Q +$$

$$- i \vartheta_Q k \partial Q - (1 - f) a \vartheta_Q k \partial Q \tag{4.28}$$

According to an optimal policy, a firm which at instant t is entirely financed from equity and produces goods with an utilization rate of 100% will maintain the production rate during the remaining period $(t, z]$ at the level it was at instant t, only when neither ∂J_- nor ∂J_+ is positive. Therefore, $K(s) = X(s) = kQ(s) = kQ(t)$ for $s \in (t, z]$ holds, only when:

$$Q(t) \leq (S')^{-1} \left(wl + \left(a + \frac{i}{1-f} \right) k \right) \tag{4.29}$$

ànd

$$Q(t) \geq (S')^{-1} \left(wl + \left(a + \frac{i}{1-f} \right) \left(1 + \frac{i\vartheta_Q}{1 - e^{-i(z-t)}} \right) k \right) \tag{4.30}$$

Inserting $t = \tau$ will give the upper and lower bounds of the production rate during a stationary final stage.

Finally, the situation with $i > (1 - f)r$, i.e. relatively expensive equity, is considered. Given a sufficiently distant planning horizon, the optimal dynamic strategy is now characterized by a stationary final stage with maximum financing from debt and full utilization of the capital assets[4], which is to say that: $K(t) = (1 + b)X(t) = kQ(t) = kQ(\tau)$ for $t \in [\tau, z]$, where τ is the instant of time when the stationary final stage is reached. Developing the necessary conditions for paths 8a and 8c produces the results that follow below. The production rate on path 8a equals:

$$Q(\tau) = (S')^{-1} \left(wl + \left(a + \frac{br}{b+1} + \frac{1}{b+1} \cdot \frac{i}{1-f} \right) k \right) \tag{4.31}$$

and the following inequalities apply for the production rate on path 8c:

$$Q(\tau) < (S')^{-1} \left(wl + \left(a + \frac{br}{b+1} + \frac{1}{b+1} \cdot \frac{i}{1-f} \right) k \right) \tag{4.32}$$

$$Q(\tau) \geq (S')^{-1} \left(wl + \left(a + \frac{br}{b+1} + \frac{1}{b+1} \cdot \frac{i}{1-f} \right) \left(1 + \frac{i\vartheta_Q}{1 - e^{-i(z-t)}} \right) k \right) \tag{4.33}$$

At the limit when $z = \infty$, the following holds:

$$Q(\tau) \geq (S')^{-1} \left(wl + \left(a + \frac{br}{b+1} + \frac{1}{b+1} \cdot \frac{i}{1-f} \right) (1 + i\vartheta_Q) k \right) \tag{4.34}$$

The economic interpretation of the upper and lower bounds of the production rate during a stationary final stage will be completely analogous with the situation in which equity is cheaper than debt.

---

[4] Assuming that: $S'(0) - wl - ak > \frac{1}{1+b} \frac{i}{1-f} + \frac{1}{1+b} r$.

4.4 Case study

In this section, numerical examples for a firm with start-up costs ($\vartheta_Q = 3$) are given, for both $i < (1-f)r$ and $i > (1-f)r$, for both low and high initial stock of capital assets. The same price function is used as was in the case study of Chapter 3:

$$P(Q(t)) = \overline{P}\left(1 - \frac{Q(t)}{\overline{Q}}\right) \tag{4.35}$$

The results are always compared with those for an identical firm without start-up costs, i.e. the basic model of Chapter 3[5].

4.4.1 The case of $i < (1-f)r$

Low initial stock of capital assets. In Figure 4.2, a series of graphs can be seen for the model with start-up costs, when the following initial condition applies: $K_0 = (b+1)X_0 = kQ_0 = 0.0036$. A simple chronological decision rule can be given only after the coupling points τ_1 and τ_4 have been determined. Since the planning horizon also has effect, now, their calculation must take into account the whole strategy from zero to z. This is different from the basic model where the coupling points, in principle, can be determined easily, i.e. successively in chronological order. The start-up costs have great consequences for the firm; for example: the final size of the stock of capital assets is roughly five times less than in the situation without any start-up costs (Figure 3.1). The value of the objective function is 68% less due to those costs (see Figure 4.4(a)).

High initial stock of capital assets. In Figure 4.3, graphs are shown for the model with start-up costs, but this time: $K_0 = (b+1)X_0 = kQ_0 = 0.18$. The differences from the basic model are less spectacular now, this is understandable because start-up costs play no part during a contraction. Crucial to the optimal strategy is the determination of the coupling point τ_1. With start-up costs, the firm begins to make replacement investments earlier; here, an optimal balance must be made between the payment of extra interest charges now and the avoidance of start-up costs later. The maximum value of the objective function is only reduced by 3% (Figure 4.4(b)).

---

[5]The following parameter values are used (see Section 3.4 for descriptions): $a = 0.1$; $b = 2$ (low initial stock of capital assets) or $b = 9$ (high initial stock of capital assets); $f = 0.4$; $i = 0.04$ or $i = 0.08$; $k = 62.5$; $r = 0.1$; $wl = 80$; $z = 50$; $p_0 = 95.263$; $\overline{Q} = 0.0625$; $\Delta t = 0.25$.

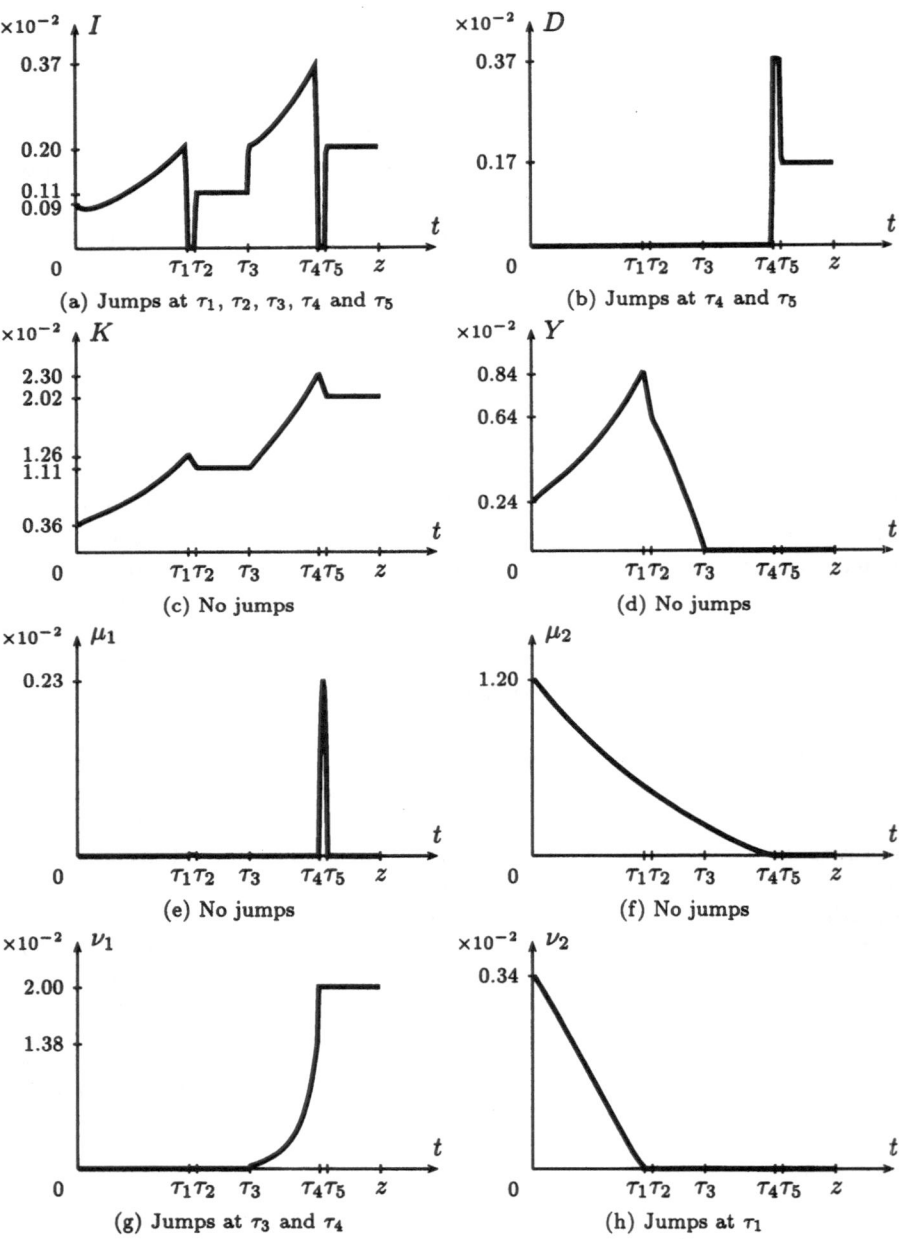

(a) Jumps at τ_1, τ_2, τ_3, τ_4 and τ_5

(b) Jumps at τ_4 and τ_5

(c) No jumps

(d) No jumps

(e) No jumps

(f) No jumps

(g) Jumps at τ_3 and τ_4

(h) Jumps at τ_1

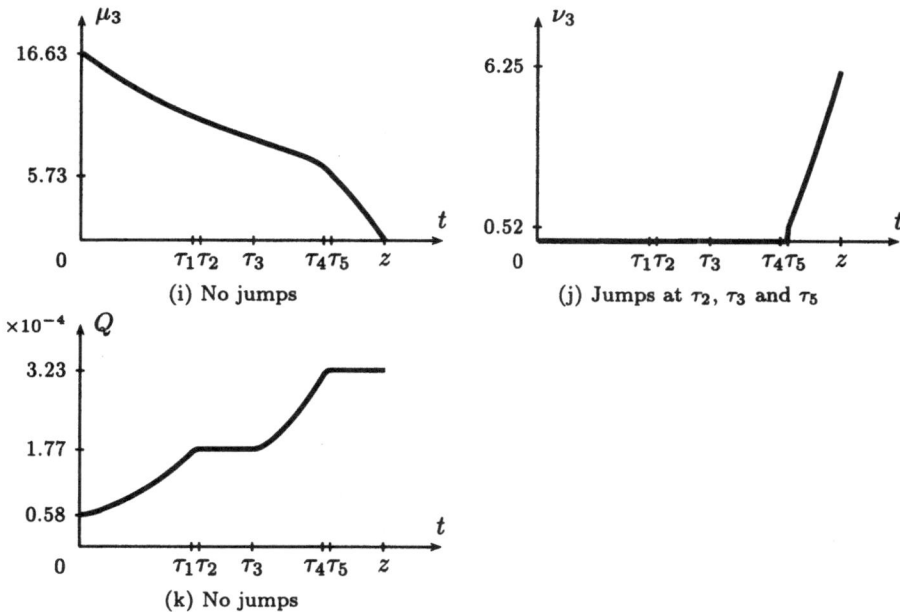

Figure 4.2 Model with start-up costs ($\vartheta_Q = 3$); $i < (1 - f)r$; $K_0 = (1 + b)X_0 = kQ_0$ low. Optimal string of paths: 6bo9bo10co2bo3bo4c.

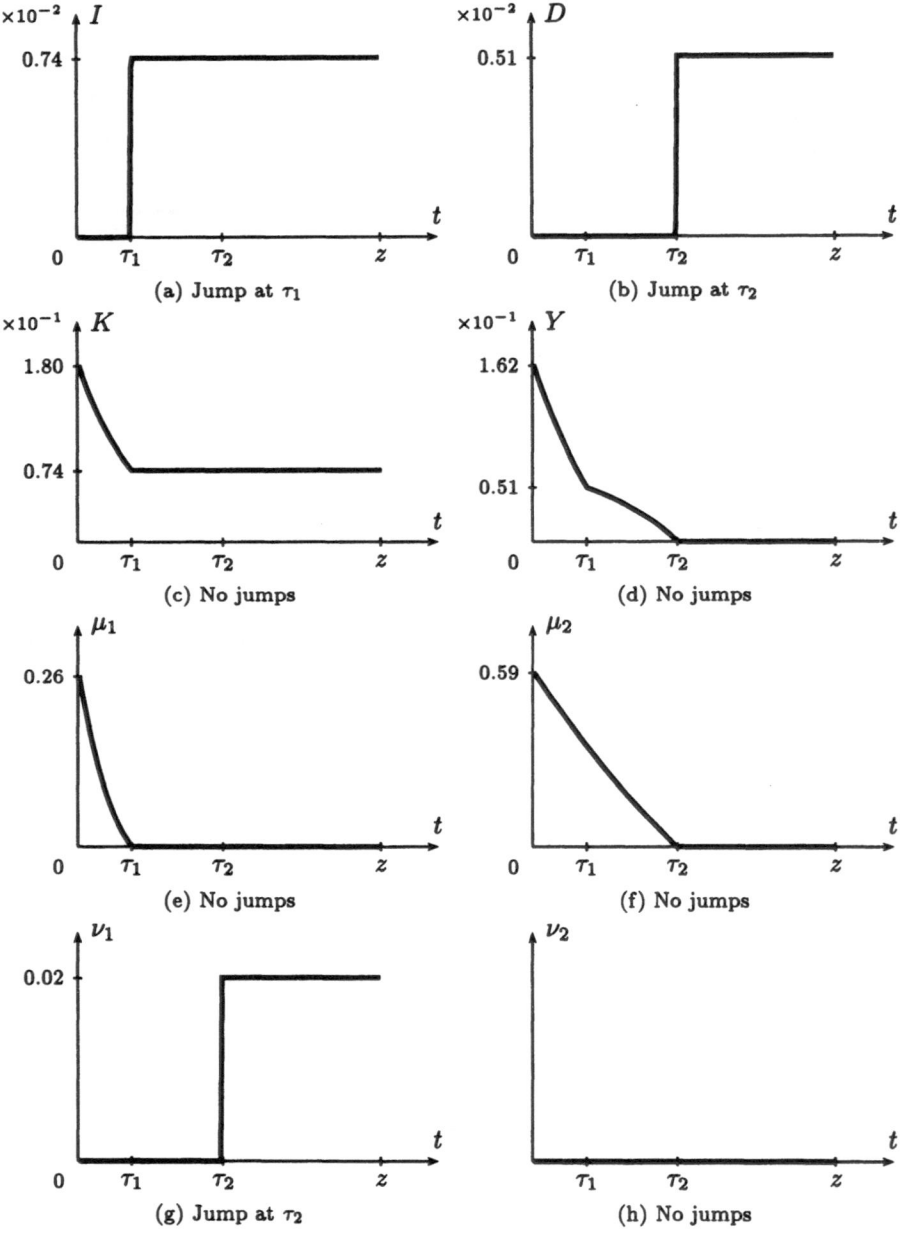

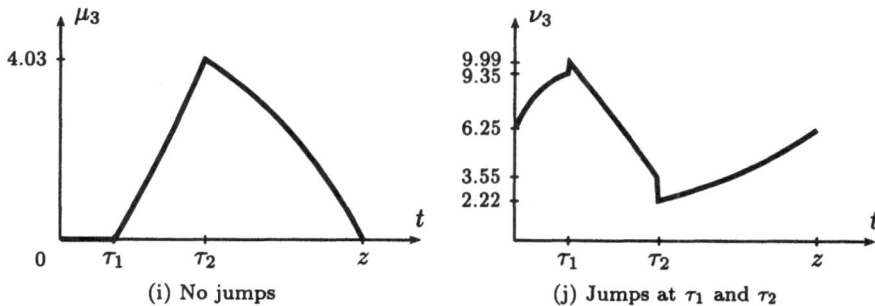

Figure 4.3 Model with start-up costs $(\vartheta_Q = 3)$; $i < (1 - f)r$; $K_0 = (1 + b)X_0 = kQ_0$ high. Optimal string of paths: 9ao10co4c.

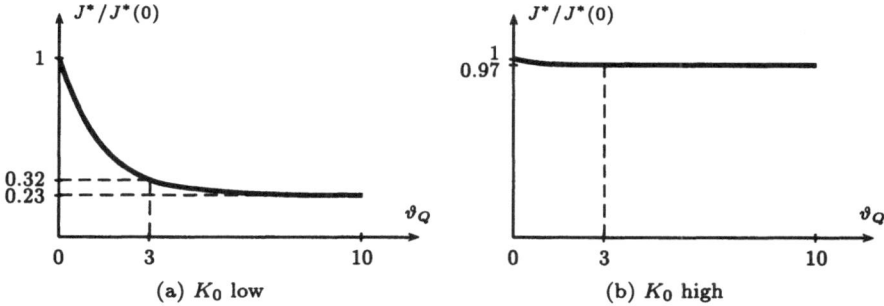

Figure 4.4 Model with start-up costs; $i < (1-f)r$: the maximum value of the objective function J^* as a function of ϑ_Q, where $J^*(0)$ is normalized at unity.

4.4.2 The case of $i > (1 - f)r$

Low initial stock of capital assets. In Figure 4.5, graphs are presented for the model with start-up costs, given that: $K_0 = (b+1)X_0 = kQ_0 = 0.0036$. The firm already finds itself on path 8c at the outset so that, all quantities except μ_3 and ν_3 are stationary.

High initial stock of capital assets. $I(t)$, $D(t)$, $K(t)$, $Y(t)$, $\lambda_i(t)$, $\mu_i(t)$ and $\nu_i(t)$ $(i = 1, 2)$ are identical to the values in the basic model. In Figure 4.6, the results are drawn for $\mu_3(t)$ and $\nu_3(t)$, given that: $K_0 = (b+1)X_0 = kQ_0 = 0.18$.

48   A MODEL WITH START-UP COSTS

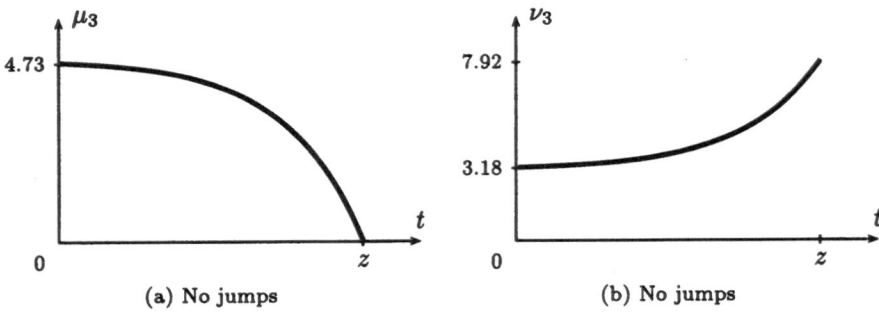

Figure 4.5 Model with start-up costs ($\vartheta_Q = 3$); $i > (1 - f)r$; $K_0 = (1 + b)X_0 = kQ_0$ low. Optimal string of paths: 8c.

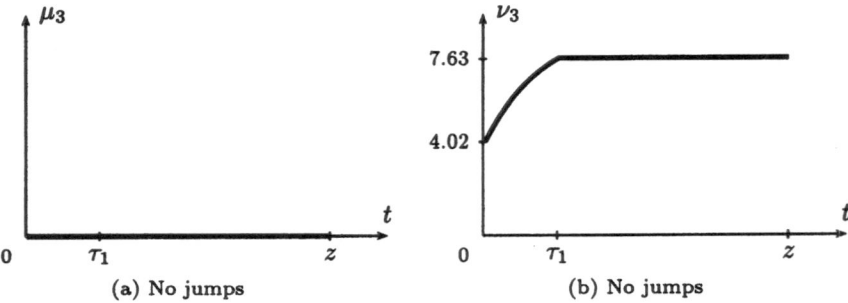

Figure 4.6 Model with start-up costs ($\vartheta_Q = 3$); $i > (1 - f)r$; $K_0 = (1 + b)X_0 = kQ_0$ high. Optimal string of paths: 7ao8a.

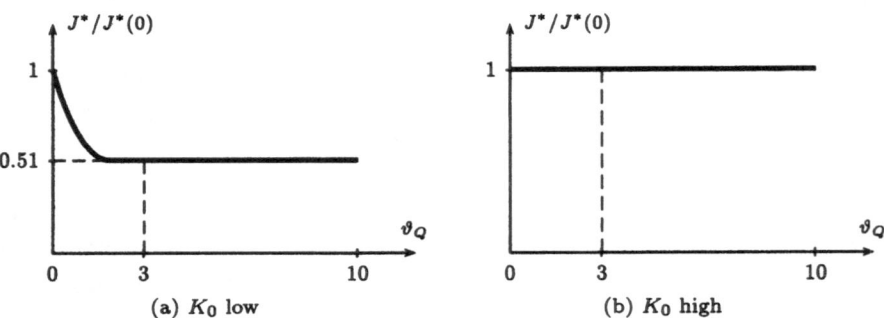

Figure 4.7 Model with start-up costs; $i > (1-f)r$: the maximum value of the objective function J^* as a function of ϑ_Q, where $J^*(0)$ is normalized at unity.

4.5   Conclusions

The existence of start-up costs in the model studied in this chapter makes finding optimal dynamic investment and dividend strategies rather more complicated.

With the basic model, the firm needs to know only the actual values of the state variables at each instant of time in order to make an optimal dynamic decision; the planning horizon z has no effect at all on deciding the investment and dividend policies.

With the model that includes start-up costs, in general at each instant of time t, the firm must review the planning horizon z, or better still, the remaining time $z - t$, when making its decisions. Since cost comes before benefit, for example, a firm that considers expanding its stock of capital assets should ascertain if the remaining period is long enough to recover the extra costs, with future returns discounted against the time preference rate of the shareholder i. Depending on the initial state, this can lead to the final value of the stock of capital assets, the equity and the production rate, as well as, the maximum value of the objective function, all being substantially lower when compared with a similar firm without any start-up costs. In addition to the characteristic time to reach the normal utilization, ϑ_Q, i and z play the most important roles. It can be very useful for the firm to be able to reduce ϑ_Q. In the case of $i = 0$ and $z = \infty$, the final values of the state variables are independent of ϑ_Q and the initial state.

Chapter 5

Models with a Business Cycle

5.1 Introduction

In this chapter, four models of the firm are examined in which an exogenous business cycle is presented by means of an explicitly time-dependent price function. The model described in the next section is actually the basic model from Chapter 3. The other three models have been derived from it, but each contains a different development. The developments are: a variable utilization rate (Section 5.3), a cash balance (Section 5.4) and an inventory of finished goods (Section 5.5), respectively. An interesting feature of these models is that jumps in in the course of the costate variables occur in certain situations. Great emphasis is put on the economic interpretation of those jumps. Finally, in Section 5.6, the most important conclusions are summarized.

5.2 The basic model

5.2.1 Description of the model

Except for the turnover function, or more precisely the price function, this model is identical to the model described in Chapter 3, where the price function only is implicitly time-dependent; whereas here, a business cycle is simulated with the aid of an explicit relationship between price and time. The problem can now be formulated as follows:

$$\max_{I(t),D(t)} \left\{ J = \int_0^z e^{-it} D(t)\, \mathrm{d}t + e^{-iz} X(z) \right\} \tag{5.1a}$$

$$\dot{K}(t) = I(t) - aK(t), \quad K(0) = K_0 > 0 \tag{5.1b}$$

$$\dot{X}(t) = (1 - f)\left\{ S(t, Q(t)) - wL(t) - aK(t) - rY(t) \right\} - D(t),$$

$$X(0) = X_0 > 0 \tag{5.1c}$$

$$Q(t) = k^{-1}K(t) \tag{5.1d}$$

$$L(t) = lQ(t) \tag{5.1e}$$

$$K(t) = X(t) + Y(t) \tag{5.1f}$$

$$Y(t) \geq 0 \tag{5.1g}$$

$$Y(t) \leq bX(t) \tag{5.1h}$$

$$I(t) \geq 0 \tag{5.1i}$$

$$D(t) \geq 0 \tag{5.1j}$$

with:

$$S(t, Q(t)) = Q(t)P(t, Q(t)) \tag{5.2}$$

and:

$$P(t, Q(t)) = \begin{cases} \overline{P}\left[e^{-gt}\dfrac{Q(t)}{Q} \right]^{-\frac{1}{\varepsilon}} & \text{if } 0 \leq t \leq \tau_u; \\[2mm] \overline{P}\left[e^{-m\tau_u}e^{(m-g)t}\dfrac{Q(t)}{Q} \right]^{-\frac{1}{\varepsilon}} & \text{if } \tau_u < t \leq \tau_d; \\[2mm] \overline{P}\left[e^{m(\tau_d-\tau_u)}e^{-gt}\dfrac{Q(t)}{Q} \right]^{-\frac{1}{\varepsilon}} & \text{if } \tau_d < t \leq z. \end{cases} \tag{5.3}$$

The price function is based on research by Nickell [1974] and Leban & Lesourne [1980, 1983], and was also used by Van Hilten [1991][1]. It is assumed here that the price elasticity of demand is greater than unity, i.e. $\varepsilon > 1$; also, that the growth and contraction rate of the price function are greater than zero, i.e. $g > 0$ and $m - g > 0$, respectively (see Figure 5.1 too). With this price function, the following equation applies:

$$\frac{\partial S}{\partial K}(t, Q(t)) = (1 - \varepsilon^{-1})k^{-1}P(t, Q(t)) \tag{5.4}$$

so that the price per product unit is constant on paths 4, 8 and 10.

For the definition of the adjoint variables, the table showing the feasible paths and the economic interpretation of a number of those paths, refer to Chapter 3. For the set of necessary conditions, see Appendix A.

In the following sections, the numerical results obtained from two case studies with the basic model are presented, namely, one for the case of cheap equity, $i < (1 - f)r$, and one for the case of expensive equity, $i > (1 - f)r$, where only

---

[1]Note that p cannot be differentiated in τ_u and τ_d. The Maximum Principle requires that all functions that arise from the model be continuously differentiable; however Van Hilten shows that the discontinuities of $\frac{\partial p}{\partial t}$ cause no problems

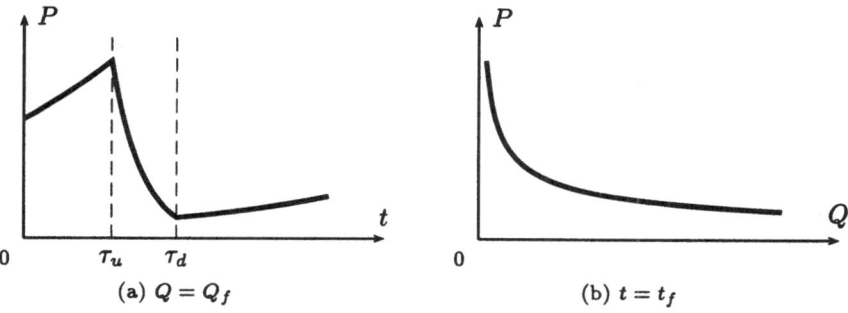

Figure 5.1 The price function (the suffix f means fixed).

the m-values, and thus the depths of the recessions, differ from one another[2]. At the start, the firm is either on path 4 in the case of $i < (1 - f)r$, or on path 8 in case of $i > (1 - f)r$, so that K_0 and X_0, respectively, are fixed:

$$K_0 = X_0 = k\overline{Q} \left[\frac{wl + \left(a + \frac{i}{1-f}\right)k}{\overline{P}(1 - \varepsilon^{-1})} \right]^{-\varepsilon} \tag{5.5}$$

and:

$$K_0 = (1 + b)X_0 = k\overline{Q} \left[\frac{wl + \left(a + \frac{1}{1+b}\frac{i}{1-f} + \frac{b}{1+b}r\right)k}{\overline{P}(1 - \varepsilon^{-1})} \right]^{-\varepsilon} \tag{5.6}$$

Parameter values are such that $(1 - f)(wlk^{-1} + a)\varepsilon^{-1} + i - g(1 - \varepsilon^{-1}) \geq 0$, so the firm can continue following either path 4 or 8 in the boom phase. The inequality stems from the requirement that $O_{vi}(t, K(t)) \geq (a + g)K(t)$ on path 4, and $O_{vi}(t, K(t)) \geq \left[a + g + b((1 - f)r - g)(1 + b)^{-1}\right]K(t)$ on path 8, with $K(t) = K_0 e^{gt}$. Further $(1 - f)wlk^{-1} - af > 0$ holds, so that a situation with a negative operating cash flow before interest cannot be excluded beforehand. For mathematical reasons, $(a + g)\varepsilon^{-1} \neq a + i$.

A recession is called *moderate* when paths 4 and 8 are no longer feasible during the recession; thus when $m > a + g$. Moreover, when the model of the firm is under optimal dynamic control, should the operating cash flow during a certain period around τ_d become less than zero, in which case equity is cheaper than debt, or less than $\frac{ab}{1+b}K(t)$, in the opposite case, then the recession is

---

[2]The other parameter values are: $i = 0.04$ or $i = 0.08$; $a = 0.1$; $b = 2$; $f = 0.4$; $k = 62.5$; $r = 0.1$; $wl = 80$; $z = 70$; $\overline{P} = 20$; $\overline{Q} = 1$; $g = 0.04$; $\varepsilon = 2$; $\tau_u = 20$; $\tau_d = 35$. In principle, the parameters are the same as those of the case study in Chapter 3 except for the business cycle parameters. (See Section 3.4).

severe. For the boundary value of m that distinguishes between a moderate and a severe recession, no analytical expression as a function of the model parameters exist.

The four case studies that follow all refer to a severe recession and they are especially interesting, because jumps occur in the course of the costate variables, which can be explained in economic terms. Since they are important quantities in this chapter, again the definitions of the operating cash flow before and after interest payments are given. Now, these have become explicitly time-dependent when compared with the corresponding definitions in Chapter 3. The operating cash flow before interest is defined as:

$$O_{vi}\big(t,K(t)\big) = (1-f)\left\{\frac{1}{k}P\left(t,\frac{K(t)}{k}\right) - \frac{wl}{k} + \frac{af}{1-f}\right\}K(t) \qquad (5.7)$$

and the operating cash flow (after interest) as:

$$O_{ni}\big(t,K(t),Y(t)\big) = O_{vi}\big(t,K(t)\big) - (1-f)rY(t) \qquad (5.8)$$

Leading from the above definition, the following expression for the partial derivative of the cash flow before interest with respect to the capital assets applies:

$$\frac{\partial O_{vi}}{\partial K}\big(t,K(t)\big) = (1-f)\left\{\frac{1-\varepsilon^{-1}}{k}P\left(t,\frac{K(t)}{k}\right) - \frac{wl}{k} + \frac{af}{1-f}\right\} \qquad (5.9)$$

This magnitude will appear frequently in later relationships for the costate variables.

5.2.2 Severe recession in case of $i < (1-f)r$ and $m < m^\star$

The meaning of $m^\star$ in the heading of this subsection will become clear after awhile. Figure 5.2 shows the graphs of optimal $I(t)$, $D(t)$, $K(t)$, $Y(t)$, $\mu_j(t)$ and $\nu_j(t)$ $(j=1,2)$, where $m = 0.3268$. The course of the costate variables is not presented explicitly, because $\lambda_1(t) = -\mu_1(t)$ and $\lambda_2(t) = 1 + \mu_2(t)$ apply for them here (see the necessary conditions in Appendix A). Now, a short explanation of the solution follows: at the start, the firm is on path 4 and it could remain there during the expansion period. However, during the recession, path 4 implies negative investing or, in other words, selling capital assets against book value. This is not allowed in the model. Consequently, the firm will have stopped investing already before τ_u and thus will leave path 4: so, an optimal balance must be made between the lack of income now and the savings of overcapacity costs later. Once the optimal value of τ_1 is known, the optimal strategy from 0 to z can be calculated in a single forward run and can be included in a simple decision rule. In Appendix C, a set of equations is given from which τ_1 and the other coupling points can be solved iteratively. The decision rule reads as follows:

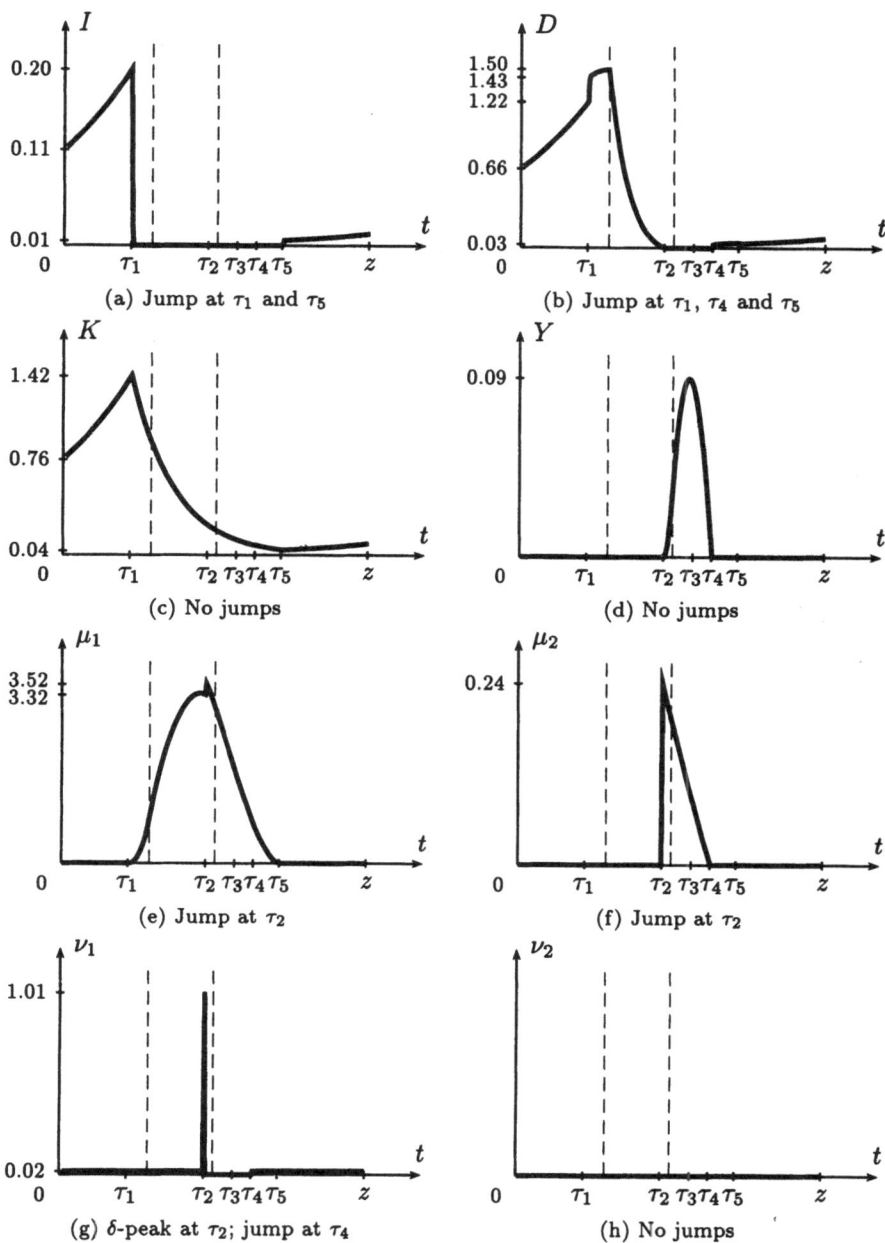

Figure 5.2 Solution of the basic model for a severe recession in the case of $i < (1-f)r$ and $m < m^\star$. The broken lines indicate the successive peak and trough in the business cycle. Optimal string of paths: 4-3⋆9o3-4. ($\Delta t = 0.25$)

1. Follow path 4 until τ_1.

2. Stop investing and pay out all the operating cash flow as dividend until it becomes negative at τ_2 (path 3).

3. Stop paying out dividend and attract debt necessary in order to pay wages and interest until a certain instant after the bottom of the recession when the operating cash flow becomes positive. Then, use it completely in order to pay off debt, which is achieved at τ_4 (path 9)[3].

4. Pay out all the operating cash flow as dividend until at τ_5 path 4 is reached (path 3).

5. Follow path 4 until z.

From Figure 5.2, it appears that a discontinuity occurs at τ_2 in both μ_1 and μ_2; therefore in the costate variables λ_1 and λ_2 too. The jumps result from a δ-peak at that time in the course of ν_1. Since Figure 5.2 gives the results for the time discretized variant of the time continuous optimization problem, for a certain discretization step, the peak in ν_1 indeed has a finite height, but this height will increase with ever smaller discretization steps, so that the surface under the peak (height $\times$ discretization stepsize) converges to the value of the jump height parameter $\eta_1(\tau_2)$. According to the necessary conditions (Appendix A) the jumps in λ_1 and λ_2, as a result of a δ-peak in ν_1, are just as high but in the opposite direction. This is logical because ν_1 is related to the constraint $K(t) - X(t) \geq 0$: an extra unit of capital assets creates just as much space down to the lower bound as that removed by an extra unit of equity.

Verheyen [1992] gives an economic explanation of the jump in λ_2 by considering the development of λ_2 over time. This is repeated below, after which the same is done for λ_1.

The course of λ_2
In general, the value of a costate variable is equal to the change in the maximum attainable value of the objective function caused by a marginal increase in the corresponding state variable. In this model, $\lambda_2(t)$ corresponds to the state variable $X(t)$. Hence, in order to interpret the development of λ_2, the change in the objective function due to an additional increase in equity at each instant of time, needs to be considered.

Period $[0, \tau_2)$, string of paths 4-3:

$$\lambda_2(t) = 1 \tag{5.10}$$

---

[3]When $(a+g)\varepsilon^{-1} - a - (1-f)r < 0$, such as for the parameter set used here, in principle, it is possible that the amount of debt 'explodes'; for the growth rate of the interest charges $(1-f)r$ is greater than the growth rate of the turnover directly after the end of the recession: $(a+g)\varepsilon^{-1} - a$. The case studies here have been chosen in order to prevent that from happening.

One extra unit of equity is used to pay out dividend. Therefore, the objective function will increase by one unit.

Period $\langle \tau_2, \tau_4]$, path 9:

$$\lambda_2(t) = e^{((1-f)r-i)(\tau_4-t)} \tag{5.11}$$

When the firm has one extra unit of equity at its disposal, it can reduce its debt, needed to finance wages and interest, by a single unit. Thus, at τ_4 the firm can pay out an amount of extra dividend equal to $e^{(1-f)r(\tau_4-t)}$, bearing in mind that $Y(t) = 0$ for $t > \tau_4$. Since the value of the costate variable is measured at an instant of time t, the extra dividend at τ_4 must be discounted to t, so that the above expression for $\lambda_2(t)$ can be obtained.

Period $[\tau_4, z]$, string of paths 3-4:

$$\lambda_2(t) = 1 \tag{5.12}$$

Once again, the extra unit of equity will be used to pay out dividend.

The course of λ_1

In the following test, $\lambda_1(t)$ will be interpreted as described in Chapter 3, thus, as the change in the maximum attainable value of the objective function discounted to t, when the firm has to acquire a unit of capital assets at instant t. For certain cases, $\lambda_1(t)$ could also be interpreted as the net present value of an *extra* investment of one unit of capital assets at that instant of time t ('net present value of marginal investment', see Kort [1989]).

The relationships shown below can easily be derived from the necessary conditions (Appendix A) using the expressions developed previously for $\lambda_2(t)$.

Period $[0, \tau_1]$, path 4:

$$\lambda_1(t) = 0 \tag{5.13}$$

The requirement that the firm must acquire one unit of capital assets at instant t is not imperative, because at t the firm is already investing 'voluntarily'.

Period $[\tau_1, \tau_2)$, path 3:

$$\lambda_1(t) = -1 + \int_t^{\tau_2} \frac{\partial O_{vi}}{\partial K}(s, K(s)) e^{-(a+i)(s-t)} ds +$$

$$e^{-i(\tau_4-t)} \int_{\tau_2}^{\tau_4} \frac{\partial O_{vi}}{\partial K}(s, K(s)) e^{-a(s-t)} e^{(1-f)r(\tau_4-s)} ds +$$

$$\int_{\tau_4}^{\tau_5} \frac{\partial O_{vi}}{\partial K}(s, K(s)) e^{-(a+i)(s-t)} ds + e^{-(a+i)(\tau_5-t)} \tag{5.14}$$

The acquisition of the unit of capital assets is financed from equity and thus is at the expense of the dividend paid out at instant t (first term). The second term is the discounted differential dividend flow between t and τ_2, as a result of the unit of capital assets being acquired at instant t; this will decrease due to wastage according to $e^{-a(s-t)}$. The third term is the discounted reduction in the dividend paid out at τ_4. For debt at instant τ_4 has increased by an amount equal to the integral of this third term as a result of the unit of capital assets acquired at t. The fourth term is analogous with the second. The final term is the discounted reduction in the investments expenditure at τ_5 which benefits the dividend paid out.

Period $\langle \tau_2, \tau_4]$, path 9:

$$\lambda_1(t) = -e^{-i(\tau_4-t)} \left[e^{(1-f)r(\tau_4-t)} - \right.$$

$$\left. \int_t^{\tau_4} \frac{\partial O_{vi}}{\partial K}(s, K(s)) e^{-a(s-t)} e^{(1-f)r(\tau_4-s)} ds \right] +$$

$$\int_{\tau_4}^{\tau_5} \frac{\partial O_{vi}}{\partial K}(s, K(s)) e^{-(a+i)(s-t)} ds + e^{-(a+i)(\tau_5-t)} \tag{5.15}$$

The firm must finance the unit of capital assets from debt, resulting in an increase in debt at τ_4 by an amount equal to the expression between square brackets. Its redemption is at the expense of the dividend paid out. The last two terms are interpreted as previously.

Period $[\tau_4, \tau_5]$, path 3:

$$\lambda_1(t) = -1 + \int_t^{\tau_5} \frac{\partial O_{vi}}{\partial K}(s, K(s)) e^{-(a+i)(s-t)} ds + e^{-(a+i)(\tau_5-t)} \tag{5.16}$$

The unit of capital assets is financed from equity and thus is at the expense of the dividend paid out (first term). Again, the last two terms can be interpreted as before.

Period $[\tau_5, z]$, path 4:

$$\lambda_1(t) = 0 \tag{5.17}$$

Interpretation is analogous with the first period.

Now the course of the costate variables has been given, expressions for the jumps at τ_2 can be derived directly:

$$\lambda_1(\tau_2^+) - \lambda_1(\tau_2^-) = 1 - e^{((1-f)r-i)(\tau_4-\tau_2)} \tag{5.18}$$

$$\lambda_2(\tau_2^+) - \lambda_2(\tau_2^-) = e^{((1-f)r-i)(\tau_4-\tau_2)} - 1 \tag{5.19}$$

This is consistent with the remark made earlier about the relative direction and height of the jumps in the costate variables.

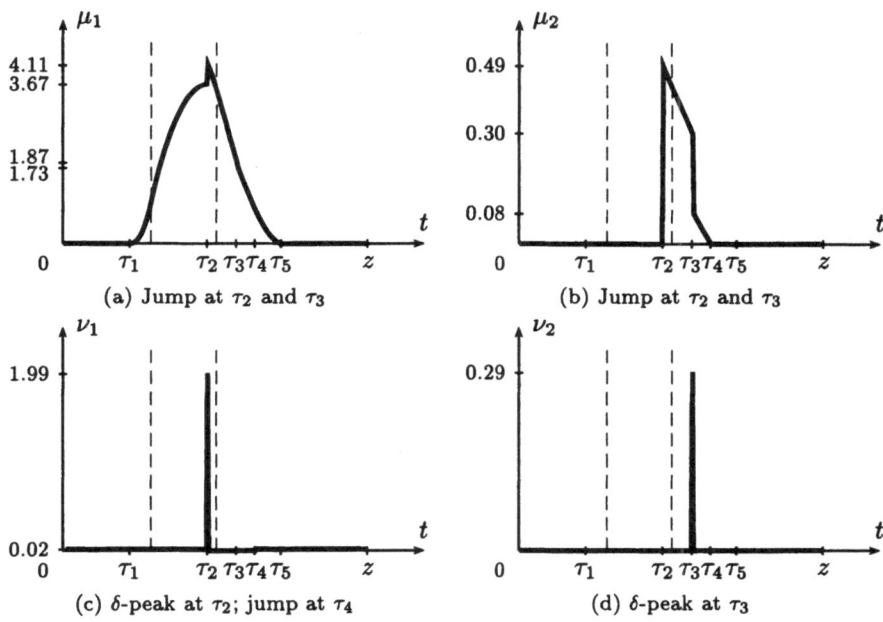

Figure 5.3 Solution of the basic model for a severe recession in the case of $i < (1 - f)r$ and $m > m^\star$. The broken lines indicate the successive peak and trough in the business cycle. Optimal string of paths: 4-3*9*9o3-4. ($\Delta t = 0.25$)

5.2.3 Severe recession in the case of $i < (1 - f)r$ and $m > m^\star$

In Figure 5.3, the graphs of optimal $\mu_j(t)$ and $\nu_j(t)$ ($j = 1, 2$) are presented for $m = 0.3276$. Graphs of $I(t)$, $D(t)$, $K(t)$ and $X(t)$ for this situation are omitted because they cannot be distinguished from the corresponding graphs in Figure 5.2. The crucial difference from the solution of the previous situation is implied in the optimal instant of stopping investments, τ_1. For $m = 0.3268$, the τ_1 found is a *free* optimum, i.e. stopping investments infinitesimally earlier or later does not necessarily lead to exceeding one or more of the bounds, but in any case, no higher value of the objective function will be involved. For $m = 0.3276$, the τ_1 found is a *boundary* optimum for which continuing to invest for an infinitesimally longer time will definitely result in a higher value of the objective function, but with due observance of the other bounds, will inevitably lead to exceeding the upper bound of debt at τ_3, and therefore is not permitted.

So that from a certain value of m the upper bound $Y(t) = bX(t)$ becomes active for exactly one instant of time (τ_3) with a value of $\tau_1 > 0$, the following condition must be satisfied (see its derivation in Appendix C):

$$\frac{wlk^{-1} + a + \frac{i}{1-f}}{(1-\varepsilon^{-1})(wlk^{-1} - \frac{af}{1-f} + \frac{b}{1+b}(\frac{a}{1-f} + r))} > 1 \tag{5.20}$$

Subsequently, the meaning of $m^\star$ becomes clear - it is the boundary value of m where the upper bound of debt just is active at τ_3. Later, it will be shown how to find this particular value by iteration. The value of $m^\star$ is not the boundary value for the firm's bankruptcy, as long as the firm still invests in the initial stage ($\tau_1 > 0$).

The fact that τ_1 is a boundary optimum now, makes the iterative determination of the coupling points much simpler than when compared with the case of $m < m^\star$. In Appendix C it is explained how this comes about and the values obtained this way are presented for the parameter set used here.

Figure 5.3 makes it clear that now two jumps appear in the course of the costate variables, at instants τ_2 and τ_3. The jump at τ_2 is again caused by a δ-peak in the course of ν_1, the jump at τ_3 by a δ-peak in the course of ν_2. From the necessary conditions it appears that a δ-peak in ν_2 causes λ_1 and λ_2, respectively, to jump in the opposite direction with the heights of these jumps in the ratio of $1 : (1 + b)$. This is logical because ν_2 is related to the constraint $(1 + b)X(t) - K(t) \geq 0$: an extra unit of equity creates $(1 + b)$ times as much space down to the lower bound as that removed by an extra unit of capital assets.

Once again, the course of the costate variables is described below, followed by expressions for the different jumps.

The course of λ_2

Apart from τ_3, because there λ_2 is also discontinuous now, the same relationships apply as those given for the case of $m < m^\star$, on the understanding that to the expression for the period $\langle \tau_2, \tau_3 \rangle$ a positive contribution:

$$\Phi\chi(t)e^{i(t-\tau_1)} \tag{5.21}$$

must be added, for which an explanation follows now.

When the firm has one extra unit of equity available somewhere in the period $\langle \tau_2, \tau_3 \rangle$, it can not only reduce its debt by one unit leading to an increase in the dividend paid out at τ_4 (such as in the case of $m < m^\star$), but additionally, it can anticipate investing more at τ_1 without implying violation of the upper bound of debt at τ_3. Since τ_1 is a boundary optimum, as stated before, this will cause an positive extra contribution to the maximum attainable value of the objective function.

In order to obtain an expression for that contribution, it must be calculated *how much* more the firm can invest at τ_1 so that, the upper bound of debt at τ_3 again becomes momentarily active (but not exceeded), knowing that it will obtain one extra unit of equity at t. This amount being a function of t represented by $\chi(t)$, comes to:

$$\chi(t) = -e^{(1-f)r(\tau_3-t)}\left[\int_{\tau_2}^{\tau_3}\frac{\partial O_{vi}}{\partial K}(s,K(s))e^{-a(s-\tau_1)}e^{(1-f)r(\tau_3-s)}ds + \right.$$

$$\left.\frac{b}{1+b}e^{-a(\tau_3-\tau_1)}\right]^{-1} \tag{5.22}$$

A comprehensive derivation is given in Appendix C.

The extra investment $\chi(t)$ at τ_1 produces a return of $\Phi\chi(t)$, discounted to τ_1, with:

$$\Phi = -1 + \int_{\tau_1}^{\tau_2}\frac{\partial O_{vi}}{\partial K}(s,K(s))e^{-(a+i)(s-\tau_1)}ds +$$

$$e^{-i(\tau_4-\tau_1)}\int_{\tau_2}^{\tau_4}\frac{\partial O_{vi}}{\partial K}(s,K(s))e^{-a(s-\tau_1)}e^{(1-f)r(\tau_4-s)}ds +$$

$$\int_{\tau_4}^{\tau_5}\frac{\partial O_{vi}}{\partial K}(s,K(s))e^{-(a+i)(s-\tau_1)}ds + e^{-(a+i)(\tau_5-\tau_1)} \tag{5.23}$$

Logically, this is the expression for $\lambda_1(\tau_1)$ in the case of $m < m^\star$, bearing in mind that it no longer equals zero, but has a positive value now, for τ_1 is a boundary optimum. Discounting to the instant of time t then leads to the additional contribution (5.21) which increases much faster with rising m than the extra dividend paid out at τ_4, and consequently, will dominate this extra dividend completely for sufficiently large m-values.

Furthermore, it is clear that the opportunity of investing more at τ_1 will disappear should the extra unit of equity become available outside the period $\langle\tau_2,\tau_3\rangle$.

The course of λ_1

Apart from τ_3, because there λ_1 is also discontinuous now, the same relationships apply as those given for the case of $m < m^\star$, on the understanding that the expressions for the period $[\tau_1,\tau_3\rangle$ must be reduced by the following positive amount:

$$\Phi\xi(t)e^{i(t-\tau_1)} \tag{5.24}$$

Here, $\xi(t)$ plays a similar role as $\chi(t)$ did previously. When the firm acquires a unit of capital assets at instant $t \in \langle\tau_1,\tau_3\rangle$, at τ_1, in anticipation, it must invest less by an amount of $\xi(t)$, otherwise, the upper bound of debt at τ_3 will be exceeded inevitably. For the period $[\tau_1,\tau_2\rangle$, the following applies:

$$\xi(t) = e^{a(t-\tau_1)} \tag{5.25}$$

which can be seen directly. Using this expression, $\lambda_1(t)$ can be written for the period $[\tau_1, \tau_2)$ more simply as:

$$\lambda_1(t) = e^{(a+i)(t-\tau_1)} - \int_{\tau_1}^{t} \frac{\partial O_{vi}}{\partial K}(s, K(s))e^{(a+i)(t-s)}ds - 1 \tag{5.26}$$

For the period $\langle \tau_2, \tau_3 \rangle$ the following expression has been derived in Appendix C:

$$\xi(t) = - \left[e^{(1-f)r(\tau_3-t)} - \int_{t}^{\tau_3} \frac{\partial O_{vi}}{\partial K}(s, K(s))e^{-a(s-t)}e^{(1-f)r(\tau_3-s)}ds - \right.$$

$$\frac{b}{1+b}e^{-a(\tau_3-t)} \Bigg] \left[\int_{\tau_2}^{\tau_3} \frac{\partial O_{vi}}{\partial K}(s, K(s))e^{-a(s-\tau_1)}e^{(1-f)r(\tau_3-s)}ds + \right.$$

$$\left. \frac{b}{1+b}e^{-a(\tau_3-\tau_1)} \right]^{-1} \tag{5.27}$$

From the above relationships for $\lambda_1(t)$ and $\lambda_2(t)$, the following expressions for the jumps can be found directly[4]:

$$\lambda_1(\tau_2^+) - \lambda_1(\tau_2^-) = 1 - e^{((1-f)r-i)(\tau_4-\tau_2)} - \Phi\chi(\tau_2)e^{i(\tau_2-\tau_1)} \tag{5.28}$$

$$\lambda_1(\tau_3^+) - \lambda_1(\tau_3^-) = \frac{\Phi\chi(\tau_3)e^{i(\tau_3-\tau_1)}}{b+1} \tag{5.29}$$

$$\lambda_2(\tau_2^+) - \lambda_2(\tau_2^-) = e^{((1-f)r-i)(\tau_4-\tau_2)} + \Phi\chi(\tau_2)e^{i(\tau_2-\tau_1)} - 1 \tag{5.30}$$

$$\lambda_2(\tau_3^+) - \lambda_2(\tau_3^-) = -\Phi\chi(\tau_3)e^{i(\tau_3-\tau_1)} \tag{5.31}$$

This is consistent with the previous observations about relative directions and heights of the jumps in the costate variables.

Finally in this subsection, it should be mentioned that $m^\star$ can be found iteratively by determining the coupling points for different m-values as described in Appendix C and subsequently calculating the value of Φ. Only for $m = m^\star$ is Φ equal to zero, whilst for $m < m^\star$, $\Phi < 0$ and for $m > m^\star$, $\Phi > 0$. So, it can be found that $m^\star = 0.3257$ (all figures being significant) for the set of parameters used here.

5.2.4   Severe recession in the case of $i > (1-f)r$ and $m < m^\circ$

The meaning of m° is equivalent to that of $m^\star$ previously, which will soon become clear. Figure 5.4 shows the graphs of optimal $I(t)$, $D(t)$, $K(t)$, $Y(t)$, $\mu_j(t)$ and $\nu_j(t)$ $(j = 1, 2)$ with $m = 0.3240$. Further, $\lambda_1(t) = -\mu_1(t)$ applies again, likewise, $\lambda_2(t) = 1+\mu_2(t)$. The following comments apply to the solution: at the start, the firm is on the 'ideal' path 8 and it could remain there during

---

[4]Verify that: $\xi(\tau_2^+) = \chi(\tau_2^+) + e^{-a(\tau_2-\tau_1)}$ and $\xi(\tau_3^-) = \chi(\tau_3^-)/(1+b)$.

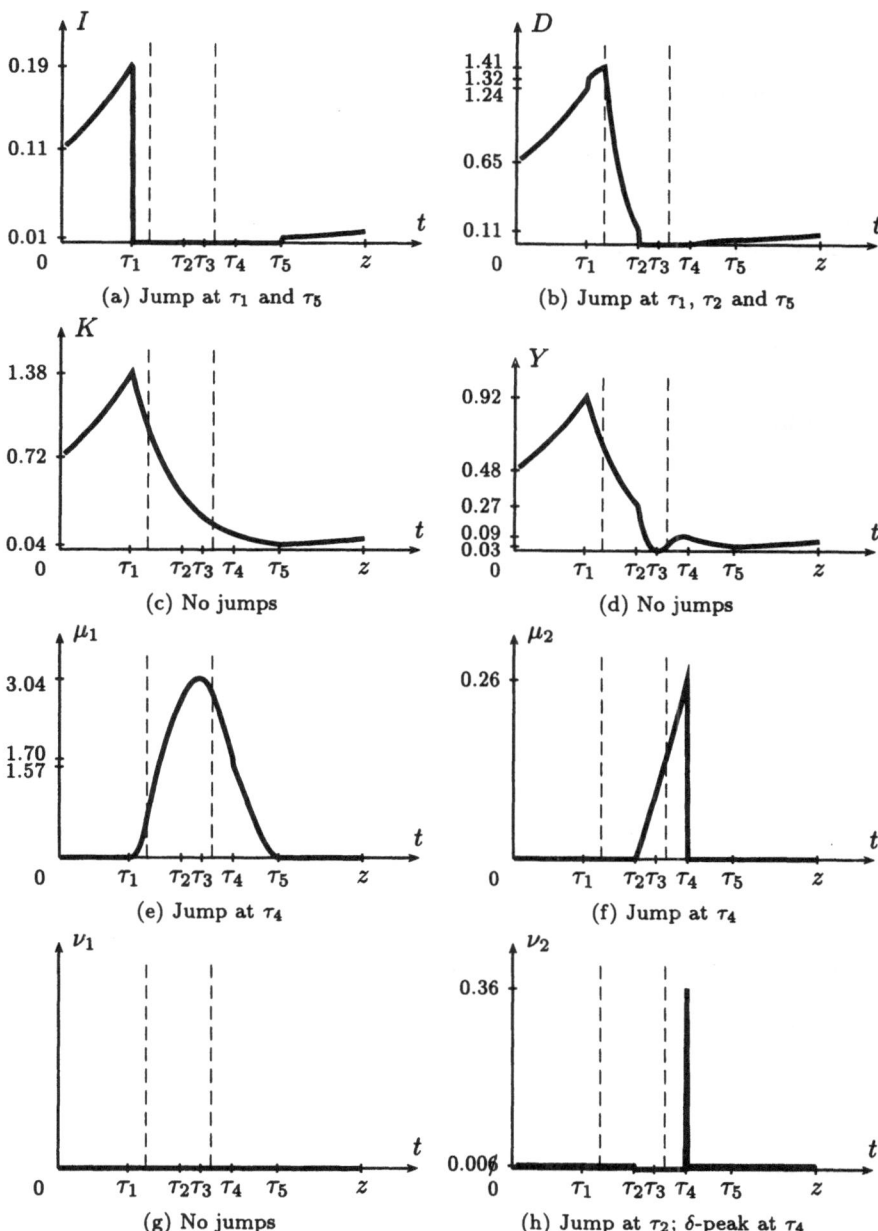

Figure 5.4 Solution of the basic model for a severe recession in the case of $i > (1 - f)r$ and $m < m^\circ$. The broken lines indicate the successive peak and trough in the business cycle. Optimal string of paths: 8-7∘9⋆7-8. ($\Delta t = 0.25$)

the expansion period. However during the recession, path 8 implies negative investing, or in other words, selling of capital assets against book value. As this is not permitted in the model, the firm will already have stopped investing before τ_u and consequently will have left path 8: an optimal balance has to be made here between lacking income now and preventing overcapacity costs later. In principle, once the optimal value of τ_1 is known, the optimal value of τ_2 is fixed: the firm chooses the instant to stop paying out dividend in order to create borrowing capacity so that, at τ_4, the instant after the end of the recession when the upper bound of debt is reached again, the operating cash flow exactly covers the obligatory redemption of debt; stopping later inevitably leads to the upper bound of debt being exceeded. Only when the optimal value of τ_2 is known too, can the optimal strategy from 0 to z be calculated in a single forward run and included in a simple decision rule:

1. Follow path 8 until τ_1.

2. Stop investing and use the operating cash flow for paying out dividend and redeeming debt until τ_2, so that the amount of debt remains maximal (path 7).

3. Stop distributing dividend and use the operating cash flow completely for paying off debt until the operating cash flow becomes negative at τ_3[5]. Attract debt necessary to pay wages and interest until the operating cash flow becomes positive shortly before τ_4. Then, use it completely in order to redeem debt until at τ_4 the amount of debt has become maximal with an operating cash flow that exactly covers the obligatory redemption of debt (path 9).

4. Use the operating cash flow for distributing dividend and redeeming debt, so that the amount of debt remains maximal, until at τ_5 path 8 is reached.

5. Follow path 8 until z.

In Appendix C a set of equations is given from which the coupling points can be determined iteratively. From Figure 5.4, it appears that a discontinuity occurs at τ_4 in the course of the costate variables, caused by a δ-peak in the course of ν_2 at that instant of time.

The course of λ_2

Again, the course of λ_2 will be explained in economic terms by considering the change in the objective function as a result of an additional increase in equity at each instant of time.

---

[5]The operating cash flow during a severe recession does not become negative by definition; for this reason, m must lie above a certain boundary value which is greater than the boundary value between a moderate and a severe recession.

Period $[0, \tau_2]$, string of paths 8-7:

$$\lambda_2(t) = 1 \tag{5.32}$$

An extra unit of equity is used to pay out dividend; therefore the objective function increases by one unit.

Period $[\tau_2, \tau_4)$, path 9:

$$\lambda_2(t) = e^{(i-(1-f)r)(t-\tau_2)} \tag{5.33}$$

When the firm has one extra unit of equity available at instant t, it is able to pay off one unit of debt. Consequently, it can anticipate paying out at τ_2 an amount of $e^{-(1-f)r(t-\tau_2)}$ as extra dividend. That will produce an extra unit of debt at t which is exactly paid off, so that the amount of debt after t will stay the same as in the original situation. Since the value of the costate variables are measured at instant t, the extra dividend paid out at τ_2 must be discounted to t in order to get the expression for $\lambda_2(t)$ above.

Period $\langle \tau_4, z]$, string of paths 7-8:

$$\lambda_2(t) = 1 \tag{5.34}$$

Once again the extra unit of equity will be used to distribute dividend.

The course of λ_1

$\lambda_1(t)$ is again interpreted as the change in the maximum attainable value of the objective function discounted to t when the firm has to acquire a unit of capital assets at t. The relationships presented below can be derived via the necessary conditions in Appendix A using the expressions for $\lambda_2(t)$ above.

First, the following definition is given:

$$y = \frac{b}{1+b}(a + (1-f)r) \tag{5.35}$$

Period $[0, \tau_1]$, path 8:

$$\lambda_1(t) = 0 \tag{5.36}$$

The requirement that the firm must acquire one unit of capital assets at instant t is not imperative, because at t the firm is already investing 'voluntarily'.

Period $[\tau_1, \tau_2]$, path 7:

$$\lambda_1(t) = \frac{-1}{1+b} + \int_t^{\tau_2} \left\{ \frac{\partial O_{vi}}{\partial K}(s, K(s)) - y \right\} e^{-(a+i)(s-t)} ds -$$

$$e^{-i(\tau_2 - t)} \left[\frac{b}{1+b} e^{-a(\tau_2 - t)} - \right.$$

$$\int_{\tau_2}^{\tau_4} \frac{\partial O_{vi}}{\partial K}(s,K(s))e^{-a(s-t)}e^{-(1-f)r(s-\tau_2)}ds -$$

$$\left. \frac{b}{1+b}e^{-a(\tau_4-t)}e^{-(1-f)r(\tau_4-\tau_2)} \right] +$$

$$\int_{\tau_4}^{\tau_5} \left\{ \frac{\partial O_{vi}}{\partial K}(s,K(s)) - y \right\} e^{-(a+i)(s-t)}ds + \frac{e^{-(a+i)(\tau_5-t)}}{1+b} \qquad (5.37)$$

The purchase of one unit of capital assets is financed from equity and debt in the ratio of $1 : (1+b)$ (first term). The second term is the discounted differential dividend flow between t and τ_2 following from the unit of capital assets acquired at instant t which decreases due to wastage according to $e^{-a(s-t)}$. So that the firm precisely reaches the upper bound of debt at τ_4, such that $O_{vi}(\tau_4,K(\tau_4)) = yK(\tau_4)$, it is forced to distribute less dividend at τ_2. The expression between square brackets represents this decrease in the dividend being distributed at τ_2. The fourth term is analogous with the second term. The last term is the discounted decrease in the investments expenditure at τ_5 which benefits the dividend paid out.

Period $[\tau_2,\tau_4)$, path 9:

$$\lambda_1(t) = -e^{i(t-\tau_2)}\left[e^{-(1-f)r(t-\tau_2)} - \right.$$

$$\int_{t}^{\tau_4} \frac{\partial O_{vi}}{\partial K}(s,K(s))e^{-a(s-t)}e^{-(1-f)r(s-\tau_2)}ds -$$

$$\left. \frac{b}{1+b}e^{-a(\tau_4-t)}e^{-(1-f)r(\tau_4-\tau_2)} \right] +$$

$$\int_{\tau_4}^{\tau_5} \left\{ \frac{\partial O_{vi}}{\partial K}(s,K(s)) - y \right\} e^{-(a+i)(s-t)}ds + \frac{e^{-(a+i)(\tau_5-t)}}{1+b} \qquad (5.38)$$

The firm must finance the unit of capital assets entirely from debt. So that the firm again precisely reaches the upper bound of debt at τ_4, such that $O_{vi}(\tau_4,K(\tau_4)) = yK(\tau_4)$, it is forced to distribute less dividend at τ_2 (expression between square brackets). Interpretation of the last two terms is the same as before.

Period $\langle\tau_4,\tau_5]$, path 7:

$$\lambda_1(t) = \frac{-1}{1+b} +$$

$$\int_{t}^{\tau_5} \left\{ \frac{\partial O_{vi}}{\partial K}(s,K(s)) - y \right\} e^{-(a+i)(s-t)}ds + \frac{e^{-(a+i)(\tau_5-t)}}{1+b} \qquad (5.39)$$

The unit of capital assets is financed from equity and debt in the ratio of $1 : (1 + b)$ (first term). The last two terms are interpreted as in the previous periods.

Period $[\tau_5, z]$, path 8:

$$\lambda_1(t) = 0 \tag{5.40}$$

Interpretation is analogous with the first period.

Now, the jumps in the costate variables at τ_4 can be derived easily:

$$\lambda_1(\tau_4^+) - \lambda_1(\tau_4^-) = \left(e^{(i-(1-f)r)(\tau_4-\tau_2)} - 1 \right) / (1 + b) \tag{5.41}$$

$$\lambda_2(\tau_4^+) - \lambda_2(\tau_4^-) = 1 - e^{(i-(1-f)r)(\tau_4-\tau_2)} \tag{5.42}$$

5.2.5   Severe recession in the case of $i > (1 - f)r$ and $m > m°$

In Figure 5.5, the graphs of optimal $\mu_j(t)$ and $\nu_j(t)$ $(j = 1, 2)$ are presented for $m = 0.3245$. Graphs of $I(t)$, $D(t)$, $K(t)$ and $X(t)$ for this situation are omitted because they cannot be distinguished from the corresponding graphs in Figure 5.4. The crucial difference from the solution in the previous situation again is implied in the optimal instant of stopping investments, τ_1. The τ_1 found for $m = 0.3240$ is a *free* optimum, which is to say that continuing to invest for infinitesimally longer or shorter will not necessarily lead to exceeding one or more bounds, but in any case, no higher value of the objective function will result. For $m = 0.3245$, τ_1 is found to be a *boundary* optimum, where it applies that an infinitesimally longer period of continuing to invest definitely implies a higher value of the objective function, but with due observance of the other bounds, it will inevitably lead to exceeding the lower bound of debt at τ_3, and therefore is not permitted. A mathematical foundation for this statement can be found in Section 1.6 of Appendix C.

In comparison with the previous subsection, now at τ_3, the instant when the cash flow becomes negative, debt has been paid off completely and consequently, the borrowing capacity is maximal: $bX(\tau_3)$. So that from a certain value of m the lower bound $Y(t) = 0$ becomes active for exactly one instant of time (τ_3) with a value of $\tau_1 > 0$, the following condition must be satisfied (derivation in Appendix C):

$$\frac{wlk^{-1} + a + \frac{1}{1+b}\frac{i}{1-f} + \frac{b}{1+b}r}{(1 - \varepsilon^{-1})(wlk^{-1} - \frac{af}{1-f} + \frac{b}{1+b}(\frac{a}{1-f} + r))} > 1 \tag{5.43}$$

Subsequently, the meaning of $m°$ becomes clear - it is the boundary value of m where the lower bound of debt just becomes active at τ_3. Later, it will be described how this particular value can be found by iteration. The value $m°$ is not the boundary value for the firm's bankruptcy, as long as the firm still invests in the initial stage.

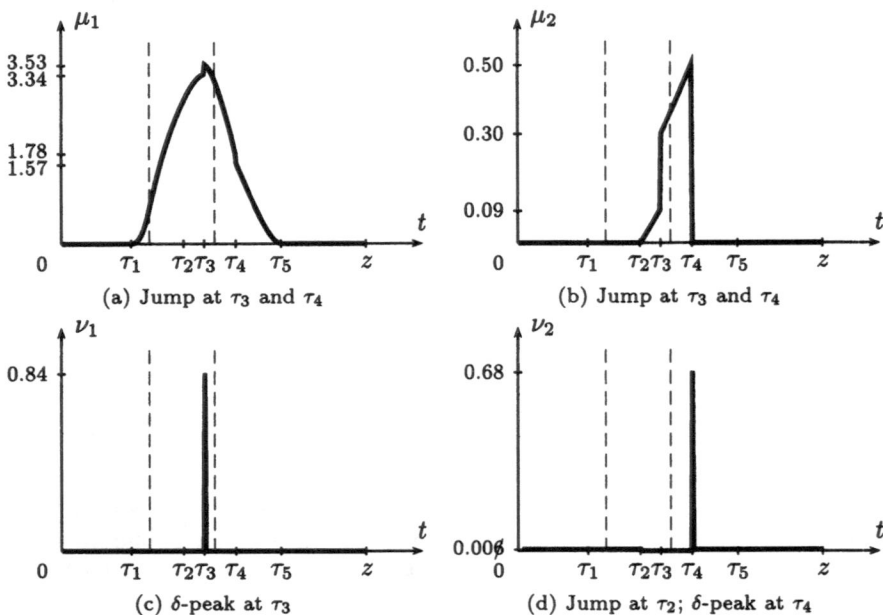

Figure 5.5 Solution of the basic model for a severe recession in the case of $i > (1-f)r$ and $m > m°$. The broken lines indicate the successive peak and trough in the business cycle. Optimal string of paths: 8-7∘9⋆9⋆7-8. ($\Delta t = 0.25$)

The fact that τ_1 is a boundary optimum now, once again makes the iterative determination of the coupling points much simpler than when compared with the case of $m < m°$. In Appendix C it is explained how this comes about and the values obtained this way are presented for the parameter set used here.

Figure 5.5 makes it clear that there are two jumps now in the course of the costate variables, at instants τ_3 and τ_4. The jump at τ_4 once again is caused by a δ-peak in the course of ν_2 and the jump at τ_3 by a δ-peak in the course of ν_1.

The course of λ_2

Apart from τ_3, because there λ_2 is also discontinuous now, the same relationships apply as those given for the case of $m < m°$, on the understanding that to the expression for the period $\langle \tau_3, \tau_4 \rangle$ a positive contribution:

$$\Psi \varrho(t)e^{i(t-\tau_1)} \tag{5.44}$$

must be added, for which an explanation follows now.

When the firm has an extra unit of equity available somewhere in the period $\langle \tau_3, \tau_4 \rangle$, it can pay out extra dividend at τ_2 - just like the case of $m < m°$. Due to that, the lower bound of debt at τ_3 will no longer be attained. Therefore, with due observance of the other bounds, the firm can anticipate investing more at τ_1 without implying violation of the lower bound of debt at τ_3. Since τ_1 is a boundary optimum, as mentioned before, this causes a positive extra contribution to the maximum attainable value of the objective function.

In order to arrive at an expression for this contribution, it must be calculated *how much* more the firm can invest at τ_1 so that, with the lower bound of debt momentarily active at τ_3, the upper bound of debt will be reached again tangentially at τ_4, knowing that it will have available at instant t one extra unit of equity. This amount, being a function of t represented by $\varrho(t)$, comes to:

$$\varrho(t) = -e^{(1-f)r(\tau_4-t)} \left[\int_{\tau_3}^{\tau_4} \frac{\partial O_{vi}}{\partial K}(s, K(s)) e^{-a(s-\tau_1)} e^{(1-f)r(\tau_4-s)} ds + \right.$$

$$\left. \frac{b}{1+b} e^{-a(\tau_4-\tau_1)} \right]^{-1} \tag{5.45}$$

A comprehensive derivation is given in Appendix C.

The extra investment $\varrho(t)$ at τ_1 produces a return of $\Psi \varrho(t)$, discounted to τ_1, with:

$$\Psi = \frac{-1}{1+b} + \int_{\tau_1}^{\tau_2} \left\{ \frac{\partial O_{vi}}{\partial K}(s, K(s)) - y \right\} e^{-(a+i)(s-\tau_1)} ds -$$

$$e^{-i(\tau_2-\tau_1)} \left[\frac{b}{1+b} e^{-a(\tau_2-\tau_1)} - \right.$$

$$\int_{\tau_2}^{\tau_4} \frac{\partial O_{vi}}{\partial K}(s, K(s)) e^{-a(s-\tau_1)} e^{-(1-f)r(s-\tau_2)} ds -$$

$$\left. \frac{b}{1+b} e^{-a(\tau_4-\tau_1)} e^{-(1-f)r(\tau_4-\tau_2)} \right] +$$

$$\int_{\tau_4}^{\tau_5} \left\{ \frac{\partial O_{vi}}{\partial K}(s, K(s)) - y \right\} e^{-(a+i)(s-\tau_1)} ds + \frac{e^{-(a+i)(\tau_5-\tau_1)}}{1+b} \tag{5.46}$$

Logically, this the expression for $\lambda_1(\tau_1)$ in the case of $m < m°$, where it should be noted that it no longer amounts to zero, but has a positive value, for τ_1 is a boundary optimum. Discounting to instant t then leads to the extra contribution in (5.44) which increases much faster with rising m than the extra dividend paid out at τ_2, and consequently, will dominate this extra dividend completely for sufficiently large m-values.

Furthermore, it is clear that the opportunity of investing more at τ_1 will disappear should the extra unit of equity become available outside the period $\langle \tau_3, \tau_4 \rangle$.

The course of λ_1

Apart from τ_3, because there λ_1 is also discontinuous now, the same relationships apply as those given for the case of $m < m^\circ$, on the understanding that the expressions for the period $[\tau_1, \tau_4)$ must be reduced by a positive amount:

$$\Psi \zeta(t) e^{i(t-\tau_1)} \tag{5.47}$$

In this, $\zeta(t)$ plays an equivalent role as $\varrho(t)$ did before. When the firm acquires one unit of capital assets at instant $t \in \langle \tau_1, \tau_4 \rangle$, at τ_1, in anticipation, it must invest less by an amount of $\zeta(t)$, otherwise, with due observance of the other bounds, the lower bound of debt at τ_3 will be exceeded inevitably. For the period $[\tau_1, \tau_3)$, the following applies:

$$\zeta(t) = e^{a(t-\tau_1)} \tag{5.48}$$

which can be seen directly. In Appendix C, it is derived that the following expression applies for the period $\langle \tau_3, \tau_4 \rangle$:

$$\zeta(t) = - \left[e^{(1-f)r(\tau_4-t)} - \int_t^{\tau_4} \frac{\partial O_{vi}}{\partial K}(s, K(s)) e^{-a(s-t)} e^{(1-f)r(\tau_4-s)} ds - \right.$$
$$\left. \frac{b}{1+b} e^{-a(\tau_4-t)} \right] \left[\int_{\tau_3}^{\tau_4} \frac{\partial O_{vi}}{\partial K}(s, K(s)) e^{-a(s-\tau_1)} e^{(1-f)r(\tau_4-s)} ds + \right.$$
$$\left. \frac{b}{1+b} e^{-a(\tau_4-\tau_1)} \right]^{-1} \tag{5.49}$$

From the above relationships for $\lambda_1(t)$ and $\lambda_2(t)$, the expressions below can be found directly for the jumps[6]:

$$\lambda_1(\tau_3^+) - \lambda_1(\tau_3^-) = -\Psi \varrho(\tau_3^+) e^{i(\tau_3-\tau_1)} \tag{5.50}$$

$$\lambda_1(\tau_4^+) - \lambda_1(\tau_4^-) = \frac{e^{(i-(1-f)r)(\tau_4-\tau_2)} + \Psi \varrho(\tau_4^-) e^{i(\tau_4-\tau_1)} - 1}{1+b} \tag{5.51}$$

$$\lambda_2(\tau_3^+) - \lambda_2(\tau_3^-) = \Psi \varrho(\tau_3^+) e^{i(\tau_3-\tau_1)} \tag{5.52}$$

$$\lambda_2(\tau_4^+) - \lambda_2(\tau_4^-) = 1 - e^{(i-(1-f)r)(\tau_4-\tau_2)} - \Psi \varrho(\tau_4^-) e^{i(\tau_4-\tau_1)} \tag{5.53}$$

This is consistent with the previous remarks about relative directions and heights of the jumps in the costate variables.

Finally in this subsection, it should be mentioned that m° can be found iteratively by determining the coupling points for different m-values as described in Appendix C and subsequently calculating the value of Ψ. Only for $m = m^\circ$ is Ψ equal to zero, whilst for $m < m^\circ$, $\Psi < 0$ and for $m > m^\circ$, $\Psi > 0$. So, it can be found that $m^\circ = 0.3227$ (all figures being significant) for the set of parameters used here.

In the sections that follow, some models of the firm are studied all of which contain a different extension with respect to the basic model.

---

[6]Verify that: $\zeta(\tau_3^+) = \varrho(\tau_3^+) + e^{-a(\tau_3-\tau_1)}$ and $\zeta(\tau_4^-) = \varrho(\tau_4^-)/(1+b)$.

5.3   A model with a variable utilization rate

5.3.1   Description of the model

In the basic model of the previous section, the production rate is fully determined by the stock of capital assets:

$$Q(t) = k^{-1}K(t) \tag{5.54}$$

The firm is 'obliged' to make full use of its capital; in other words, the utilization
rate is always equal to 100%. The following expression applies for the necessary
amount of labour:

$$L(t) = lQ(t) = lk^{-1}K(t) \tag{5.55}$$

In this section, it is no longer necessary for the utilization rate to equal unity.
The production rate, along with investments and dividend, will be the third
freely adjustable control variable (within certain bounds); logically, the upper
and lower bound of which are:

$$Q(t) \le k^{-1}K(t) \tag{5.56}$$

and

$$Q(t) \ge 0 \tag{5.57}$$

respectively.

Furthermore, it is assumed that the wage costs remain proportional to the
production rate. Labour can be recruited or dismissed without incurring any
expenses. The complete formulation of the firm model then proceeds in the
following way:

$$\max_{I(t),D(t),Q(t)} \left\{ J = \int_0^z e^{-it} D(t)\,dt + e^{-iz} X(z) \right\} \tag{5.58a}$$

$$\dot{K}(t) = I(t) - aK(t), \quad K(0) = K_0 \tag{5.58b}$$

$$\dot{X}(t) = (1-f)\left\{ S(t,Q(t)) - wL(t) - aK(t) - rY(t) \right\} - D(t),$$

$$X(0) = X_0 \tag{5.58c}$$

$$L(t) = lQ(t) \tag{5.58d}$$

$$K(t) = X(t) + Y(t) \tag{5.58e}$$

$$Y(t) \ge 0 \tag{5.58f}$$

$$Y(t) \le bX(t) \tag{5.58g}$$

$$I(t) \geq 0 \tag{5.58h}$$

$$D(t) \geq 0 \tag{5.58i}$$

$$Q(t) \geq 0 \tag{5.58j}$$

$$Q(t) \leq k^{-1}K(t) \tag{5.58k}$$

It is shown in Appendix C that the optimization problem (5.58) satisfies the required constraint qualification, so that Theorem 2.1 for the derivation of the necessary conditions can be applied. For this purpose, the Hamiltonian and Lagrangian are defined as follows ($\lambda_0 = 1$, see Observation 2.1):

$$\mathcal{H}(t, K, X, I, D, Q, \lambda_1, \lambda_2) = D + \lambda_1[I - aK] +$$

$$\lambda_2\left[(1 - f)\{S(t, Q) - wlQ - aK - r(K - X)\} - D\right] \tag{5.59}$$

and:

$$\mathcal{L}(t, K, X, I, D, Q, \lambda_1, \lambda_2, \mu_1, \mu_2, \mu_3, \mu_4, \nu_1, \nu_2) =$$

$$\mathcal{H}(t, K, X, I, D, Q, \lambda_1, \lambda_2) + \mu_1 I + \mu_2 D +$$

$$\mu_3 Q + \mu_4[k^{-1}K - Q] + \nu_1[K - X] + \nu_2[(1 + b)X - K] \tag{5.60}$$

respectively, where:

$\lambda_1(t)$: costate variable of capital assets

$\lambda_2(t)$: costate variable of equity

$\mu_1(t)$: Lagrange multiplier for lower bound of investment rate (5.58h)

$\mu_2(t)$: Lagrange multiplier for lower bound of dividend rate (5.58i)

$\mu_3(t)$: Lagrange multiplier for lower bound of production rate (5.58j)

$\mu_4(t)$: Lagrange multiplier for upper bound of production rate (5.58k)

$\nu_1(t)$: Lagrange multiplier for lower bound of debt (5.58f)

$\nu_2(t)$: Lagrange multiplier for upper bound of debt (5.58g)

The set of necessary conditions that results from applying Theorem 2.1 is given in Appendix C, where it is shown further that the necessary conditions are sufficient too.

In comparison with the basic model, two extra constraints arise which cannot be active at the same time however (because $K(t) \geq K_0 e^{-at} > 0$). This means that each path of the basic model, in principle, divides into three paths for the model with a variable utilization rate. The designation of the paths for the latter model comes about in the following way:

path xa if $\mu_3(t) = 0 \wedge \mu_4(t) > 0$, so that $Q(t) = k^{-1} K(t)$

path xb if $\mu_3(t) = 0 \wedge \mu_4(t) = 0$, so that $0 \le Q(t) \le k^{-1} K(t)$

path xc if $\mu_3(t) > 0 \wedge \mu_4(t) = 0$, so that $Q(t) = 0$

with: $x = 1, \ldots, 12$ the path numbers from Table 3.1. From the necessary conditions of Appendix C, it follows simply that:

$$\mu_4(t) = \mu_3(t) + (1-f)\left\{\frac{\partial S}{\partial Q}(t, Q(t)) - wl\right\}(1 + \mu_2(t)) \tag{5.61}$$

On the paths xb ($x = 1, \ldots, 12$) therefore, it holds that:

$$\frac{\partial S}{\partial Q}(t, Q(t)) = wl \tag{5.62}$$

Expressed in words: the marginal returns from production are equal to the marginal *variable* costs of production. On paths xa, the marginal returns from production are greater than the marginal variable costs of production; while, on paths xc, they are less ($x = 1, \ldots, 12$). The paths xc, $x = 1, \ldots, 12$ can be excluded since for the price function (5.3), it holds that:

$$\frac{\partial S}{\partial Q}(t, 0) = \infty \tag{5.63}$$

The firm can always adjust its production rate to a positive value so that (5.62) applies, since solving this equation leads to:

$$Q(t) = \overline{Q}\left[\frac{wl}{\overline{P}(1 - \varepsilon^{-1})}\right]^{-\varepsilon}\begin{cases} e^{gt} & \text{if } t \le \tau_u; \\ e^{m\tau_u - (m-g)t} & \text{if } \tau_u \le t \le \tau_d; \\ e^{-m(\tau_d - \tau_u) - gt} & \text{if } t \ge \tau_d. \end{cases} \tag{5.64}$$

One thing and the other means that, from the strict concavity requirement of turnover as a function of the production rate, in an optimal strategy, the operating cash flow before interest is positive throughout the business cycle regardless of the depth of the recession:

$$(1-f)\left\{S(t, Q(t)) - wlQ(t) + \frac{af}{1-f}K(t)\right\} > 0 \tag{5.65}$$

Consquently, it should be noted that definition (5.7) of $O_{vi}(t, K(t))$, as the operating cash flow before interest, here applies only for full utilization of the capital assets. For the model with a variable utilization rate, $Q(t)$, along with t and $K(t)$, formally is the third independent variable which determines the value of the operating cash flow before interest.

In Appendix C, it is shown that half of the twentyfour remaining paths can be excluded once more. Table 5.1 contains the twelve paths which may appear in an optimal string.

Table 5.1 The twelve paths which may appear in an optimal string for the model with a variable utilization rate. The final column contains the conditions, if any, that must apply.

	μ_1	μ_2	μ_3	μ_4	ν_1	ν_2	
path 2a	0	+	0	+	+	0	
path 2b	0	+	0	0	+	0	
path 3a	+	0	0	+	+	0	only when $i < (1-f)r$
path 3b	+	0	0	0	+	0	only when $i < (1-f)r$
path 4a	0	0	0	+	+	0	only when $i < (1-f)r$
path 6a	0	+	0	+	0	+	
path 7a	+	0	0	+	0	+	only when $i > (1-f)r$
path 7b	+	0	0	0	0	+	only when $i > (1-f)r$
path 8a	0	0	0	+	0	+	only when $i > (1-f)r$
path 9a	+	+	0	+	0	0	
path 9b	+	+	0	0	0	0	
path 10a	0	+	0	+	0	0	

In the next subsections, the numerical results of three case studies are discussed. One refers to a moderate recession in the case of equity being cheaper than debt. The other two refer to a moderate and a severe recession, respectively, in the case of equity being more expensive than debt. Possibly with the exception of the m-values, the parameter values are unchanged with respect to the case studies presented in the previous section. This applies for the initial values of the state variables too.

5.3.2 Moderate recession in the case of $i < (1-f)r$

In Figure 5.6, the optimal $D(t)$, $kQ(t)/K(t)$, $\mu_1(t)$ and $\mu_4(t)$ are depicted graphically for $m = 0.4$. The courses of K and I do not deviate principally from those for the basic model in Subsection 5.2.2. Further, $Y(t) = \mu_2(t) = \mu_3(t) = \nu_2(t) = 0$, $\nu_1(t) = (1-f)r - i$ $\lambda_1(t) = -\mu_1(t)$ and $\lambda_2(t) = 1$ hold for the whole planning period. Since the operating cash flow before interest is always positive regardless the value of m, the firm is never forced to attract debt in order to pay wages. This means that here the case of a severe recession does not occur and thus, that the firm will never be bankrupt. The term 'moderate recession' in the heading of this subsection alludes to the occurence of a period where nothing is invested in an optimal strategy (see also Subsection 5.2.1).

The optimal strategy is entirely fixed by the optimal value for τ_1. In Appendix C, a set of equations is given from which the coupling points can be calculated. The decision rule then reads as follows:

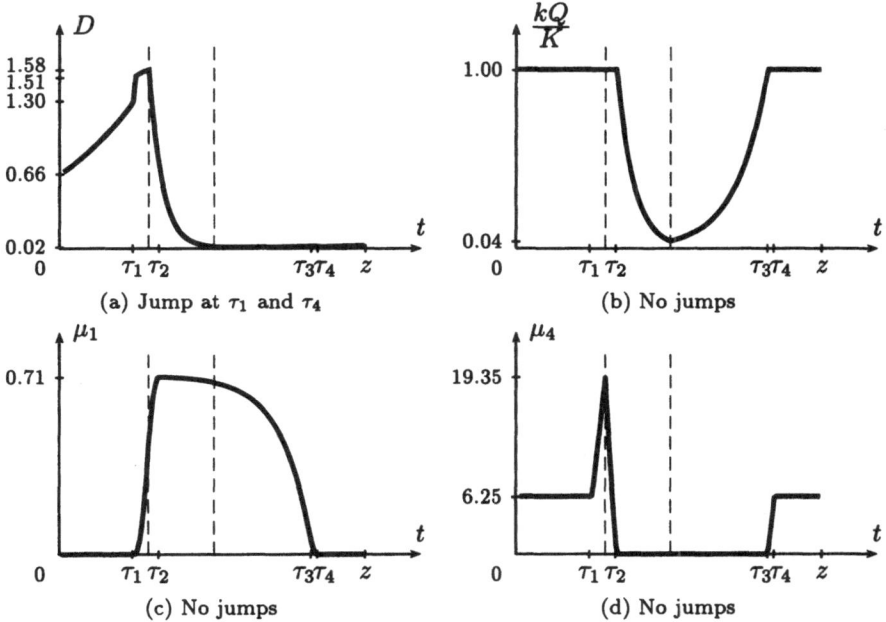

Figure 5.6 Solution of the model with a variable utilization rate for a moderate recession in the case of $i < (1 - f)r$. The broken lines indicate the successive
peak and trough in the business cycle. Optimal string of paths: 4a-3a-3b-
3a-4a. ($\Delta t = 0.5$)

1. Follow path 4a until τ_1.

2. Stop investing and pay out all the operating cash flow as dividend at full
   utilization of the production resources until τ_2 when the marginal returns
   from production become equal to the marginal variable costs (path 3a).

3. Distribute the operating cash flow entirely as dividend at a production
   rate that is adjusted to maintain the equality of marginal returns and
   marginal variable costs, whereby the utilization rate falls at first before
   rising again from τ_d, until τ_3 when full utilization is restored (path 3b).

4. Distribute all the operating cash flow as dividend at full utilization of the
   production resources until path 4a is reached at τ_4 (path 3a).

5. Follow path 4a until z.

Where the course of the costate variables is concerned, it was already estab-
lished that $\lambda_2(t) = 1$ during the entire planning period: one extra unit of equity

at instant t is used directly for distributing dividend. The development of λ_1 over time will be studied next.

The course of λ_1

During the periods $[0, \tau_1]$ and $[\tau_4, z]$, the company is already investing 'voluntarily' so that $\lambda_1(t) = 0$ applies then (path 4a).

Period $[\tau_1, \tau_2]$: path 3a.

$$\lambda_1(t) = -1 + \int_t^{\tau_2} \frac{\partial O_{vi}}{\partial K}(s, K(s)) e^{-(a+i)(s-t)} ds +$$

$$\int_{\tau_2}^{\tau_3} af e^{-(a+i)(s-t)} ds +$$

$$\int_{\tau_3}^{\tau_4} \frac{\partial O_{vi}}{\partial K}(s, K(s)) e^{-(a+i)(s-t)} ds + e^{-(a+i)(\tau_4-t)} \tag{5.66}$$

The unit of capital assets is financed from equity (first term). Between t and τ_2, this unit is fully utilized; consequently the meanwhile familiar expression of the integral of the discounted dividend flow appears (second term). Likewise, the third term is the integral of the discounted dividend flow, but now between τ_2 and τ_3. The difference from the period $[t, \tau_2]$ is that the remainder of the unit acquired is completely unused, so that the operating cash flow, which is distributed entirely as dividend, increases by an amount of $af e^{-a(s-t)}$. The fourth term is analogous with the second term. The last term is the reduction in the investments expenditure at τ_4 which benefits the dividend paid out.

The expressions for the other periods need no further explanation.

Period $[\tau_2, \tau_3]$: path 3b.

$$\lambda_1(t) = -1 + \int_t^{\tau_3} af e^{-(a+i)(s-t)} ds +$$

$$\int_{\tau_3}^{\tau_4} \frac{\partial O_{vi}}{\partial K}(s, K(s)) e^{-(a+i)(s-t)} ds + e^{-(a+i)(\tau_4-t)} \tag{5.67}$$

Period $[\tau_3, \tau_4]$: path 3a.

$$\lambda_1(t) = -1 + \int_t^{\tau_4} \frac{\partial O_{vi}}{\partial K}(s, K(s)) e^{-(a+i)(s-t)} ds + e^{-(a+i)(\tau_4-t)} \tag{5.68}$$

5.3.3 Moderate recession in the case of $i > (1-f)r$

In Figure 5.7, the optimal $D(t)$, $kQ(t)/K(t)$, $\mu_1(t)$ and $\mu_4(t)$ are depicted graphically for $m = 0.34$. The courses of K and I do not principally deviate

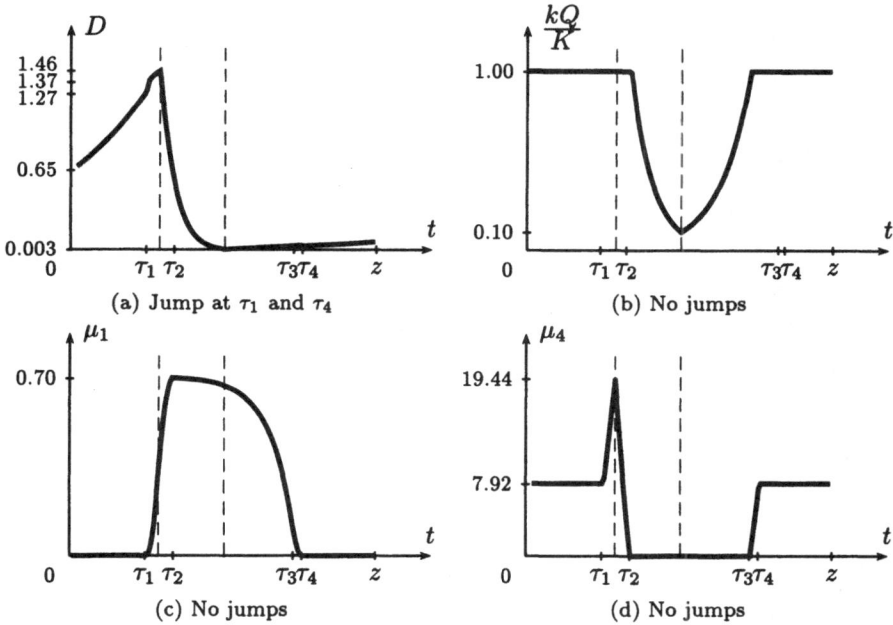

Figure 5.7 Solution of the model with a variable utilization rate for an moderate recession in the case of $i > (1 - f)r$. The broken lines indicate the successive
peak and trough in the business cycle. Optimal string of paths: 8a-7a-7b-
7a-8a. ($\Delta t = 0.5$)

from those for the basic model in Subsection 5.2.4. Furthermore, throughout the whole planning period the following apply: $Y(t) = \frac{b}{1+b}K(t)$, $\mu_2(t) =$
$\mu_3(t) = \nu_1(t) = 0$, $\nu_2(t) = \frac{1}{1+b}(i - (1 - f)r)$, $\lambda_1(t) = -\mu_1(t)$, $\lambda_2(t) = 1$. During
the whole period where nothing is invested the operating cash flow after in-
terest is greater than the mandatory redemption of debt $\frac{ab}{1+b}K(t)$, so that the
firm can continue to distribute dividend (definition of a moderate recession). In
contrast with the case of equity being cheaper than debt, the situation of a severe recession will occur from a certain m-value when equity is more expensive
than debt, as will be shown in the next subsection.

Again, the optimal strategy is entirely fixed by the optimal value for τ_1. In
Appendix C, a set of equations is given from which the coupling points can be
calculated. The decision rule now reads as follows:

1. Follow path 8a until τ_1.

2. Stop investing and use the operating cash flow at full utilization of the
   production resources for distributing dividend and redeeming debt so that

the amount of debt remains maximal, until at τ_2, the marginal returns from production become equal to the marginal variable costs (path 7a).

3. Use the operating cash flow for distributing dividend and redeeming debt so that the amount of debt remains maximal, at a production rate that is adjusted to maintain the equality of marginal returns and marginal variable costs, whereby the utilization rate falls at first before rising again from τ_d, until τ_3 when full utilization is restored (path 7b).

4. Use the operating cash flow at full utilization of the production resources for distributing dividend and redeeming debt so that the amount of debt remains maximal, until path 8a is reached at τ_4 (path 7a).

5. Follow path 8a until z.

Where the course of the costate variables is concerned, again $\lambda_2(t) = 1$ holds during the whole planning period. The development of λ_1 over time is studied below.

The course of λ_1
During the periods $[0, \tau_1]$ and $[\tau_4, z]$, the firm is already investing 'voluntarily' so that $\lambda_1(t) = 0$ applies then (path 8a).
Period $[\tau_1, \tau_2]$: path 7a.

$$\lambda_1(t) = \frac{-1}{1+b} + \int_t^{\tau_2} \left\{ \frac{\partial O_{vi}}{\partial K}(s, K(s)) - y \right\} e^{-(a+i)(s-t)} ds +$$

$$\int_{\tau_2}^{\tau_3} (af - y) e^{-(a+i)(s-t)} ds +$$

$$\int_{\tau_3}^{\tau_4} \left\{ \frac{\partial O_{vi}}{\partial K}(s, K(s)) - y \right\} e^{-(a+i)(s-t)} ds + \frac{e^{-(a+i)(\tau_4-t)}}{1+b} \qquad (5.69)$$

The unit of capital assets is financed from equity and debt in the ratio of $1 : b$ (first term). Between t and τ_2, this unit is fully utilized; consequently the familiar expression for the integral of the discounted dividend flow (second term) will appear. Likewise, the third term is the integral of the discounted dividend flow, but now between τ_2 and τ_3. This differs from the period $[t, \tau_2]$ because the remainder of the unit acquired is completely unused, so that the operating cash flow after mandatory redemption of debt, which is distributed entirely as dividend, increases by an amount of $(af - y)e^{-a(s-t)}$. Interpretation of the fourth term is analogous with that of the second. The last term is the reduction in the investments expenditure at τ_4 which will benefit the dividend paid out.

The expressions for the other periods need no further explanation.

Period $[\tau_2, \tau_3]$: path 7b.

$$\lambda_1(t) = \frac{-1}{1+b} + \int_t^{\tau_3} (af - y)e^{-(a+i)(s-t)}ds +$$

$$\int_{\tau_3}^{\tau_4} \left\{ \frac{\partial O_{vi}}{\partial K}(s, K(s)) - y \right\} e^{-(a+i)(s-t)}ds + \frac{e^{-(a+i)(\tau_4-t)}}{1+b} \qquad (5.70)$$

Period $[\tau_3, \tau_4]$: path 7a.

$$\lambda_1(t) = \frac{-1}{1+b} + \int_t^{\tau_4} \left\{ \frac{\partial O_{vi}}{\partial K}(s, K(s)) - y \right\} e^{-(a+i)(s-t)}ds +$$

$$\frac{e^{-(a+i)(\tau_4-t)}}{1+b} \qquad (5.71)$$

5.3.4 Severe recession in the case of $i > (1-f)r$

In Figure 5.8 the optimal $D(t)$, $Y(t)$, $\mu_1(t)$, $\mu_2(t)$ and $\nu_2(t)$ are depicted graphically for $m = 0.4$. The courses of the other variables are not fundamentally changed with regard to the previous subsection. Once more, the optimal strategy is fixed by the optimal value for the instant when to stop investing, τ_1. Even though the firm has a certain preference for maximal debt financing, it is obliged, given the optimal value for τ_1, to pay off extra debt from a certain instant τ_3 instead of continuing to pay out dividend. The reason is that otherwise the operating cash flow inevitably some time later will not be sufficient to pay off the required minimum amount of debt (bankruptcy).

However, the firm is never forced to redeem its debt completely: since, as recorded earlier, the operating cash flow before interest remains positive all the time, a certain amount of debt can always be present without causing the cash flow after interest to become negative. Therefore, a critical value m° does not exist[7]. In view of the firm being confronted with a rising business cycle during the period $[0, \tau_u]$, which is not effected by the chosen m-value and where the operating cash flow, in principle, is large enough to redeem debt completely, the firm will never go bankrupt no matter how severe the recession.

In Appendix C, a set of equations is given from which the coupling points can be calculated. The decision rule then runs as follows:

1. Follow path 8a until τ_1.

2. Stop investing and use the operating cash flow at full utilization of the production resources for distributing dividend and redeeming debt so that the amount of debt remains maximal, until at τ_2 the marginal returns from production become equal to the marginal variable costs (path 7a).

---

[7] The equality: $\frac{af}{1-f} = \frac{b}{1+b}r$ applies for the chosen parameter set (coincidentally), so that the operating cash flow after interest can even remain positive with the maximum amount of debt.

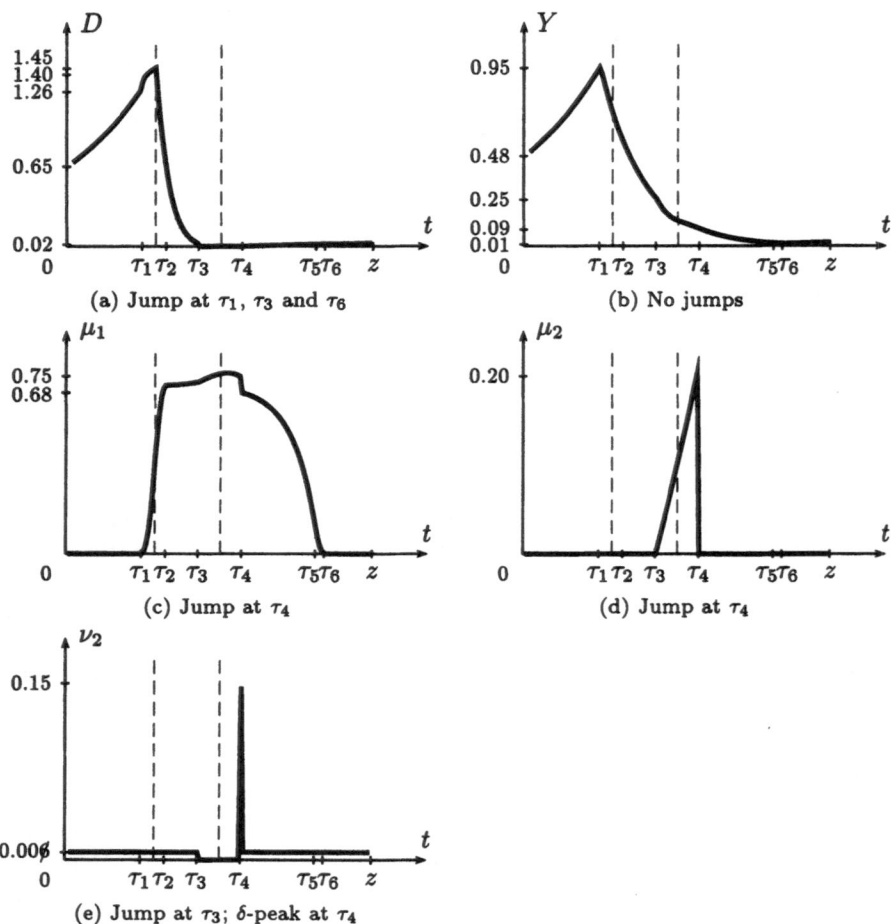

Figure 5.8 Solution of the model with a variable utilization rate for a severe recession in the case of $i > (1 - f)r$. The broken lines indicate the suuccessive peak and trough in the business cycle. Optimal string of paths: 8a-7a-7bo9b⋆7b-7a-8a. ($\Delta t = 0.5$)

3. Use the operating cash flow until τ_3 for distributing dividend and redeeming debt so that the amount of debt remains maximal, at a production rate that is adjusted to maintain the equality of marginal returns and marginal variable costs, whereby the utilization rate falls (path 7b).

4. Use all the operating cash flow for redeeming debt at a production rate that is adjusted to maintain the equality of marginal returns and marginal

variable costs, whereby the solvability increases at first, but subsequently falls, until τ_4 when the upper bound of debt is reached again at an operating cash flow that exactly covers the mandatory redemption of debt (path 9b).

5. Use the operating cash flow for distributing dividend and redeeming debt so that the amount of debt remains maximal, at a production rate that is adjusted to maintain the equality of marginal returns and marginal variable costs, until at τ_5 full utilization is reached (path 7b).

6. Use the operating cash flow at full utilization of the production resources for distributing dividend and redeeming debt so that the amount of debt remains maximal until path 8a is reached at τ_6 (path 7a).

7. Follow path 8a until z.

An expression in τ_1 and the model parameters for the boundary value of m between a moderate and a severe recession can be obtained by putting the operating cash flow after interest and mandatory redemption of debt equal to zero at the bottom of the recession, τ_d, with the maximum amount of debt (path 7b):

$$(1 - f)\left\{ S\left(\tau_d, Q(\tau_d)\right) - wlQ(\tau_d) + \frac{af}{1 - f}K(\tau_d)\right\} - yK(\tau_d) = 0 \qquad (5.72)$$

Hereby applies:

$$K(\tau_d) = k\overline{Q}\left[\frac{wl + \left(a + \frac{1}{1+b}\frac{i}{1-f} + \frac{b}{1+b}r\right)k}{\overline{P}\left(1 - \varepsilon^{-1}\right)}\right]^{-\varepsilon} e^{g\tau_1 - a(\tau_d - \tau_1)} \qquad (5.73)$$

and:

$$Q(\tau_d) = \overline{Q}\left[\frac{wl}{\overline{P}\left(1 - \varepsilon^{-1}\right)}\right]^{-\varepsilon} e^{m\tau_u - (m - g)\tau_d} \qquad (5.74)$$

These are obtained by using expressions (5.6) and (5.64), respectively.

The course of the costate variables is studied below, after which an expression will be given for the associated jumps at τ_4.

The course of λ_2

Apart from the coupling points, relationships and related interpretations for $\lambda_2(t)$ are identical with those in Subsection 5.2.4 for the basic model.

Period $[0, \tau_3]$: string of paths 8a-7a-7b

$$\lambda_2(t) = 1 \qquad (5.75)$$

One extra unit of equity is used directly for distributing dividend; therefore, the objective function increases by one.

Period $[\tau_3, \tau_4)$: path 9b

$$\lambda_2(t) = e^{(i-(1-f)r)(t-\tau_3)} \tag{5.76}$$

The extra unit of equity is used to pay off debt, whereupon, at τ_3, the firm anticipates distributing extra dividend by an amount of $e^{-(1-f)r(t-\tau_3)}$ so that the state variables remain unchanged after t.

Period $\langle \tau_4, z]$: string of paths 7b-7a-8a

$$\lambda_2(t) = 1 \tag{5.77}$$

Once more, the extra unit of equity will be used for distributing dividend.

The course of λ_1

During the periods $[0, \tau_1]$ and $[\tau_6, z]$, the firm is investing voluntarily so that the requirement to acquire a unit of capital assets is not mandatory then: $\lambda_1(t) = 0$ (path 8a).

Period $[\tau_1, \tau_2]$: path 7a

$$\lambda_1(t) = \frac{-1}{1+b} + \int_t^{\tau_2} \left\{ \frac{\partial O_{vi}}{\partial K}(s, K(s)) - y \right\} e^{-(a+i)(s-t)} ds +$$

$$\int_{\tau_2}^{\tau_3} (af - y) e^{-(a+i)(s-t)} ds -$$

$$e^{-i(\tau_3-t)} \left[\frac{b}{1+b} e^{-a(\tau_3-t)} - \int_{\tau_3}^{\tau_4} af e^{-a(s-t)} e^{-(1-f)r(s-\tau_3)} ds - \right.$$

$$\left. \frac{b}{1+b} e^{-a(\tau_4-t)} e^{-(1-f)r(\tau_4-\tau_3)} \right] + \int_{\tau_4}^{\tau_5} (af - y) e^{-(a+i)(s-t)} ds +$$

$$\int_{\tau_5}^{\tau_6} \left\{ \frac{\partial O_{vi}}{\partial K}(s, K(s)) - y \right\} e^{-(a+i)(s-t)} ds + \frac{e^{-(a+i)(\tau_6-t)}}{1+b} \tag{5.78}$$

The purchase of one unit of capital assets is financed from equity and debt in the ratio of $1 : b$ (first term). The second and third term are integrals of the discounted dividend flow and as such, have already occurred in the previous subsection. The expression between square brackets represents how much less dividend the firm is obliged to distribute at τ_3, so that the upper bound of debt is exactly reached at τ_4 but not exceeded. The interpretations of the fifth and sixth term are analogous with those for the second and the third. The final term is the discounted reduction in the investments expenditure at τ_6 which will benefit the dividend paid out.

Period $[\tau_2, \tau_3]$: path 7b

$$\lambda_1(t) = \frac{-1}{1+b} + \int_t^{\tau_3} (af - y)e^{-(a+i)(s-t)}ds -$$

$$e^{-i(\tau_3-t)}\left[\frac{b}{1+b}e^{-a(\tau_3-t)} - \int_{\tau_3}^{\tau_4} afe^{-a(s-t)}e^{-(1-f)r(s-\tau_3)}ds -\right.$$

$$\left.\frac{b}{1+b}e^{-a(\tau_4-t)}e^{-(1-f)r(\tau_4-\tau_3)}\right] + \int_{\tau_4}^{\tau_5} (af-y)e^{-(a+i)(s-t)}ds +$$

$$\int_{\tau_5}^{\tau_6}\left\{\frac{\partial O_{vi}}{\partial K}(s, K(s)) - y\right\}e^{-(a+i)(s-t)}ds + \frac{e^{-(a+i)(\tau_6-t)}}{1+b} \tag{5.79}$$

Interpretation is analogous with the previous period.

Period $[\tau_3, \tau_4)$: path 9b

$$\lambda_1(t) = -e^{i(t-\tau_3)}\left[e^{-(1-f)r(t-\tau_3)} - \int_t^{\tau_4} afe^{-a(s-t)}e^{-(1-f)r(s-\tau_3)}ds -\right.$$

$$\left.\frac{b}{1+b}e^{-a(\tau_4-t)}e^{-(1-f)r(\tau_4-\tau_3)}\right] + \int_{\tau_4}^{\tau_5} (af-y)e^{-(a+i)(s-t)}ds +$$

$$\int_{\tau_5}^{\tau_6}\left\{\frac{\partial O_{vi}}{\partial K}(s, K(s)) - y\right\}e^{-(a+i)(s-t)}ds + \frac{e^{-(a+i)(\tau_6-t)}}{1+b} \tag{5.80}$$

The unit of capital assets is entirely financed from debt. The interpretations of the resulting terms remain unchanged.

Period $\langle\tau_4, \tau_5]$: path 7b.

$$\lambda_1(t) = \frac{-1}{1+b} + \int_t^{\tau_5} (af-y)e^{-(a+i)(s-t)}ds +$$

$$\int_{\tau_5}^{\tau_6}\left\{\frac{\partial O_{vi}}{\partial K}(s, K(s)) - y\right\}e^{-(a+i)(s-t)}ds + \frac{e^{-(a+i)(\tau_6-t)}}{1+b} \tag{5.81}$$

The purchase of one unit of capital assets again is financed from equity and debt in the ratio of $1 : b$. Interpretation is known already.

Period $[\tau_5, \tau_6]$: path 7a.

$$\lambda_1(t) = \frac{-1}{1+b} + \int_t^{\tau_6}\left\{\frac{\partial O_{vi}}{\partial K}(s, K(s)) - y\right\}e^{-(a+i)(s-t)}ds +$$

$$\frac{e^{-(a+i)(\tau_6-t)}}{1+b} \tag{5.82}$$

Interpretation needs no further explanation.

The jumps at τ_4 in the costate variables now can be simply derived:

$$\lambda_1(\tau_4^+) - \lambda_1(\tau_4^-) = \left(e^{(i-(1-f)r)(\tau_4-\tau_3)} - 1\right)/(1+b) \qquad (5.83)$$

$$\lambda_2(\tau_4^+) - \lambda_2(\tau_4^-) = 1 - e^{(i-(1-f)r)(\tau_4-\tau_3)} \qquad (5.84)$$

5.4   A model with a cash balance

5.4.1   Description of the model

According to the basic model of Section 5.2, in which no cash balance is included, the firm has, in principle, three alternatives available for spending its operating cash flow, namely:

- investing,

- distributing dividend,

- redeeming debt.

Of these three, the first two alternatives can be adjusted freely within certain bounds; the third is fixed by the following identity:

$$O_{ni}\big(t, K(t), Y(t)\big) + \dot{Y}(t) - I(t) - D(t) = 0 \qquad (5.85)$$

This identity implies that the *net* cash flow is always equal to zero.

In this section, a model of the firm is studied in which a cash balance, indicated by $M(t)$, is included next to capital on the assets side of the balance sheet. So, the firm has a fourth alternative for spending its operating cash flow, namely:

- supplementing the cash balance.

Therefore, the following identity holds:

$$O_{ni}\big(t, K(t), Y(t)\big) + \dot{Y}(t) - I(t) - D(t) = \dot{M}(t) \qquad (5.86)$$

Supplementing the cash balance has been chosen as the third control variable in addtion to investing and distributing dividend, so the redemption of debt is fixed via identity (5.86). Furthermore, the firm will receive no interest on the cash balance: the cash interest rate is always assumed to be zero and for this reason, it is not included in the model of the firm. Consequently, the optimal strategy will not differ principally from the case with a positive cash interest rate, as long as it is lower than the pretax costs of equity and debt, $\frac{i}{1-f}$ and r respectively.

The complete formulation of the model can now be presented as follows:

$$\max_{I(t),D(t),\dot{M}(t)} \left\{ J = \int_0^z e^{-it} D(t)\, dt + e^{-iz} X(z) \right\} \tag{5.87a}$$

$$\dot{K}(t) = I(t) - aK(t), \quad K(0) = K_0 \tag{5.87b}$$

$$\dot{X}(t) = (1 - f)\left\{ S\big(t, Q(t)\big) - wL(t) - aK(t) - rY(t) \right\} - D(t),$$
$$X(0) = X_0 \tag{5.87c}$$

$$M(0) = M_0 \tag{5.87d}$$

$$Q(t) = k^{-1} K(t) \tag{5.87e}$$

$$L(t) = lQ(t) \tag{5.87f}$$

$$K(t) + M(t) = X(t) + Y(t) \tag{5.87g}$$

$$Y(t) \geq 0 \tag{5.87h}$$

$$Y(t) \leq bX(t) \tag{5.87i}$$

$$M(t) \geq 0 \tag{5.87j}$$

$$I(t) \geq 0 \tag{5.87k}$$

$$D(t) \geq 0 \tag{5.87l}$$

In Appendix C, it is shown that the optimization problem (5.87) satifies the required constraint qualification, so that Theorem 2.1 for deriving the necessary conditions can be applied. For this purpose, the Hamiltonian and Lagrangian are defined as follows ($\lambda_0 = 1$, see Observation 2.1):

$$\mathcal{H}(t, K, X, M, I, D, \dot{M}, \lambda_1, \lambda_2, \lambda_3) = D + \lambda_1 \left[I - aK \right] +$$
$$\lambda_2 \left[(1 - f)\left\{ S(t, k^{-1}K) - wlk^{-1}K - aK - \right.\right.$$
$$\left.\left. r(K + M - X) \right\} - D \right] + \lambda_3 \dot{M} \tag{5.88}$$

and:

$$\mathcal{L}(t, K, X, M, I, D, \dot{M}, \lambda_1, \lambda_2, \lambda_3, \mu_1, \mu_2, \nu_1, \nu_2, \nu_3) =$$
$$\mathcal{H}(t, K, X, M, I, D, \dot{M}, \lambda_1, \lambda_2, \lambda_3) + \mu_1 I + \mu_2 D +$$
$$\nu_1 \left[K + M - X \right] + \nu_2 \left[(1 + b)X - K - M \right] + \nu_3 M \tag{5.89}$$

respectively, where:

$\lambda_1(t)$: costate variable of capital assets

$\lambda_2(t)$: costate variable of equity

$\lambda_3(t)$: costate variable of cash balance

$\mu_1(t)$: Lagrange multiplier for lower bound of investment rate (5.87k)

$\mu_2(t)$: Lagrange multiplier for lower bound of dividend rate (5.87l)

$\nu_1(t)$: Lagrange multiplier for lower bound of debt (5.87h)

$\nu_2(t)$: Lagrange multiplier for upper bound of debt (5.87i)

$\nu_3(t)$: Lagrange multiplier for lower bound of cash balance (5.87j)

Economic interpretations of $\lambda_1(t)$ and $\lambda_2(t)$ have already been given in Chapter 3. For $\lambda_3(t)$, it follows now:

- $\lambda_3(t)$ is the change in the maximum attainable value of the objective function should the firm have to add one unit of money to its cash balance at instant t.

It follows directly that this requirement is not imperative for those periods where the cash balance grows in an optimal strategy; so λ_3 is equal to zero there. However, that holds for the other periods too. Since $\dot{M}(t)$ is entirely unlimited, the unit of money added to the cash balance at t can be used for the intended purposes instantaneously, so that the strategy and consequently, the value of the objective function, remain unchanged. This is an essential difference from the situation in which the firm must acquire one unit of capital assets at a certain instant when it is not required in an optimal strategy. That unit of capital assets cannot be cancelled (e.g. sold) instantaneously, resulting in a negative value of λ_1.

The set of necessary conditions that result after applying Theorem 2.1 is given in Appendix C, where it is shown further that the necessary conditions are sufficient too.

In comparison with the basic model, one extra constraint arises; therefore, in principle, each path of the basic model will divide into two paths for the model with cash. The designation of the paths for the latter model comes about in the following way:

path xa if $\nu_3(t) > 0$, so that $M(t) = 0$

path xb if $\nu_3(t) = 0$, so that $M(t) \geq 0$

with: $x = 1, \ldots, 12$ the path numbers from Table 3.1. In Appendix C, it is shown that fourteen of these twentyfour paths can be excluded. For example, a situation where a cash balance and debt are present at the same time will never occur in an optimal strategy. The same applies for simultaneously holding a cash balance and distributing dividend. Table 5.2 contains the ten paths which may form part of an optimal string. Path 1b and 2b are the only ones where

Table 5.2 The ten paths which may appear in an optimal string for the model with a cash balance. The last column contains the conditions, if any, that must apply.

	μ_1	μ_2	ν_1	ν_2	ν_3	
path 1b	+	+	+	0	0	
path 2a	0	+	+	0	+	
path 2b	0	+	+	0	0	
path 3a	+	0	+	0	+	only when $i < (1-f)r$
path 4a	0	0	+	0	+	only when $i < (1-f)r$
path 6a	0	+	0	+	+	
path 7a	+	0	0	+	+	only when $i > (1-f)r$
path 8a	0	0	0	+	+	only when $i > (1-f)r$
path 9a	+	+	0	0	+	
path 10a	0	+	0	0	+	

a cash balance exceeding zero can arise, the others correspond to paths of the basic model.

In the following subsections, the numerical results from the four case studies are discussed. Once again, they always involve a severe recession; in the first two cases, equity is cheaper than debt; in the last two, the situation is reversed. With the exception of the m-values, the parameter values are unchanged with respect to the case studies discussed before. This applies to K_0 and X_0 as well; moreover, $M_0 = 0$ has been chosen for all the cases.

5.4.2 Severe recession in the case of $i < (1-f)r$ and $m < m^*$

The meaning of m^* in this heading will appear to be the same as for the basic model. Figure 5.9 shows the graphs for optimal $D(t)$, $Y(t)$, $M(t)$, $\mu_1(t)$, $\mu_2(t)$ and $\nu_j(t)$ ($j = 1, 2, 3$), where $m = 0.335$. The course of I and K does not fundamentally deviate from that for the basic model in the corresponding situation shown in Figure 5.2 of Section 5.2. The course of $\dot{M}$ is not given because it can deduced quite simply from the graph for M. Furthermore, it holds that: $\lambda_1(t) = -\mu_1(t)$, $\lambda_2(t) = 1 + \mu_2(t)$ and $\lambda_3(t) = 0$ (see the necessary conditions in Appendix C). In contrast to the basic model, where the optimal strategy from 0 to z can be calculated in a single forward run and can be included in a simple decision rule once the optimal value of τ_1 is known, for the model with a cash balance, the optimal value of τ_2 needs to be known too. In Appendix C, a set of equations is given from which the coupling points can be calculated. The decision rule now reads as follows:

1. Follow path 4a until τ_1.

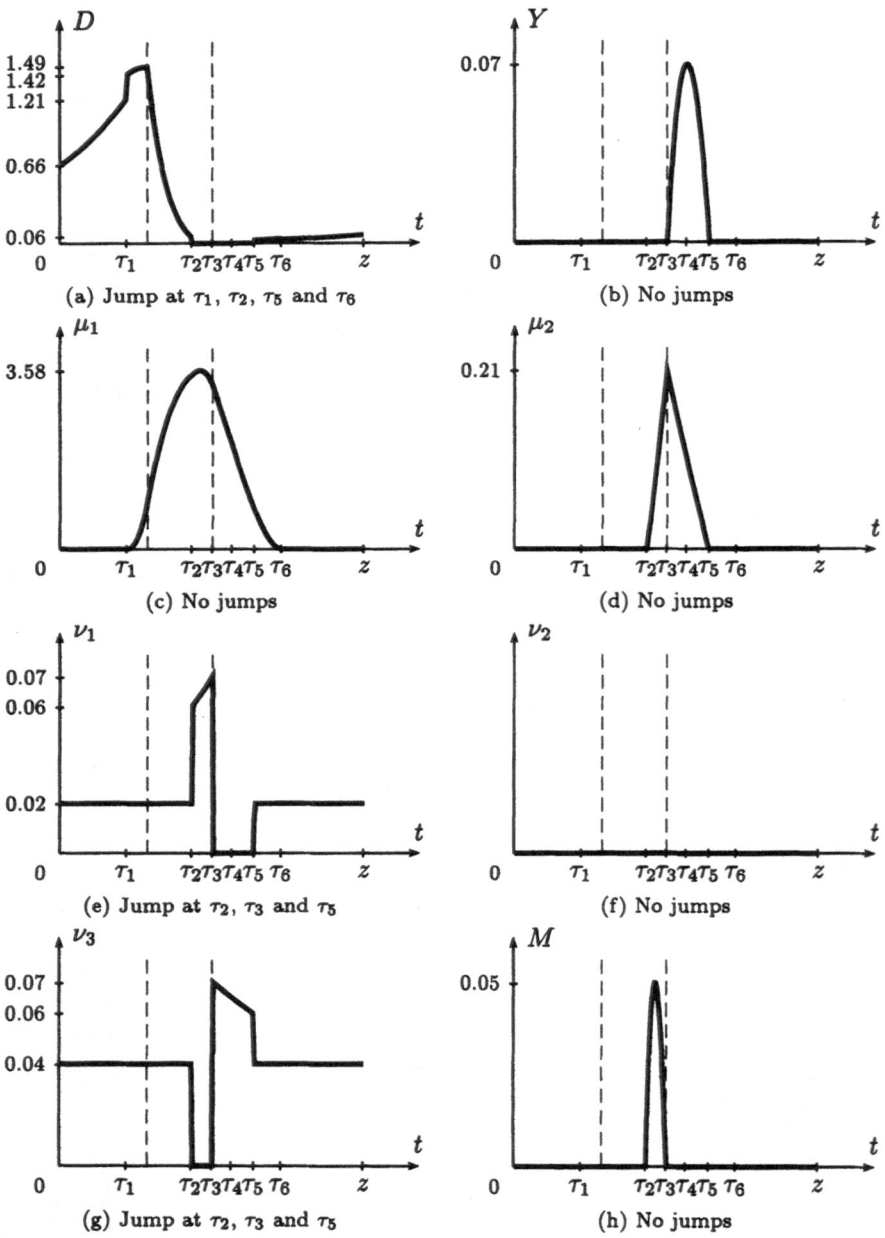

Figure 5.9 Solution of the model with a cash balance for a severe recession in the case of $i < (1-f)r$ and $m < m^\star$. The broken lines indicate the successive peak and trough in the business cycle. Optimal string of paths: 4a-3ao1bo9ao3a-4a. ($\Delta t = 0.25$)

2. Stop investing and pay out all the operating cash flow as dividend until τ_2 (path 3a).

3. Stop paying out dividend; as long as the operating cash flow remains positive, use it to build up a cash balance. As soon as the operating cash flow becomes negative, pay wages from cash until the cash balance is depleted at τ_3 (path 1b).

4. Attract debt necessary to pay wages and interest until a certain instant after the bottom of the recession when the operating cash flow becomes positive again. Then, use it entirely to redeem debt, which is completed at τ_5 (path 9a).

5. Pay out all the operating cash flow as dividend until path 4a is reached at τ_6 (path 3a).

6. Follow path 4a until z.

From Figure 5.9, it appears that no discontinuities occur in μ_1 and μ_2; therefore, the costate variables too are continuous everywhere. From the necessary conditions in Appendix C, it follows directly that a δ-peak in ν_1, like the one that occurred in the equivalent case for the basic model, now, would imply an opposite (negative) δ-peak in ν_3, so that the lower bound $\nu_3(t) \geq 0$ would be exceeded momentarily. Thus, in an optimal strategy when equity is cheaper than debt with m-values greater than the boundary value of a severe recession, the firm holds a cash balance during a certain period. For m-values smaller than the boundary value of a severe recession, the firm distributes dividend during the whole planning period in the absence of a cash balance (string of paths: 4a-3a-4a).

The development over time of the costate variables of capital assets and equity is studied below.

The course of λ_2

At each instant of time, the change in the maximum attainable value of the objective function arising from an extra increase in equity is considered.

Period $[0, \tau_2]$, string of paths 4a-3a:

$$\lambda_2(t) = 1 \tag{5.90}$$

One extra unit of equity is used for paying out dividend; therefore, the objective function increases by one unit.

Period $[\tau_2, \tau_3]$, path 1b:

$$\lambda_2(t) = e^{i(t-\tau_2)} \tag{5.91}$$

When the firm gets one extra unit of equity at its disposal, it can expand the cash balance needed for paying the wages by one unit. In anticipation, at τ_2 the firm pays out an extra unit of dividend so that the state variables will remain unchanged after instant t. Discounting to t gives the relationship above.

Period $[\tau_3, \tau_5]$, path 9a:

$$\lambda_2(t) = e^{((1-f)r-i)(\tau_5-t)} \tag{5.92}$$

One extra unit of equity is used for paying off debt. The expression above is the dividend increase at τ_5 (discounted to t), which is the result of that.

Period $[\tau_5, z]$, string of paths 3a-4a:

$$\lambda_2(t) = 1 \tag{5.93}$$

Again, the extra unit of equity is now used for paying out dividend.

Since λ_2 is continuous everywhere, the expressions (5.91) and (5.92) can be made equal to each other after inserting $t = \tau_3$. This produces the following relationship between τ_2, τ_3 and τ_5 which will be used for determining the coupling points (see Appendix C):

$$i(\tau_3 - \tau_2) = ((1 - f)r - i)(\tau_5 - \tau_3) \tag{5.94}$$

Therefore, during the period $[\tau_2, \tau_3]$ the following alternative expression and interpretation of $\lambda_2(t)$ hold:

$$\lambda_2(t) = e^{(1-f)r(\tau_5-\tau_3)-i(\tau_5-t)} \tag{5.95}$$

As a consquence of having an extra unit of equity which the firm uses for supplementing its cash balance, the firm needs to attract less debt after τ_3. The reduction in debt at τ_5 amounts to $e^{(1-f)r(\tau_5-\tau_3)}$ and benefits the dividend at that instant. Discounting to t produces the expression above for $\lambda_2(t)$.

Also during the period $[\tau_3, \tau_5]$, an alternative expression and interpretation of $\lambda_2(t)$ is possible:

$$\lambda_2(t) = e^{i(t-\tau_2)-(1-f)r(t-\tau_3)} \tag{5.96}$$

Anticipating the extra unit of equity at t, which will be used for paying off debt, at τ_2 the firm distributes extra dividend amounting to $e^{-(1-f)r(t-\tau_3)}$, so again, the state variables remain unchanged after instant t. Discounting to t then gives the alternative relationship.

The course of λ_1

Again, $\lambda_1(t)$ is seen as the change discounted to t of the maximum attainable value of the objective function when the firm must acquire a unit of capital assets at instant t. With the aid of (5.94), it is also possible to give different expressions and related interpretations of $\lambda_1(t)$, which all fit into the view just repeated. Below, one expression per period will be presented with its interpretation.

The relationships can be derived directly from the necessary conditions in Appendix C and making use of the expressions for $\lambda_2(t)$ above.

Period $[0, \tau_1]$, path 4a:

$$\lambda_1(t) = 0 \tag{5.97}$$

The requirement that the firm must acquire a unit of capital assets at t is not imperative, because at t the firm is already investing 'voluntarily'.

Period $[\tau_1, \tau_2]$, string of paths 4a-3a:

$$\lambda_1(t) = -1 + \int_t^{\tau_2} \frac{\partial O_{vi}}{\partial K}(s, K(s))e^{-(a+i)(s-t)}ds +$$

$$e^{-i(\tau_5-t)} \left[e^{(1-f)r(\tau_5-\tau_3)} \int_{\tau_2}^{\tau_3} \frac{\partial O_{vi}}{\partial K}(s, K(s))e^{-a(s-t)}ds + \right.$$

$$\left. \int_{\tau_3}^{\tau_5} \frac{\partial O_{vi}}{\partial K}(s, K(s))e^{-a(s-t)}e^{(1-f)r(\tau_5-s)}ds \right] +$$

$$\int_{\tau_5}^{\tau_6} \frac{\partial O_{vi}}{\partial K}(s, K(s))e^{-(a+i)(s-t)}ds + e^{-(a+i)(\tau_6-t)} \tag{5.98}$$

The purchase of one unit of capital assets is financed from equity and thus, is at the expense of the dividend distributed at instant t (first term). The second term is the discounted differential dividend flow between t and τ_2, arising from the unit of capital assets acquired at t which decreases as a result of wastage according to $e^{-a(s-t)}$. The third main term is the discounted reduction in distributed dividend at τ_5. For the amount of debt at instant τ_5 has increased by an amount equal to the expression between square brackets as a result of the unit of capital assets. The interpretation of the next to last term is analogous with that of the second. The final term is the discounted reduction in the investments expenditure at τ_6 which benefits the dividend distributed.

Period $[\tau_2, \tau_3]$, path 1b:

$$\lambda_1(t) = e^{-i(\tau_5-t)} \left[-e^{(1-f)r(\tau_5-\tau_3)} + \right.$$

$$e^{(1-f)r(\tau_5-\tau_3)} \int_t^{\tau_3} \frac{\partial O_{vi}}{\partial K}(s, K(s))e^{-a(s-t)}ds +$$

$$\left. \int_{\tau_3}^{\tau_5} \frac{\partial O_{vi}}{\partial K}(s, K(s))e^{-a(s-t)}e^{(1-f)r(\tau_5-s)}ds \right] +$$

$$\int_{\tau_5}^{\tau_6} \frac{\partial O_{vi}}{\partial K}(s, K(s))e^{-(a+i)(s-t)}ds + e^{-(a+i)(\tau_6-t)} \tag{5.99}$$

The purchase of one unit of capital assets now is financed from cash. Hereby, the amount of debt at τ_5 increases and, thus, the amount of dividend at τ_5 reduces by a sum equal to the expression between square brackets. The interpretation of the last two terms has already been given for the previous period.

Period $[\tau_3, \tau_5]$, path 9a:

$$\lambda_1(t) = -e^{-i(\tau_5-t)} \left[e^{(1-f)r(\tau_5-t)} - \right.$$

$$\left. \int_t^{\tau_5} \frac{\partial O_{vi}}{\partial K}(s, K(s)) e^{-a(s-t)} e^{(1-f)r(\tau_5-s)} ds \right] +$$

$$\int_{\tau_5}^{\tau_6} \frac{\partial O_{vi}}{\partial K}(s, K(s)) e^{-(a+i)(s-t)} ds + e^{-(a+i)(\tau_6-t)} \qquad (5.100)$$

Financing the unit of capital assets takes place with debt and results in a discounted reduction in the dividend at τ_5 equal to the first main term.

Period $[\tau_5, \tau_6]$, path 3a:

$$\lambda_1(t) = -1 + \int_t^{\tau_6} \frac{\partial O_{vi}}{\partial K}(s, K(s)) e^{-(a+i)(s-t)} ds + e^{-(a+i)(\tau_6-t)} \qquad (5.101)$$

The finance for the unit of capital assets comes from equity (first term).

Period $[\tau_6, z]$, path 4a:

$$\lambda_1(t) = 0 \qquad (5.102)$$

Interpretation is analogous with the first period.

5.4.3 Severe recession in the case of $i < (1 - f)r$ and $m > m^*$

In Figure 5.10, the graphs for $\mu_1(t)$, $\mu_2(t)$, $\nu_2(t)$ and $\nu_3(t)$ are given for $m = 0.35$. The course of the other variables has not changed principally from Figure 5.9. The crucial difference from the solution in the previous situation, is implied in the optimal instants of stopping to invest and stopping to pay out dividend, τ_1 and τ_2 respectively. For $m < m^*$, the combination (τ_1, τ_2) is found to be a *free* optimum; that is to say, an infinitesimally shorter or longer time for investing and/or distributing dividend will not necessarily lead to exceeding one or more bounds, but in any case no higher value of the objective function will be involved. For $m > m^*$, the combination (τ_1, τ_2) is found to be a *boundary* optimum. Continued investment for an infinitesimally longer time at fixed τ_2 now results in a higher value of the objective function, but will inevitably lead to exceeding the upper bound of debt at τ_3, and therefore is not permitted. An infinitesimally longer time distributing dividend at fixed τ_1 will have the same effect.

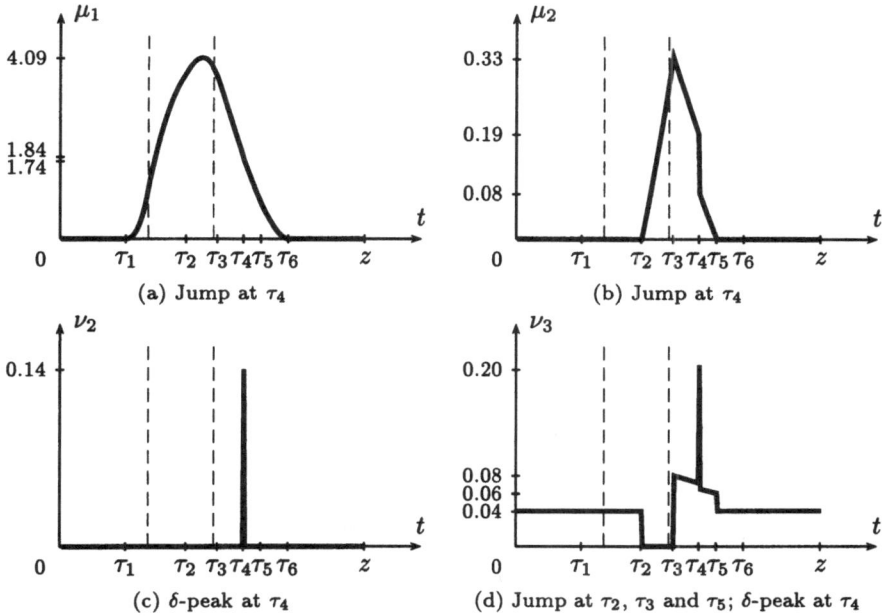

Figure 5.10 Solution the model with a cash balance for a severe recession in the case of $i < (1 - f)r$ and $m > m^*$. The broken lines indicate the successive peak and trough in the business cycle. Optimal string of paths: 4a-3ao1bo9a⋆9ao3a-4a. ($\Delta t = 0.25$)

Yet, the optimal instant of stopping investments, τ_1, can be seen as a free optimum: continuing to invest longer need not necessarily lead to exceeding the upper bound of debt at τ_3, because a smaller τ_2 can be chosen, and, for these reasons, will not result in a higher value of the objective function. According to this reasoning, the value of τ_2 is fixed implicitly by the value of τ_1 via the requirement that: $Y(\tau_4) = bX(\tau_4)$ and $\dot{Y}(\tau_4) = b\dot{X}(\tau_4)$.

In Appendix C, a set of equations is given from which the coupling points for this case can be determined iteratively. The m-value, for which $\tau_2 \approx 0$ is an approximation of the critical m-value at which the firm will not be bankrupt.

Figure 5.10 makes it clear that a jump appears in the course of λ_1 and λ_2 at instant τ_4 which is caused by a δ-peak in the course of ν_2 at that instant. In the course of ν_3, a similar δ-peak occurs which 'neutralizes' the effect on λ_3 of the first δ-peak mentioned, so that λ_3 remains equal to zero everywhere, and thus is continuous everywhere (see the necessary conditions in Appendix C). The jump in λ_1 is again in the opposite direction and smaller by a factor $(1 + b)$ when compared with the jump in λ_2.

Below, the course of λ_1 and λ_2 is examined again.

The course of λ_2

As a result of the discontinuity at τ_4, the relationship (5.94) between τ_2, τ_3 and τ_5 is no longer valid here. This means that the alternative expression (5.95) with its associated interpretation cannot be maintained for the period $[\tau_2, \tau_3]$. Since τ_2 is a boundary optimum now, an extra unit of dividend distributed at τ_2 and discounted to t generates more than $e^{(1-f)r(\tau_5 - \tau_3)}$ extra dividend paid out at τ_5 and discounted to t, in contrast to the previous subsection where τ_2 is a free optimum and the extra income is the same for both alternatives.

For comparative reasons, during the period $[\tau_3, \tau_4)$, exactly the alternative expression (5.96) applies; however for the period $\langle \tau_4, \tau_5]$, the opportunity to pay out extra dividend at τ_2 is excluded because it implies that the upper bound of debt would be exceeded at τ_4. Therefore, expression (5.91) must apply here.

The expressions with interpretations for the periods which have not been explained here, are the same as those for the case of $m < m^*$ in the previous subsection.

The course of λ_1

For the periods $[0, \tau_1]$ and $\langle \tau_4, z]$, the expressions with interpretations given in the previous subsection for the case of $m < m^*$ apply. The other periods are discussed below.

Period $[\tau_1, \tau_2]$, path 3a:

$$\lambda_1(t) = -1 + \int_t^{\tau_2} \frac{\partial O_{vi}}{\partial K}(s, K(s)) e^{-(a+i)(s-t)} ds +$$

$$e^{-i(\tau_2 - t)} \left[\int_{\tau_2}^{\tau_3} \frac{\partial O_{vi}}{\partial K}(s, K(s)) e^{-a(s-t)} ds + \right.$$

$$\int_{\tau_3}^{\tau_4} \frac{\partial O_{vi}}{\partial K}(s, K(s)) e^{-a(s-t)} e^{-(1-f)r(s-\tau_3)} ds +$$

$$\left. \frac{b}{1+b} e^{-a(\tau_4 - t)} e^{-(1-f)r(\tau_4 - \tau_3)} \right] -$$

$$e^{-i(\tau_5 - t)} \left[\frac{b}{1+b} e^{-a(\tau_4 - t)} e^{(1-f)r(\tau_5 - \tau_4)} - \right.$$

$$\left. \int_{\tau_4}^{\tau_5} \frac{\partial O_{vi}}{\partial K}(s, K(s)) e^{-a(s-t)} e^{(1-f)r(\tau_5 - s)} ds \right] +$$

$$\int_{\tau_5}^{\tau_6} \frac{\partial O_{vi}}{\partial K}(s, K(s)) e^{-(a+i)(s-t)} ds + e^{-(a+i)(\tau_6 - t)} \qquad (5.103)$$

The first and last two terms occur in the expression for $\lambda_1(t)$ too in the case of $m < m^*$; in the previous subsection, their interpretations are described. So

that the firm, after acquiring a unit of capital assets, again reaches the upper
bound of debt at τ_4 exactly for one instant without exceeding that bound, it
must distribute less dividend at τ_2. The expression between the first pair of
square brackets is the negative change in dividend distributed at τ_2 which is
discounted to t. The expression between the second pair of square brackets
is the increase in debt at τ_5 which deviates from the previous expression for
the increase in debt at τ_5 in the case of $m < m^*$, due to the reduced dividend
distributed at τ_2.

Period $[\tau_2, \tau_3]$, path 1b:

$$\lambda_1(t) = e^{i(t-\tau_2)}\left[-1 + \int_t^{\tau_3} \frac{\partial O_{vi}}{\partial K}(s, K(s))e^{-a(s-t)}ds + \right.$$

$$\int_{\tau_3}^{\tau_4} \frac{\partial O_{vi}}{\partial K}(s, K(s))e^{-a(s-t)}e^{-(1-f)r(s-\tau_3)}ds +$$

$$\left. \frac{b}{1+b}e^{-a(\tau_4-t)}e^{-(1-f)r(\tau_4-\tau_3)}\right] -$$

$$e^{-i(\tau_5-t)}\left[\frac{b}{1+b}e^{-a(\tau_4-t)}e^{(1-f)r(\tau_5-\tau_4)} - \right.$$

$$\left. \int_{\tau_4}^{\tau_5} \frac{\partial O_{vi}}{\partial K}(s, K(s))e^{-a(s-t)}e^{(1-f)r(\tau_5-s)}ds\right] +$$

$$\int_{\tau_5}^{\tau_6} \frac{\partial O_{vi}}{\partial K}(s, K(s))e^{-(a+i)(s-t)}ds + e^{-(a+i)(\tau_6-t)} \qquad (5.104)$$

The first main term is the discounted decrease in dividend distributed at τ_2.
The other terms are unchanged from those given for the previous period.

Period $[\tau_3, \tau_4)$, path 9a:

$$\lambda_1(t) = e^{i(t-\tau_2)}\left[-e^{-(1-f)r(t-\tau_3)} + \right.$$

$$\int_t^{\tau_4} \frac{\partial O_{vi}}{\partial K}(s, K(s))e^{-a(s-t)}e^{-(1-f)r(s-\tau_3)}ds +$$

$$\left. \frac{b}{1+b}e^{-a(\tau_4-t)}e^{-(1-f)r(\tau_4-\tau_3)}\right] -$$

$$e^{-i(\tau_5-t)}\left[\frac{b}{1+b}e^{-a(\tau_4-t)}e^{(1-f)r(\tau_5-\tau_4)} - \right.$$

$$\left. \int_{\tau_4}^{\tau_5} \frac{\partial O_{vi}}{\partial K}(s, K(s))e^{-a(s-t)}e^{(1-f)r(\tau_5-s)}ds\right] +$$

$$\int_{\tau_5}^{\tau_6} \frac{\partial O_{vi}}{\partial K}(s, K(s)) e^{-(a+i)(s-t)} ds + e^{-(a+i)(\tau_6-t)} \qquad (5.105)$$

The interpretation is analogous with that for the previous period.

From the relationships for $\lambda_1(t)$ and $\lambda_2(t)$ given above, the following expressions for the jumps can be found directly:

$$\lambda_1(\tau_4^+) - \lambda_1(\tau_4^-) = \frac{e^{i(\tau_3-\tau_2)-((1-f)r-i)(\tau_4-\tau_3)} - e^{((1-f)r-i)(\tau_5-\tau_4)}}{1+b} \qquad (5.106)$$

$$\lambda_2(\tau_4^+) - \lambda_2(\tau_4^-) = e^{((1-f)r-i)(\tau_5-\tau_4)} - e^{i(\tau_3-\tau_2)-((1-f)r-i)(\tau_4-\tau_3)} \qquad (5.107)$$

This is consistent with the remark made earlier that a δ-peak in the course of ν_2 causes a jump in λ_1 and λ_2 at the same time, although the jumps are in opposite directions and in the ratio of $1:(1 + b)$.

In concluding this subsection, it should be mentioned that m^* can be determined iteratively in two ways. The first is by iteration to determine the coupling points for different m-values via the set of equations from Appendix C.3.3; the value of m^* required is the m-value where: $Y(\tau_4) = bX(\tau_4)$. The second is by iteration to determine the coupling points for different m-values via the set of equations from Appendix C.3.4; the unique m-value at which the jumps described above are exactly zero, is the value of m^* required.

5.4.4   Severe recession in the case of $i > (1 - f)r$ and $m < m^\circ$

In an optimal strategy when debt is more expensive than equity, the firm will never make use of the extra spending alternative to supplement its cash for m-values smaller than m°: $Y(t) > 0$ and $M(t) = \dot{M}(t) = 0$, $t \in [0, z]$. The solution of the model with cash, thus, is in fact identical to that for the basic model. For the development over time of the common variables and its discussion, the reader is referred to Subsection 5.2.4. The course of $\nu_3(t)$ for $m = 0.324$ is illustrated in Figure 5.11, from which it appears that a δ-peak occurs at τ_4. This δ-peak 'neutralizes' the effect on λ_3 of the δ-peak at the same instant in ν_2, so that λ_3 remains equal to zero everywhere (also see the previous subsection).

5.4.5   Severe recession in the case of $i > (1 - f)r$ and $m > m^\circ$

In Figure 5.12, the graphs for the optimal $D(t)$, $Y(t)$, $M(t)$, $\mu_1(t)$, $\mu_2(t)$ and $\nu_j(t)$ $(j = 1, 2, 3)$ with $m = 0.35$ are shown. The course of I and K does not fundamentally deviate from that for the basic model shown in Figure 5.4. The course of $\dot{M}$ can simply be deduced from that of M. Once again, $\lambda_1(t) = -\mu_1(t)$, $\lambda_2(t) = 1 + \mu_2(t)$ and $\lambda_3(t) = 0$ all apply. There are no essential differences with respect to the previous subsection. Arising from an opportunity to build up a cash balance, the optimal instant to stop investing τ_1 is still a

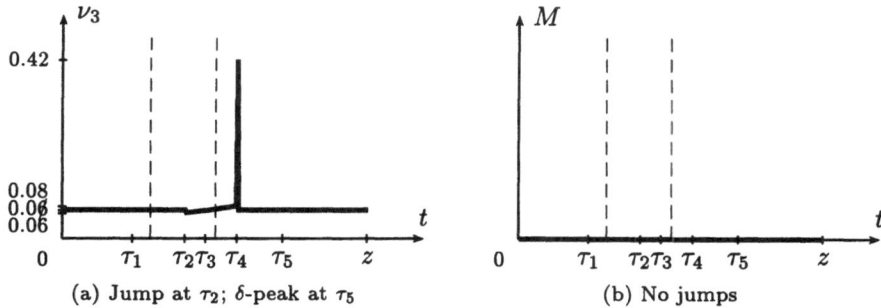

Figure 5.11 Solution of the model with a cash balance for a severe recession in the case of $i > (1-f)r$ and $m < m°$. The broken lines indicate the successive peak and trough in the business cycle. Optimal string of paths: 8a-7ao9a⋆7a-8a. ($\Delta t = 0.25$)

free optimum. The optimal instant to stop distributing dividend is determined again by the requirement that, given the optimal value of τ_1, at τ_5 the firm exactly reaches the upper bound of debt at an operating cash flow which just covers the mandatory redemption of debt.

For m-values greater than $m°$, this requirement automatically implies a period with a positive cash balance. In Appendix C, a set of equations is given from which the coupling points can be calculated. The decision rule now reads as follows:

1. Follow path 8a until τ_1.

2. Stop investing and use the operating cash flow for paying out dividend and redeeming debt until τ_2, so that the amount of debt remains maximal (path 7a).

3. Stop distributing dividend and use the operating cash flow entirely for paying off debt until no more exists at τ_3 (path 9a).

4. Use the operating cash flow, as long as it is positive, for building up a cash balance; then from the instant that it becomes negative, pay the wages from that cash balance until it is fully depleted at τ_4 (path 1b).

5. Attract debt necessary to pay wages and interest until a certain instant after the bottom of the recession when the operating cash flow becomes positive; then use it entirely in order to pay off debt until at τ_5 the upper bound of debt is reached at an operating cash flow that just covers the mandatory redemption of debt (path 9a).

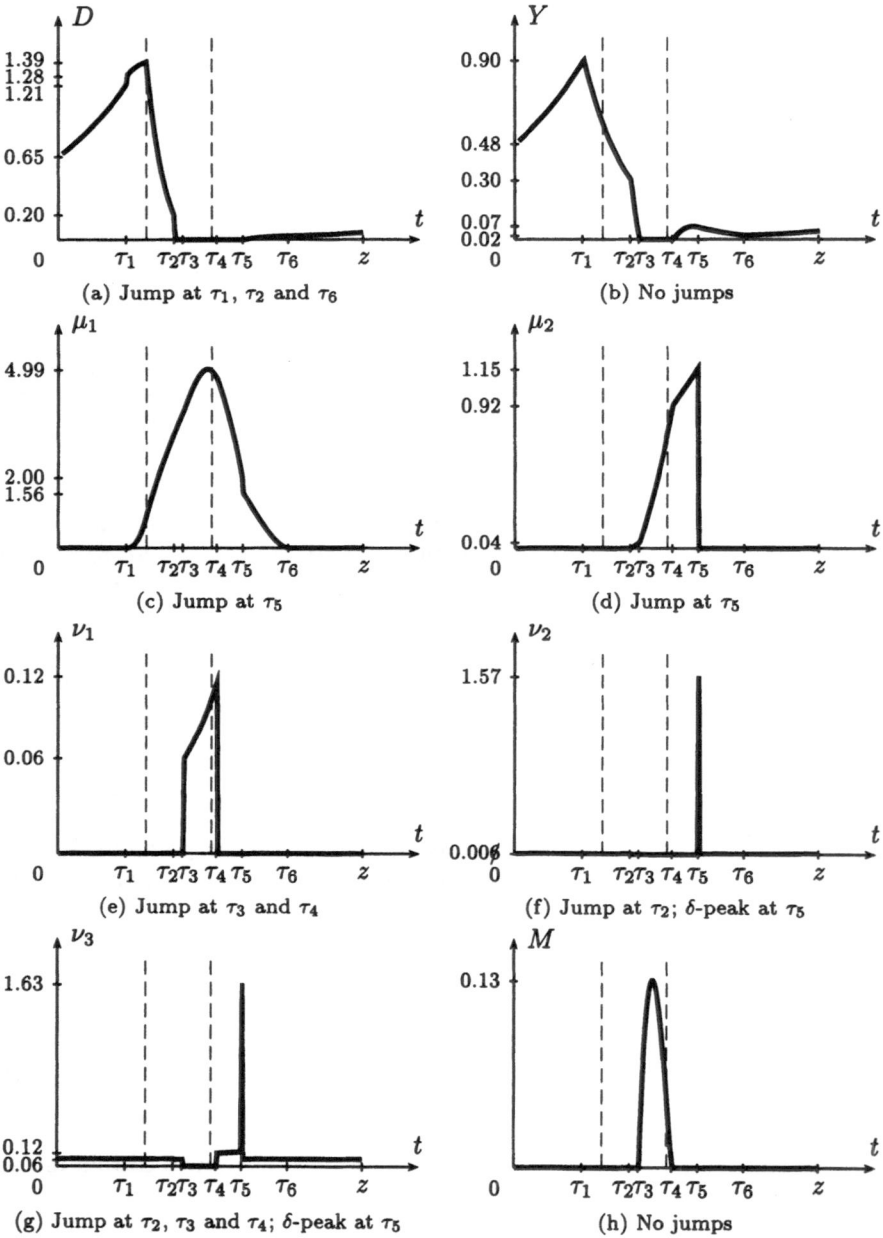

Figure 5.12 Solution of the model with a cash balance for a severe recession in the case of $i > (1 - f)r$ and $m > m°$. The broken lines indicate the successive peak and trough in the business cycle. Optimal string of paths: 8a-7a∘9a∘1b∘9a⋆7a-8a. $(\Delta t = 0.25)$

6. Use the operating cash flow for distributing dividend and redeeming debt so that the amount of debt remains maximal until path 8a is reached at τ_6 (path 7a).

7. Follow path 8a until z.

Not only economically does it become clear that the δ-peak, like that which arises in the course of ν_1 for the basic model in Subsection 5.2.5, is not forthcoming here. Also, this follows mathematically directly from the necessary conditions as mentioned already in Subsection 5.4.2.

Again, the development of λ_1 and λ_2 over time is examined below, afterwards, expressions for the jumps at τ_5 will be presented.

The course of λ_2

At each instant of time, the change in the maximum attainable value of the objective function arising from an additional increase in equity by one unit, is considered.

During the periods $[0, \tau_2]$ and $\langle \tau_5, z]$, one extra unit of equity is used directly for paying out dividend; therefore the objective function increases by one: $\lambda_2(t) = 1$. For the other periods, expressions of $\lambda_2(t)$ are shown which always represent the amount of dividend discounted to t that the firm in anticipation of getting an additional unit of equity at t can pay out extra at τ_2, so that the state variables remain unchanged after t. Without further explanation, the following relationships are given.

Period $[\tau_2, \tau_3]$, path 9a:

$$\lambda_2(t) = e^{(i-(1-f)r)(t-\tau_2)} \tag{5.108}$$

Period $[\tau_3, \tau_4]$, path 1b:

$$\lambda_2(t) = e^{i(t-\tau_2)-(1-f)r(\tau_3-\tau_2)} \tag{5.109}$$

Period $[\tau_4, \tau_5\rangle$, path 9a:

$$\lambda_2(t) = e^{i(t-\tau_2)-(1-f)r((\tau_3-\tau_2)+(t-\tau_4))} \tag{5.110}$$

The course of λ_1

Consider at each instant $t \in [0, z]$, the change discounted to t in the maximum attainable value of the objective function should the firm have to acquire a unit of capital assets at t. This requirement is not imperative for the periods $[0, \tau_1]$ and $[\tau_6, z]$ in which the firm is already investing 'voluntarily' so that $\lambda_1(t) = 0$ applies then (path 8a). For the period in which the firm does not invest, the following expressions and interpretations apply:

Period $[\tau_1, \tau_2]$, path 7a:

$$\lambda_1(t) = \frac{-1}{1+b} + \int_t^{\tau_2} \left\{ \frac{\partial O_{vi}}{\partial K}(s, K(s)) - y \right\} e^{-(a+i)(s-t)} ds -$$

$$e^{-i(\tau_2-t)} \left[\frac{b}{1+b} e^{-a(\tau_2-t)} - \right.$$

$$\int_{\tau_2}^{\tau_3} \frac{\partial O_{vi}}{\partial K}(s, K(s)) e^{-a(s-t)} e^{-(1-f)r(s-\tau_2)} ds -$$

$$e^{-(1-f)r(\tau_3-\tau_2)} \int_{\tau_3}^{\tau_4} \frac{\partial O_{vi}}{\partial K}(s, K(s)) e^{-a(s-t)} ds -$$

$$e^{-(1-f)r(\tau_3-\tau_2)} \int_{\tau_4}^{\tau_5} \frac{\partial O_{vi}}{\partial K}(s, K(s)) e^{-a(s-t)} e^{-(1-f)r(s-\tau_4)} ds -$$

$$\left. \frac{b}{1+b} e^{-a(\tau_5-t)} e^{-(1-f)r((\tau_3-\tau_2)+(\tau_5-\tau_4))} \right] +$$

$$\int_{\tau_5}^{\tau_6} \left\{ \frac{\partial O_{vi}}{\partial K}(s, K(s)) - y \right\} e^{-(a+i)(s-t)} ds + \frac{e^{-(a+i)(\tau_6-t)}}{1+b} \qquad (5.111)$$

The unit of capital assets is financed from equity and debt in the ratio of $1:b$. Financing from equity is at the expense of dividend (first term). The second term gives the integral of the discounted differential dividend flow between t and τ_2 arising from the unit of capital assets. The expression between square brackets is positive and it represents how much less dividend the firm must distribute at τ_2, so that the upper bound of debt is precisely reached at τ_5, but not exceeded. The next to last term is analogous with the second. The last term is the discounted reduction in the investments expenditure at τ_6 which will benefit the dividend distributed.

Period $[\tau_2, \tau_3]$, path 9a:

$$\lambda_1(t) = -e^{i(t-\tau_2)} \left[e^{-(1-f)r(t-\tau_2)} - \right.$$

$$\int_t^{\tau_3} \frac{\partial O_{vi}}{\partial K}(s, K(s)) e^{-a(s-t)} e^{-(1-f)r(s-\tau_2)} ds -$$

$$e^{-(1-f)r(\tau_3-\tau_2)} \int_{\tau_3}^{\tau_4} \frac{\partial O_{vi}}{\partial K}(s, K(s)) e^{-a(s-t)} ds -$$

$$e^{-(1-f)r(\tau_3-\tau_2)} \int_{\tau_4}^{\tau_5} \frac{\partial O_{vi}}{\partial K}(s, K(s)) e^{-a(s-t)} e^{-(1-f)r(s-\tau_4)} ds -$$

$$\left. \frac{b}{1+b} e^{-a(\tau_5-t)} e^{-(1-f)r((\tau_3-\tau_2)+(\tau_5-\tau_4))} \right] +$$

$$\int_{\tau_5}^{\tau_6} \left\{ \frac{\partial O_{vi}}{\partial K}(s, K(s)) - y \right\} e^{-(a+i)(s-t)} ds + \frac{e^{-(a+i)(\tau_6-t)}}{1+b} \qquad (5.112)$$

The unit of capital assets is entirely financed from debt. Interpretation of the expression between square brackets is the same as for the previous period. The last two terms are unchanged from those given in the previous period.

Period $[\tau_3, \tau_4]$, path 1b:

$$\lambda_1(t) = -e^{i(t-\tau_2)} \left[e^{-(1-f)r(\tau_3-\tau_2)} - \right.$$

$$e^{-(1-f)r(\tau_3-\tau_2)} \int_t^{\tau_4} \frac{\partial O_{vi}}{\partial K}(s, K(s)) e^{-a(s-t)} ds -$$

$$e^{-(1-f)r(\tau_3-\tau_2)} \int_{\tau_4}^{\tau_5} \frac{\partial O_{vi}}{\partial K}(s, K(s)) e^{-a(s-t)} e^{-(1-f)r(s-\tau_4)} ds -$$

$$\left. \frac{b}{1+b} e^{-a(\tau_5-t)} e^{-(1-f)r((\tau_3-\tau_2)+(\tau_5-\tau_4))} \right] +$$

$$\int_{\tau_5}^{\tau_6} \left\{ \frac{\partial O_{vi}}{\partial K}(s, K(s)) - y \right\} e^{-(a+i)(s-t)} ds + \frac{e^{-(a+i)(\tau_6-t)}}{1+b} \qquad (5.113)$$

The unit of capital assets is entirely financed from cash. The interpretation proceeds in the same way as before.

Period $[\tau_4, \tau_5)$, path 9a:

$$\lambda_1(t) = -e^{i(t-\tau_2)} \left[e^{-(1-f)r((\tau_3-\tau_2)+(t-\tau_4))} - \right.$$

$$e^{-(1-f)r(\tau_3-\tau_2)} \int_t^{\tau_5} \frac{\partial O_{vi}}{\partial K}(s, K(s)) e^{-a(s-t)} e^{-(1-f)r(s-\tau_4)} ds -$$

$$\left. \frac{b}{1+b} e^{-a(\tau_5-t)} e^{-(1-f)r((\tau_3-\tau_2)+(\tau_5-\tau_4))} \right] +$$

$$\int_{\tau_5}^{\tau_6} \left\{ \frac{\partial O_{vi}}{\partial K}(s, K(s)) - y \right\} e^{-(a+i)(s-t)} ds + \frac{e^{-(a+i)(\tau_6-t)}}{1+b} \qquad (5.114)$$

The unit of capital assets is entirely financed from debt. The interpretation proceeds as previously.

Period $\langle \tau_5, \tau_6]$, path 7a:

$$\lambda_1(t) = \frac{-1}{1+b} +$$

$$\int_t^{\tau_6} \left\{ \frac{\partial O_{vi}}{\partial K}(s, K(s)) - y \right\} e^{-(a+i)(s-t)} ds + \frac{e^{-(a+i)(\tau_6-t)}}{1+b} \qquad (5.115)$$

The unit of capital assets is financed form equity and debt in the ratio of $1 : b$. The expression is self-explanatory.

From the relationships for $\lambda_1(t)$ and $\lambda_2(t)$ above, the following expressions for the jumps at τ_5 can be found directly:

$$\lambda_1(\tau_5^+) - \lambda_1(\tau_5^-) = \frac{e^{i(\tau_5-\tau_2)-(1-f)r((\tau_3-\tau_2)+(\tau_5-\tau_4))} - 1}{1+b} \qquad (5.116)$$

$$\lambda_2(\tau_5^+) - \lambda_2(\tau_5^-) = 1 - e^{i(\tau_5-\tau_2)-(1-f)r((\tau_3-\tau_2)+(\tau_5-\tau_4))} \qquad (5.117)$$

This is consistent with the remark made earlier that a δ-peak in the course of ν_2 causes a jump in λ_1 and λ_2 at the same time, although the jumps are in opposite directions and in the ratio of $1:(1+b)$.

5.5   A model with an inventory of finished goods

5.5.1   Description of the model

In the basic model from Section 5.2, the firm has no opportunity to hold an inventory of finished goods. Everything that is produced will be sold directly.

In this section, a model of the firm will be studied in which the holding of an inventory of finished goods is an option so that the sales rate no longer need to be equal to the production rate. It is assumed that no extra costs occur when holding inventory (existing stores). Furthermore, there is no valuation of inventory on the balance sheet, i.e. the firm values its inventory at zero. As a consequence the book value of equity and, therefore, also the maximum amount of debt the firm is allowed to attract are lower than in a case of positive inventory valuation. Thus, the assumption implies that the firm has a conservative debt policy.

The complete formulation of the model now becomes:

$$\max_{I(t),D(t),Q(t)} \left\{ J = \int_0^z e^{-it}D(t)\,dt + e^{-iz}X(z) \right\} \qquad (5.118a)$$

$$\dot{K}(t) = I(t) - aK(t), \quad K(0) = K_0 \qquad (5.118b)$$

$$\dot{X}(t) = (1-f)\left\{ S(t,Q(t)) - wL(t) - aK(t) - rY(t) \right\} - D(t),$$

$$X(0) = X_0 \qquad (5.118c)$$

$$\dot{V}(t) = k^{-1}K(t) - Q(t), \quad V(0) = V_0 \qquad (5.118d)$$

$$L(t) = lk^{-1}K(t) \qquad (5.118e)$$

$$K(t) = X(t) + Y(t) \qquad (5.118f)$$

$$Y(t) \geq 0 \tag{5.118g}$$

$$Y(t) \leq bX(t) \tag{5.118h}$$

$$V(t) \geq 0 \tag{5.118i}$$

$$I(t) \geq 0 \tag{5.118j}$$

$$D(t) \geq 0 \tag{5.118k}$$

$$Q(t) \geq 0 \tag{5.118l}$$

Within these equations, $Q(t)$ no longer represents the production rate but the amount of finished goods sold per unit of time (sales rate); The production rate will always be equal to $k^{-1}K(t)$.

In Appendix C, it is shown that the optimization problem (5.118) satisfies the required constraint qualification, so that Theorem 2.1 for deriving the necessary conditions can be applied. For this purpose, the Hamiltonian and Lagrangian respectively, are defined as follows ($\lambda_0 = 1$, see Observation 2.1):

$$\mathcal{H}(t, K, X, V, I, D, Q, \lambda_1, \lambda_2, \lambda_3) = D + \lambda_1[I - aK] +$$

$$\lambda_2 \left[(1 - f)\{S(t, Q) - wlk^{-1}K - aK - r(K - X)\} - D \right] +$$

$$\lambda_3 \left[k^{-1}K - Q \right] \tag{5.119}$$

and:

$$\mathcal{L}(t, K, X, V, I, D, Q, \lambda_1, \lambda_2, \lambda_3, \mu_1, \mu_2, \mu_3, \nu_1, \nu_2, \nu_3) =$$

$$\mathcal{H}(t, K, X, V, I, D, Q, \lambda_1, \lambda_2, \lambda_3) + \mu_1 I + \mu_2 D +$$

$$\mu_3 Q + \nu_1[K - X] + \nu_2[(1 + b)X - K] + \nu_3 V \tag{5.120}$$

where:

$\lambda_1(t)$: costate variable of capital assets

$\lambda_2(t)$: costate variable of equity

$\lambda_3(t)$: costate variable of finished goods inventory

$\mu_1(t)$: Lagrange multiplier for lower bound of investment rate (5.118j)

$\mu_2(t)$: Lagrange multiplier for lower bound of dividend rate (5.118k)

$\mu_3(t)$: Lagrange multiplier for lower bound of sales rate (5.118l)

$\nu_1(t)$: Lagrange multiplier for lower bound of debt (5.118g)

$\nu_2(t)$: Lagrange multiplier for upper bound of debt (5.118h)

$\nu_3(t)$: Lagrange multiplier for lower bound of finished goods inventory
(5.118i)

The economic interpretations of $\lambda_1(t)$ and $\lambda_2(t)$ have been given already in Chapter 3. The interpretation of $\lambda_3(t)$ follows now:

- $\lambda_3(t)$ is the change in the maximum attainable value of the objective function when the firm gets one extra unit of finished goods available at instant t.

The set of necessary conditions resulting from the use of Theorem 2.1 is presented in Appendix C, where it is shown further that the necessary conditions are sufficient too.

Compared with the basic model, two extra constraints arise, which means that in principle, each path of the basic model divides into four paths for the model with an inventory of finished goods. The designation of the paths for the latter model comes about in the following way:

path xa if $\mu_3(t) = 0 \wedge \nu_3(t) > 0$, so that $Q(t) \geq 0$, $V(t) = 0$

path xb if $\mu_3(t) = 0 \wedge \nu_3(t) = 0$, so that $Q(t) \geq 0$, $V(t) \geq 0$

path xc if $\mu_3(t) > 0 \wedge \nu_3(t) = 0$, so that $Q(t) = 0$, $V(t) \geq 0$

path xd if $\mu_3(t) > 0 \wedge \nu_3(t) > 0$, so that $Q(t) = 0$, $V(t) = 0$

with: $x = 1, \ldots, 12$ the path number from Tabel 3.1. One of the necessary conditions from Appendix C reads:

$$\lambda_3(t) = (1 - f)\frac{\partial S}{\partial Q}(t, Q(t))\lambda_2(t) + \mu_3(t) \tag{5.121}$$

Following directly from the chosen price function (5.3), the paths with $Q(t) = 0$ (paths xc and xd with $x = 1, \ldots, 12$) imply an infinite value for $\lambda_3(t)$ and are excluded for this reason[8].

In Appendix C it is shown that nine of the twenty four remaining paths can be excluded once more. Table 5.3 contains the fifteen paths that may form part of an optimal string.

With the knowledge that $\mu_3(t) = 0$ for the whole planning period, expression (5.121) can be simplified to:

$$\lambda_3(t) = (1 - f)\frac{\partial S}{\partial Q}(t, Q(t))\lambda_2(t) \tag{5.122}$$

Interpretation: one extra unit of inventory of finished goods at t is sold directly and it produces an amount of:

$$(1 - f)\frac{\partial S}{\partial Q}(t, Q(t))$$

---

[8]The paths xd ($x = 1, \ldots, 12$) can endure no longer than one instant anyway; for, if $Q(t) = 0$ then $\dot{V}(t) = k^{-1}K(t) \geq k^{-1}K_0 e^{-at} > 0$.

Table 5.3 The fifteen paths which may appear in an optimal string for the model with an inventory of finished goods. The final column contains the conditions, if any, that must apply.

	μ_1	μ_2	μ_3	ν_1	ν_2	ν_3	
path 1b	+	+	0	+	0	0	
path 2a	0	+	0	+	0	+	
path 2b	0	+	0	+	0	0	
path 3a	+	0	0	+	0	+	only when $i < (1-f)r$
path 3b	+	0	0	+	0	0	only when $i < (1-f)r$
path 4a	0	0	0	+	0	+	only when $i < (1-f)r$
path 5b	+	+	0	0	+	0	
path 6a	0	+	0	0	+	+	
path 6b	0	+	0	0	+	0	
path 7a	+	0	0	0	+	+	only when $i > (1-f)r$
path 7b	+	0	0	0	+	0	only when $i > (1-f)r$
path 8a	0	0	0	0	+	+	only when $i > (1-f)r$
path 9a	+	+	0	0	0	+	
path 9b	+	+	0	0	0	0	
path 10a	0	+	0	0	0	+	

so that the situation is entirely comparable with that in which the firm at t gets that amount available as extra equity. The expression and interpretation above are valid only for $t \in [0, z)$. At instant z, a jump occurs in λ_3: an extra unit of inventory of finished goods is worthless at the end of the planning period, because neither will it be sold nor will it be valued on the balance sheet, thus:

$$\lambda_3(z^+) - \lambda_3(z^-) = -(1-f)\frac{\partial S}{\partial Q}(z, Q(z)) \qquad (5.123)$$

In the next subsections the numerical results of two case studies are discussed. The first concerns a severe recession in the case that equity is cheaper than debt and, despite that, the upper bound of debt becomes active; the second concerns a severe recession in the case that equity is more expensive than debt and, despite that, the lower bound of debt becomes active.

With respect to the fixed set of parameter values in Chapter 3, two parameters are different: $a = 0.06$ and $i = 0.055$ (cheap equity) or $i = 0.065$ (expensive equity). The motivation for these changes is the following assumption:

$$\min\{i, (1-f)r\} > (a+g)\varepsilon^{-1} \qquad (5.124)$$

which is made in order to temper the stimulus to hold an inventory of finished goods somewhat. The assumption is necessary in order that the paths 3a, 7a and 9a $(V(t) = 0)$ are may appear in an optimal string during the ascending stages of the business cycle (see Appendix C).

5.5.2   Severe recession in the case of $i < (1 - f)r$ and $m > m^\star$

Figure 5.13 illustrates the graphs for optimal $D(t)$, $Q(t)$, $Y(t)$, $V(t)$, $\mu_1(t)$, $\mu_2(t)$, $\nu_j(t)$ $(j = 1, 2, 3)$ and $\lambda_3(t)$, with $m = 0.29$. The course of K and I does not differ principally from that in Subsection 5.2.2 for the basic model. Furthermore, $\lambda_1(t) = -\mu_1(t)$, $\lambda_2(t) = 1 + \mu_2(t)$ and $\mu_3(t) = 0$ apply. The optimal instant of stopping to invest, τ_1, is not a boundary optimum in the sense that τ_1 can become larger without the upper bound of debt being exceeded inevitably at τ_6. To that end, the strategy for the sales rate must be adjusted however. The dividend strategy can be seen as being fixed entirely by investments and sales rate.

In Appendix C, a set of equations is given from which the coupling points can be calculated. A decision rule can be formulated as follows:

- Follow path 4a until τ_1.

- Stop investing and distribute the operating cash flow entirely as dividend at a sales rate equal to the production rate, until τ_2 (path 3a).

- Adjust the sales rate so that the price per unit of goods sold discounted to τ_2 against the cost of equity remains constant, whereby inventory arises; distribute all the operating cash flow as dividend until it becomes zero at τ_3 (path 3b).

- Adjust the sales rate so that the operating cash flow exactly remains zero, whereby the inventory of finished goods grows further at first, but then reduces, until τ_4 (path 1b).

- Adjust the sales rate so that the price per unit of goods sold discounted to τ_4 against the cost of debt remains constant, whereby the inventory reduces further, and attract debt necessary to pay wages and interest, until at τ_5 the inventory has entirely disappeared (path 9b).

- Attract more debt at a sales rate equal to the production rate, until a certain instant after the bottom of the recession when the operating cash flow becomes positive. Then, use it completely to pay off debt until no more exists at τ_7 (string of paths 9a$\star$9a).

- Distribute the operating cash flow entirely as dividend until path 4a is reached at τ_8 (path 3a).

- Follow path 4a until z.

Next, the development over time of the costate variables of equity and inventory of finished goods, respectively, will be studied.

The course of λ_2

Consider at each instant of time the change in the maximum attainable value of the objective function when the firm has one extra unit of equity at its disposal.

Period $[0, \tau_3]$, string of paths 4ao3ao3b:

$$\lambda_2(t) = 1 \tag{5.125}$$

The firm pays out the extra unit of equity directly as dividend.

Period $[\tau_3, \tau_4]$, path 1b:

$$\lambda_2(t) = \frac{\dfrac{\partial S}{\partial Q}(\tau_3, Q(\tau_3))}{\dfrac{\partial S}{\partial Q}(t, Q(t))} e^{i(t-\tau_3)} \tag{5.126}$$

When the firm has available one additional unit of equity at t, it anticipates this, on the one hand, by increasing the sales at τ_3 by:

$$\left[(1-f)\frac{\partial S}{\partial Q}(t, Q(t))\right]^{-1}$$

units and paying out the extra returns as dividend, and on the other hand, by reducing the sales at t by the same number of units[9]. The reduced returns at t are exactly compensated by the extra unit of equity, whereby the state variables remain unchanged after t.

Period $[\tau_4, \tau_6)$, string of paths 9bo9a:

$$\lambda_2(t) = \frac{\dfrac{\partial S}{\partial Q}(\tau_3, Q(\tau_3))}{\dfrac{\partial S}{\partial Q}(\tau_4, Q(\tau_4))} e^{-(1-f)r(t-\tau_4)} e^{i(t-\tau_3)} \tag{5.127}$$

When the firm has available at t an extra unit of equity, it anticipates this, on the one hand, by increasing the sales at τ_3 by:

$$\left[(1-f)\frac{\partial S}{\partial Q}(\tau_4, Q(\tau_4))\right]^{-1} e^{-(1-f)r(t-\tau_4)}$$

units and paying out the extra returns as dividend, and on the other hand, by reducing the sales at τ_4 by the same number of units. The result is that the firm must attract $e^{-(1-f)r(t-\tau_4)}$ units of extra debt at τ_4, which at t is paid off exactly with the extra unit of equity, so that the state variables remain unchanged after t.

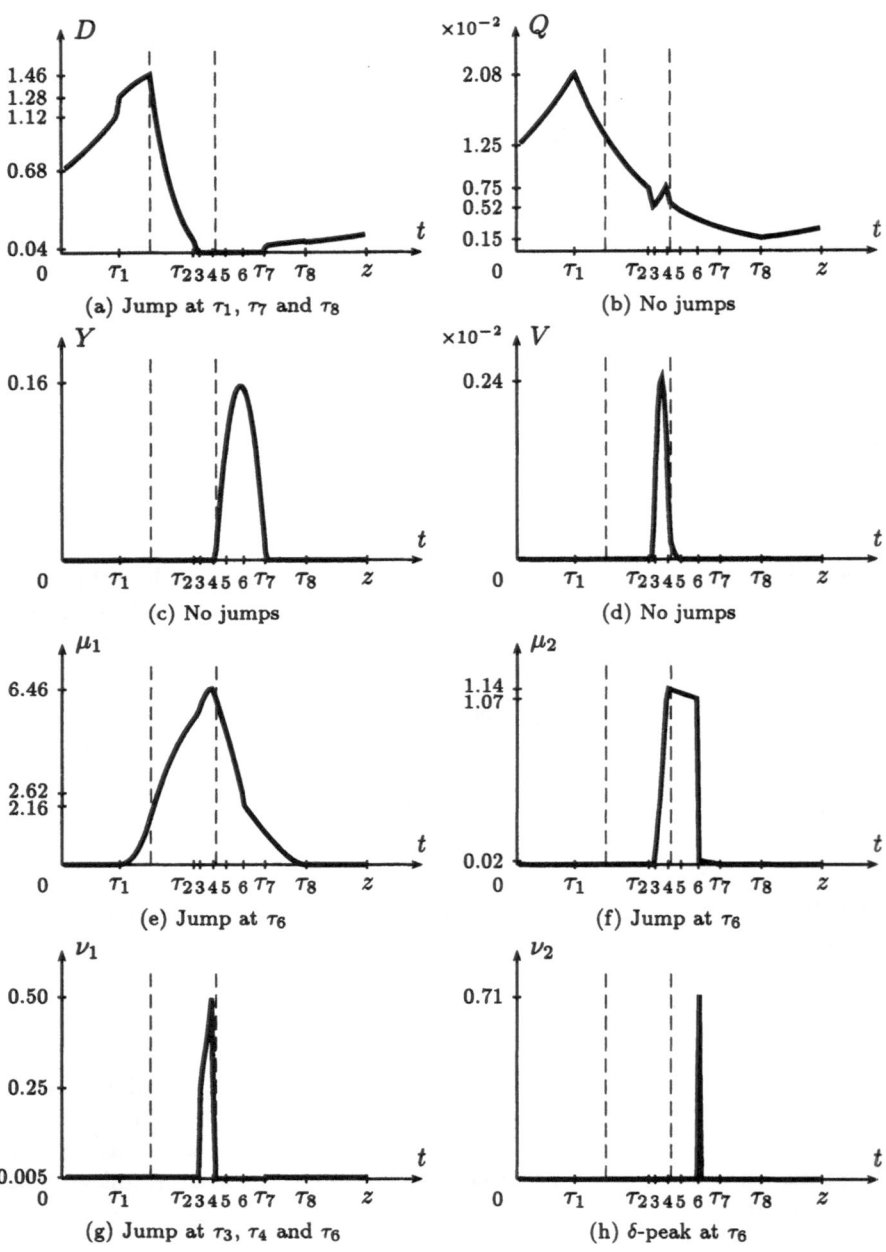

(a) Jump at τ_1, τ_7 and τ_8

(b) No jumps

(c) No jumps

(d) No jumps

(e) Jump at τ_6

(f) Jump at τ_6

(g) Jump at τ_3, τ_4 and τ_6

(h) δ-peak at τ_6

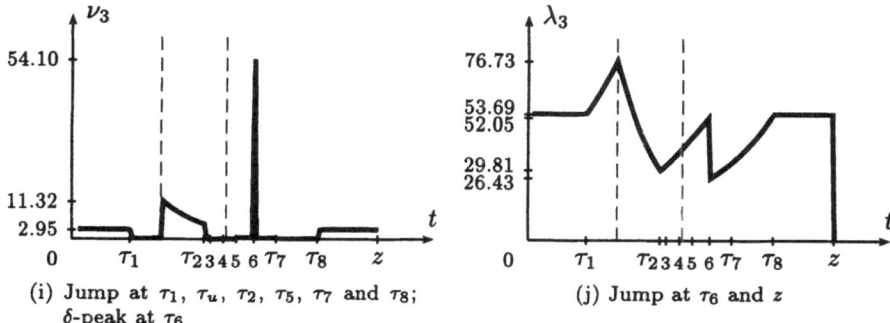

(i) Jump at τ_1, τ_u, τ_2, τ_5, τ_7 and τ_8;
δ-peak at τ_6

(j) Jump at τ_6 and z

Figure 5.13 Solution of the model with an inventory of finished goods for a severe recession in the case of $i < (1-f)r$ and $m < m^*$. The broken lines indicate the successive peak and trough in the business cycle. Optimal string of paths: 4ao3ao3bo1bo9bo9a⋆9ao3ao4a. ($\Delta t = 0.5$)

Period $\langle \tau_6, \tau_7 \rangle$, path 9a:

$$\lambda_2(t) = e^{((1-f)r-i)(\tau_7-t)} \tag{5.128}$$

The firm uses the extra unit of equity at t in order to redeem debt. This results in a reduction in debt at τ_7 amounting to $e^{(1-f)r(\tau_7-t)}$ and an increase in the dividend distributed at that instant by the same amount.

Period $[\tau_7, z]$, string of paths 3ao4a:

$$\lambda_2(t) = 1 \tag{5.129}$$

The firm distributes the extra unit of equity directly as dividend.

The course of λ_3

Consider at each instant of time the change in the maximum attainable value of the objective function when the firm gets available an extra unit of inventory of finished goods.

Now the relationships and interpretations are known for $\lambda_2(t)$, for $\lambda_3(t)$, in principle, it will be sufficient to refer to equation (5.122) and its explanation. Yet for the period in which the firm holds an inventory of finished goods, an alternative expression and interpretation are given.

---

[9]Instead of τ_3, τ_2 can be read as well, since the following applies:

$$\frac{\partial S}{\partial Q}\big(\tau_3, Q(\tau_3)\big) = \frac{\partial S}{\partial Q}\big(\tau_2, Q(\tau_2)\big)e^{i(\tau_3-\tau_2)}$$

Period $[\tau_2, \tau_5]$, string of paths 3b∘1b∘9b:

$$\lambda_3(t) = (1 - f)\frac{\partial S}{\partial Q}(\tau_2, Q(\tau_2))e^{i(t-\tau_2)} \tag{5.130}$$

The firms holds the extra unit of finished goods at t in stock. However, in anticipation of this, the firm sells one unit more than normal at τ_2 and distributes the returns as dividend, whereby the state variables remain unchanged after t.

From the necessary conditions with the aid of the relationships above for $\lambda_2(t)$ and $\lambda_3(t)$, now, expressions for $\lambda_1(t)$ can be derived directly. They will be left out here, although expressions for the jump at τ_6 in the three costate variables will follow next:

$$\lambda_1(\tau_6^+) - \lambda_1(\tau_6^-) = -\frac{\lambda_2(\tau_6^+) - \lambda_2(\tau_6^-)}{1 + b} \tag{5.131}$$

$$\lambda_2(\tau_6^+) - \lambda_2(\tau_6^-) = e^{((1-f)r-i)(\tau_7-\tau_6)} -$$

$$\frac{\dfrac{\partial S}{\partial Q}(\tau_3, Q(\tau_3))}{\dfrac{\partial S}{\partial Q}(\tau_4, Q(\tau_4))}e^{-(1-f)r(\tau_6-\tau_4)}e^{i(\tau_6-\tau_3)} \tag{5.132}$$

$$\lambda_3(\tau_6^+) - \lambda_3(\tau_6^-) = (1 - f)\frac{\partial S}{\partial Q}(\tau_6, Q(\tau_6))\left(\lambda_2(\tau_6^+) - \lambda_2(\tau_6^-)\right) \tag{5.133}$$

The value of $m^\star$ can be found iteratively by determining the coupling points and subsequently calculating the height of one of the jumps, for different m-values. The jumps equal zero only when $m = m^\star$, whilst they are positive when $m > m^\star$, or negative when $m < m^\star$.

This subsection will be concluded with two observations. An inventory of finished goods larger than zero occurs as soon as m is larger than the critical m-value for an severe recession. This is plausible because otherwise, a δ-piek would appear in the course of ν_1 like that for the basic model in Subsection 5.2.2. Next to a positive jump in $\lambda_2(t)$, that δ-peak would lead to positive jump in $\lambda_3(t)$ as well. Then, the latter would imply a negative δ-peak in the course of $\nu_3(t)$ (see the necessary conditions in Appendix C). In the case of m larger than the critical m-value for a severe recession but smaller than $m^\star$, the optimal string of paths is: 4a∘3a∘3b∘1b∘9b∘9a∘3a∘4a. From this, it appears that no jumps occur in the costate variables. In Appendix C, for this situation too, a set of equations is given from which the coupling points can be calculated.

From a certain $m > m^\star$, the coupling points τ_5 and τ_6 coincide. Then, the optimal string of paths becomes: 4a∘3a∘3b∘1b∘9b⋆9a∘3a∘4a.

5.5.3 Severe recession in the case of $i > (1 - f)r$ and $m > m°$

Figure 5.14 the graphs for the optimal $D(t)$, $Q(t)$, $Y(t)$, $V(t)$, $\mu_1(t)$, $\mu_2(t)$, $\nu_j(t)$ ($j = 1, 2, 3$) and $\lambda_3(t)$, when $m = 0.29$. The course of K and I does not deviate substantially from that in Subsection 5.2.4 for the basic model. Furthermore, $\lambda_1(t) = -\mu_1(t)$, $\lambda_2(t) = 1 + \mu_2(t)$ and $\mu_3(t) = 0$ apply. Again, the optimal instant to stop investing, τ_1, is not a boundary optimum in the sense that τ_1 can be larger without the upper limit of debt being exceeded inevitably at τ_7. To that end, the strategy for the dividend and/or sales rate must be adjusted however.

In Appendix C, a set of equations is given from which the coupling points can be calculated. A decision rule can be formulated as follows:

- Follow path 8a until τ_1

- Stop investing; use the operating cash flow, at a sales rate equal to the production rate, until τ_2 for distributing dividend and redeeming debt so that the amount of debt remains maximal (path 7a).

- Stop distributing dividend and use the operating cash flow, at a sales rate equal to the production rate, until τ_3, completely for redeeming debt (path 9a).

- Adjust the sales rate so that the marginal returns from sales discounted to τ_3 against the cost of debt remain constant, whereby an inventory of finished goods arises; use the operating cash flow entirely for redeeming debt, until both become zero at τ_4 (path 9b).

- Adjust the sales rate so that the operating cash flow exactly remains equal to zero, whereby the inventory of finished goods grows further at first, but then reduces, until τ_5 (path 1b).

- Adjust the sales rate so that the marginal returns from sales discounted to τ_5 against the cost of debt remains constant, whereby the inventory falls further; attract debt necessary to pay wages and interest, until τ_6 when the inventory has disappeared completely (path 9b).

- Attract more debt at a sales rate equal to the production rate, until a certain instant after the bottom of the recession when the operating cash flow becomes positive. Now, use it completely for redeeming debt until τ_7 when the amount of debt becomes maximal at an operating cash flow that exactly covers the obligatory redemption of debt (path 9a).

- Use the operating cash flow, at a sales rate equal to the production rate, for distributing dividend and redeeming debt so that the amount of debt remains maximal, until path 8a is reached at τ_8 (path 7a).

- Follow path 8a until z.

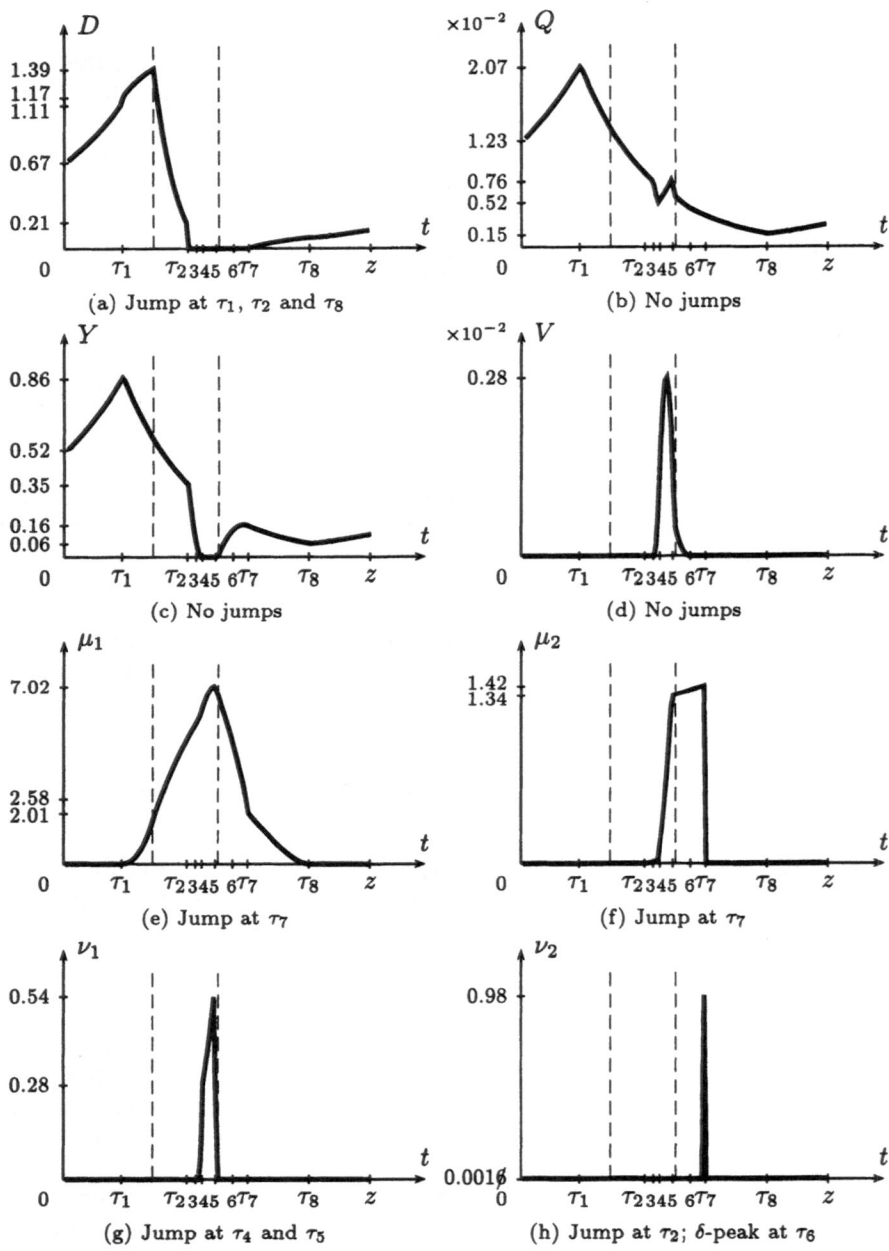

(a) Jump at τ_1, τ_2 and τ_8

(b) No jumps

(c) No jumps

(d) No jumps

(e) Jump at τ_7

(f) Jump at τ_7

(g) Jump at τ_4 and τ_5

(h) Jump at τ_2; δ-peak at τ_6

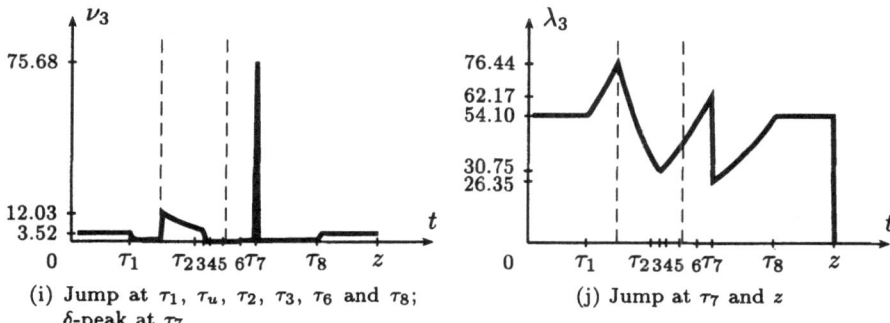

(i) Jump at τ_1, τ_u, τ_2, τ_3, τ_6 and τ_8;
δ-peak at τ_7

(j) Jump at τ_7 and z

Figure 5.14 Solution of the model with an inventory of finished goods for a severe recession in the case of $i > (1 - f)r$ and $m > m^\circ$. The broken lines indicate the successive peak and trough in the business cycle. Optimal string of paths: 8ao7ao9ao9bo1bo9bo9a$\star$7ao8a. ($\Delta t = 0.5$)

Next, the development over time of the costate variables of equity and inventory of finished goods will be examined.

The course of λ_2

Consider the change in the maximum attainable value of the objective function at each instant of time, when the firm gets available one extra unit of equity.

Period $[0, \tau_2]$, string of paths 8ao7a:

$$\lambda_2(t) = 1 \tag{5.134}$$

The firm distributes the extra unit of equity directly as dividend.

Period $[\tau_2, \tau_4]$, string of paths 9bo9a:

$$\lambda_2(t) = e^{(i-(1-f)r)(t-\tau_2)} \tag{5.135}$$

When the firm gets available one additional unit of equity at t, it anticipates this by distributing an extra amount of dividend equal to $e^{-(1-f)r(t-\tau_2)}$ at τ_2, which is at the expense of redeeming debt at that time. The extra unit of debt at t resulting from this action is exactly paid off with the extra unit of equity.

Period $[\tau_4, \tau_5]$, path 1b:

$$\lambda_2(t) = \frac{\dfrac{\partial S}{\partial Q}(\tau_3, Q(\tau_3))}{\dfrac{\partial S}{\partial Q}(t, Q(t))} e^{-(1-f)r(\tau_3-\tau_2)} e^{i(t-\tau_2)} \tag{5.136}$$

When the firm gets available one extra unit of equity at t, it anticipates this by distributing extra dividend at τ_2 amounting to:

$$\frac{\dfrac{\partial S}{\partial Q}(\tau_3, Q(\tau_3))}{\dfrac{\partial S}{\partial Q}(t, Q(t))} e^{-(1-f)r(\tau_3 - \tau_2)}$$

which is at the expense of redeeming debt. Therefore, the increase in debt at τ_3 amounts to:

$$\frac{\dfrac{\partial S}{\partial Q}(\tau_3, Q(\tau_3))}{\dfrac{\partial S}{\partial Q}(t, Q(t))}$$

and is redeemed with the extra returns from an increase in sales by:

$$\left[(1-f)\frac{\partial S}{\partial Q}(t, Q(t))\right]^{-1}$$

units. Subsequently the sales at t are reduced by the same number, where the lost returns are exactly compensated by the extra unit of equity which the firm gets available; therefore the state variables remain unchanged after t.

Period $[\tau_5, \tau_7)$, string of paths 9bo9a:

$$\lambda_2(t) = \frac{\dfrac{\partial S}{\partial Q}(\tau_3, Q(\tau_3))}{\dfrac{\partial S}{\partial Q}(\tau_5, Q(\tau_5))} e^{-(1-f)r(\tau_3 - \tau_2 + t - \tau_5)} e^{i(t-\tau_2)} \tag{5.137}$$

When the firm gets available one extra unit of equity at t, it anticipates this by distributing extra dividend at τ_2 amounting to:

$$\frac{\dfrac{\partial S}{\partial Q}(\tau_3, Q(\tau_3))}{\dfrac{\partial S}{\partial Q}(\tau_5, Q(\tau_5))} e^{-(1-f)r(\tau_3 - \tau_2 + t - \tau_5)}$$

which is at the expense of redeeming debt. Therefore, the increase in debt at at τ_3 amounts to:

$$\frac{\dfrac{\partial S}{\partial Q}(\tau_3, Q(\tau_3))}{\dfrac{\partial S}{\partial Q}(\tau_5, Q(\tau_5))} e^{-(1-f)r(t - \tau_5)}$$

and is redeemed with the extra returns from an increase in sales by:

$$\left[(1-f)\frac{\partial S}{\partial Q}(\tau_5, Q(\tau_5))\right]^{-1} e^{-(1-f)r(t-\tau_5)}$$

units. Subsequently the sales at τ_5 are reduced by the same number, whereby $e^{-(1-f)r(t-\tau_5)}$ of extra debt has to be attracted. As a result of this, the amount of debt at t has been increased by one unit that is exactly paid off with the extra unit of equity which the firm gets available; therefore, the state variables remain unchanged after t.

Period $\langle \tau_7, z]$, string of paths 7a○8a:

$$\lambda_2(t) = 1 \tag{5.138}$$

The firm distributes the extra unit of equity directly as dividend.

The course of λ_3

Consider changes in the maximum attainable value of the objective function at each instant of time, when the firm gets available one extra unit of inventory of finished goods.

After first referring back to expression (5.122) and its interpretation, once again an alternative expression and interpretation will be given for the period in which the firm holds an inventory of finished goods.

Period $[\tau_3, \tau_6]$, string of paths 9b○1b○9b:

$$\lambda_3(t) = (1-f)\frac{\partial S}{\partial Q}(\tau_3, Q(\tau_3))e^{-(1-f)r(\tau_3-\tau_2)}e^{i(t-\tau_2)} \tag{5.139}$$

The firm holds the extra unit of finished goods at t in stock. However, anticipating this the firm distributes extra dividend at τ_2 amounting to:

$$(1-f)\frac{\partial S}{\partial Q}(\tau_3, Q(\tau_3))e^{-(1-f)r(\tau_3-\tau_2)}$$

which is at the expense of redeeming debt at that instant. Hence, the increase in debt at τ_3 amounts to:

$$(1-f)\frac{\partial S}{\partial Q}(\tau_3, Q(\tau_3))$$

and is redeemed with the returns from the selling of one extra unit of goods. The reduction in the inventory by one unit resulting from this, is compensated at t with the extra unit of inventory which the firm gets available; therefore, the state variables remain unchanged afterwards.

From the necessary conditions, with the aid of the relationships above for $\lambda_2(t)$ and $\lambda_3(t)$, now, expressions for $\lambda_1(t)$ can be derived directly. They will be omitted here, although expressions for the jump at τ_7 in the three costate variables will be given:

$$\lambda_1(\tau_7^+) - \lambda_1(\tau_7^-) = -\frac{\lambda_2(\tau_7^+) - \lambda_2(\tau_7^-)}{1+b} \tag{5.140}$$

$$\lambda_2(\tau_7^+) - \lambda_2(\tau_7^-) = 1 -$$

$$\frac{\dfrac{\partial S}{\partial Q}\left(\tau_3, Q(\tau_3)\right)}{\dfrac{\partial S}{\partial Q}\left(\tau_5, Q(\tau_5)\right)} e^{-(1-f)r(\tau_3-\tau_2+\tau_7-\tau_5)} e^{i(\tau_7-\tau_2)} \tag{5.141}$$

$$\lambda_3(\tau_7^+) - \lambda_3(\tau_7^-) = (1-f)\frac{\partial S}{\partial Q}\left(\tau_7, Q(\tau_7)\right)\left(\lambda_2(\tau_7^+) - \lambda_2(\tau_7^-)\right) \tag{5.142}$$

The value of m° can be found iteratively by determining the coupling points and subsequently calculating the height of one of the jumps, for different m-values. The jumps equal zero only when $m = m^\circ$, whilst they are positive when $m > m^\circ$, or negative when $m < m^\circ$.

This subsection closes with two observations. An inventory of finished goods larger than zero does not occur when $m < m^\circ$; then, the optimal strategy is the same as for the basic model in Subsection 5.2.4.

From a certain $m > m^\circ$, the coupling points τ_6 and τ_7 coincide. Then, the optimal string of paths becomes: 8a-7a○9a○9b○1b○9b⋆7a-8a.

5.6   Conclusions

Severe recession in the case of cheap equity

The optimal investment and dividend strategy for the basic model is entirely fixed by the optimal instant of stopping to invest, τ_1, that already comes before the start of the recession (τ_u). An optimal balance must be made here between lacking income now and avoiding overcapacity costs later. Inherent in an *severe* recession is the fact that the operating cash flow becomes negative at a certain instant τ_2 during the recession. This compels the firm to attract expensive debt in order to settle its commitments. From the time when the operating cash flow rises above zero again, that comes after the end of the recession (τ_d), it is fully appropiated in order to redeem debt which will be accomplished at τ_4. As known already, a jump occurs at τ_2 in the costate variables of capital assets and equity resulting from the change in financing costs.

For a sufficiently severe recession, the size of debt becomes maximal precisely at one instant $\tau_3 \in \langle \tau_d, \tau_4 \rangle$: $Y(\tau_3) = bX(\tau_3)$, without causing the boundary case of bankruptcy being reached, since at the start of the planning period investments are made still ($\tau_1 > 0$). The instant of stopping to invest now has become a *boundary* optimum: with due observance of the other bounds, continuing to invest beyond τ_1 inevitably leads to exceeding the maximum debt permitted at τ_3. One thing and the other cause an extra jump to appear at both τ_2 and τ_3 in the costate variables. In essence, the economic explanation is that the firm uses the opportunity to continue investing beyond τ_1 should it get an extra unit of equity available between τ_2 and τ_3, and, that the firm is forced to cease investing before τ_1 should it be obliged to acquire an unit of capital assets between τ_2 and τ_3. In both events, this will have consequences for the maximum value available of the objective function, just because τ_1 is a boundary optimum. Since the boundary optimal value of τ_1 moves further from the free optimum in the absence of an upper bound of debt with rising severity of the recession, the heights of the jumps at both τ_2 and τ_3 increase quickly so that they dominate the effect of the changed financing costs on the jump at τ_2 completely.

When the basic model is extended with a variable utilization rate, an optimal adjustment of it implies that the operating cash flow before interest always remains positive regardless of the severity of the recession, so that a *severe* recession never occurs here. This means that τ_1 is always a free optimum[10] and the costate variables are always continuous.

When the basic model is extended with a cash balance or a finished goods inventory, τ_1 is always a free optimum, even if the upper bound of debt is reached after the end of the recession for precisely one instant of time. The firm can continue investing without exceeding that upper bound by building up a larger cash balance or finished goods inventory in time. As long as the upper bound of debt is reached nowhere, the instant τ_2, where building up the cash balance or finished goods inventory begins, is likewise a free optimum; hence, the costate variables are continuous everywhere. When the upper bound of debt is reached for exactly one instant of time after the end of an sufficiently severe recession, τ_2 becomes a boundary optimum for a fixed optimal value of τ_1: with due observance of the other bounds, distributing extra dividend beyond τ_2 inevitably leads to exceeding the upper bound of debt later. The costate variables of capital assets, equity and finished goods inventory all show a jump at the instant when the upper bound of debt is reached. In essence, the economic explanation is that the firm uses the opportunity to distribute extra dividend beyond τ_2 should it get available one extra unit of equity or finished goods inventory during the period between τ_2 and the instant where the upper bound of debt is reached; and, that the firm is forced to cease distributing dividend before τ_2 should it be obliged to acquire one unit of capital assets in the period mentioned. This has consequences for the maximum attainable value of the objective function, just because τ_2 is a boundary optimum.

---

[10]Provided, $\tau_1 > 0$. Since this condition is so trivial, it will be omitted hereafter.

Severe recession in the case of expensive equity

Once again, the optimal investment and dividend strategy for the basic model is completely fixed by the value of τ_1 ($< \tau_u$). Unless the firm ceases maximum debt financing in time, it will be bankrupt during the recession at the instant that the operating cash flow no longer covers the mandatory redemption of debt. This prompts the firm to cease distributing dividend at a certain instant τ_2 when the operating cash flow still exceeds the mandatory redemption, and to spend it entirely on redeeming debt in order to create a borrowing capacity for the 'severe times' that are coming. Here, the firm chooses τ_2 so that the mandatory redemption of debt is exactly covered by the operating cash flow at a certain instant τ_4 ($> \tau_d$) when the upper bound of debt is reached again. As mentioned earlier, a jump occurs at τ_4 in the costate variables of capital assets and equity as a result of the change in financing costs.

For a sufficiently severe recession, the size of the borrowing capacity becomes momentarily maximal at instant τ_3: $Y(\tau_3) = 0$, without causing the boundary case of bankruptcy being reached, since at the start of the planning period investments are made still ($\tau_1 > 0$). The instant of ceasing to invest now has become a *boundary* optimum again: with due observance of the other bounds, continued investing leads inevitably to exceeding the upper bound of debt at τ_3. One thing and the other causes an extra jump to appear both at τ_3 and τ_4 in the costate variables. In essence, the economic explanation again is that the firm uses the opportunity to continue investing beyond τ_1 should it get an extra unit of equity available between τ_3 and τ_4, and, that it is forced to cease investing before τ_1 should it have to acquire a unit of capital assets between τ_3 and τ_4. Since the boundary optimal value of τ_1 moves further away from the free optimum in the absence of a lower bound of debt with rising severity of the recession, the heights of the jumps both at τ_3 and τ_4 increase quickly, so that they dominate the effect of the changed financing costs on the jump at τ_4 completely.

When the basic model is extended with a variabele utilization rate, an optimal adjustment of it implies that the operating cash flow before interest always remains positive regardless of the severity of the recession, so that the lower bound of debt is reached nowhere. This means that τ_1 always is a free optimum and the costate variables show a jump at the instant after the end of the recession when the upper bound of debt is reached tangentially. The same explanation applies as for the jump in the basic model when the lower bound of debt is not reached.

When the basic model is extended with a cash balance or finished goods inventory, the firm only makes use of it in the case of a sufficiently severe recession whereby the lower bound of debt is reached. Then, no extra jump appears in the costate variables because τ_1 is not a boundary optimum anymore: continuing to invest for longer is possible by building up a larger cash balance or finished goods inventory for the 'severe times' that will come.

Chapter 6

A Model with Increasing Returns to Scale, an Experience Curve and a Production Life Cycle

6.1 Introduction

In this chapter, a model of the firm is studied which is an elaborated version of the basic model in Chapter 3. Essentially, it is refined in two places, the first concerns the production function of the model which describes the relationship between the production rate and the minimum quantity of production factors required. The second refinement concerns the price function which deals with the returns per product unit as a function of the sales rate (equal to the production rate) and time.

6.2 Description of the model

6.2.1 The production function

In the basic model, there are two production factors, capital K and labour L, according to a Leontief technology with constant returns to scale. The production function is expressed as:

$$Q = \min\left\{\frac{K}{k}, \frac{L}{l}\right\} \tag{6.1}$$

In many industries, for example the chemical industry, however, the production costs increase less than proportional with a rising production rate. The productivity of the production factors increases as the scale of production becomes larger, although, in general, the size of the increase differs for each of the production factors. The literature on this subject speaks of increasing returns to scale, or economies of scale.

The production function of the model in this chapter is again based on a Leontief technology, although now with a third production factor, namely, raw materials G, and with increasing returns to scale for all the production factors. The production function is represented by:

$$Q = \overline{Q} \min \left\{ \left(\frac{G}{\overline{G}} \right)^{\frac{1}{\pi_G}}, \left(\frac{K}{\overline{K}} \right)^{\frac{1}{\pi_K}}, \left(\frac{L}{\overline{L}} \right)^{\frac{1}{\pi_L}} \right\} \tag{6.2}$$

where: $\overline{Q}, \overline{K}, \overline{G}$ and $\overline{L}$ are reference values; π_G, π_K and π_L $(0 < \pi_G, \pi_K, \pi_L < 1)$ are the productivity coefficients for raw materials, capital and labour respectively, each of which may have a different value, in general. Explicit modelling of the production factor raw materials is not essential for the basic model, because it can be assumed to be incorporated into the factor labour without damaging the generality, as the productivity coefficients of both factors are equal to unity (constant returns to scale).

Assuming that the firm always executes an efficient production plan[1], the following expressions for capital assets (K), raw materials (G) and labour (L) can be derived from equation (6.2):

$$K = \overline{K} \left(\frac{Q}{\overline{Q}} \right)^{\pi_K} \tag{6.3}$$

$$G = \overline{G} \left(\frac{Q}{\overline{Q}} \right)^{\pi_G} \tag{6.4}$$

$$L = \overline{L} \left(\frac{Q}{\overline{Q}} \right)^{\pi_L} \tag{6.5}$$

The implications of these equations are that an increased production rate of 1% requires π_G% extra raw materials, π_K% extra capital assets and π_L% extra labour (first order estimating).

6.2.2   The price function

In the basic model of Chapter 3, the price that the firm receives for its product sales is only implicitly dependent of time. When the firm fixes its sales rate, in the course of time, it will always receive the same price. This is not very realistic.

In this chapter, a price function is presented which will reflect reality more closely in many cases; it is assumed to be composed as follows:

$$P\bigl(t, Q(t)\bigr) = P_a(t) \left(1 - \frac{Q(t)}{U(t)} \right) \tag{6.6}$$

---

[1]A production plan is *efficient* if there is no way to produce more output with the same inputs or to produce the same output with less inputs (Varian [1984]).

where: $P_a(t)$ is the price at instant of time t, if the firm sells nothing, so that $Q(t) = 0$; and $U(t)$ is the total market sales of all producers aggregated at instant of time t, which is always assumed to equal the total market production (no inventories). $P_a(t)$ and $U(t)$ are autonomous functions of time which means that the firm cannot influence them. For that reason, $P_a(t)$ in the following text is called the autonomous price function. The quotient of $Q(t)$ and $U(t)$ represents the firm's market share. Equation (6.6) shows that expanding the market share is at the expense of the price received, or, put the other way around, that expanding the market share can be achieved only by selling at a lower asking price.

The autonomous price is divided into the autonomous added value per product unit (time-variable) and the raw materials costs per product unit for the reference production rate $\overline{Q}$ (constant):

$$P_a(t) = T(t) + \frac{v\overline{G}}{\overline{Q}} \tag{6.7}$$

where: v is the price per unit raw materials. The autonomous added value per product unit is modelled as the so-called experience or learning curve:

$$T(t) = \overline{T}\left(\frac{E(t)}{\overline{E}}\right)^{-1/\beta}, \qquad 1/\beta > 0 \tag{6.8}$$

with:

$$E(t) = \int_{-\infty}^{t} U(s)\mathrm{d}s \tag{6.9}$$

Expressed in words: set out on logarithmic axes, the connection between the autonomous added value per product unit and the total accumulated market production ('experience') is represented by a straight line with a slope of $-1/\beta$. Such modelling is supported by many empirical studies including those of the Boston Consulting Group [1970] where usually a value for $1/\beta$ was found in the interval $[0.2, 0.3]$. In Bekker [1991], a theoretical foundation for the experience curve is given and a value of 0.3069 for $1/\beta$ is calculated[2].

Whilst the accumulated production in equation (6.8) refers to the whole market, each individual producer passes through its own experience curve with regard to its cost price minus supplies. In this model however, instead of modelling the cost price minus supplies on the basis an experience curve, a specific productivity profit per individual cost item is introduced (increasing returns to scale, see previous subsection). Using this, the firm must 'enter the battle' against the autonomously declining added value obtained from the market.

---

[2]This value relates to capital assets of which the lifetime is Weibull-distributed. The form parameter of that distribution is $\beta = (1 - \ln 2)^{-1}$. Bekker deduced that $1/\beta$ is a capital elasticity corresponding to that in a Cobb-Douglas production function.

The development over time of the total market sales of a product (number sold per time unit) can often be brought into a model using a production life cycle like that introduced by the sociologist G. Tarde (for more information see - De Jong [1985]). In that life cycle, four stages are distinguished:

1. The introduction or development stage, in which both sales rate and sales growth are low still;

2. The expansion or growth stage, in which the sales rate grows quickly;

3. The maturation or satiation stage, in which the sales growth decreases strongly and ultimately even stagnates;

4. The decline or contraction stage, in which the sales rate crumbles off, caused mainly by the introduction of subsitutes on to the market.

The final stage can last a long time actually, or it need not occur at all, for example, when new applications are found for obsolete products ('recycling'). The first three stages imply an S-shaped curve for the total market sales as a function of time, which can be described well by the so-called logistic curve. Then, $U(t)$ is the solution of the following differential equation:

$$\vartheta_U \dot{U}(t) = U(t) \left(1 - \frac{U(t)}{U_\infty} \right), \quad 0 < U(0) = U_0 < U_\infty \tag{6.10}$$

This equation says that, in the beginning of the production life cycle, the total sales rate grows exponentially and gradually changes to an asymptotic growth until the limiting value U_∞ with ϑ_U as the characteristic time period. Solving the differential equation gives:

$$U(t) = \frac{U_\infty}{1 + e^{(\tau_{50\%} - t)\vartheta_U^{-1}}} \tag{6.11}$$

where:

$$\tau_{50\%} = \vartheta_U \ln \left(\frac{U_\infty}{U_0} - 1 \right) \tag{6.12}$$

is the instant of time when the total market sales amounts to half of the limiting value U_∞ and the sales growth is maximal. Note that the logistical curve is symmetrical with respect to this point of inflection. After integration, the following is obtained for the accumulated total market sales:

$$E(t) = -\vartheta_U U_\infty \ln \left(1 - \frac{U(t)}{U_\infty} \right) \tag{6.13}$$

According to the literature, with the aid of the parameters ϑ_U, U_∞ and $\tau_{50\%}$, a good fit can be obtained for many market growth figures (Martino [1972]).

Finally, this subsection ends by presenting Figure 6.1 which shows successive graphs for: the experience curve, the production life cycle, the price as a function of time at three fixed values of the sales rate, and the price as a function of the sales rate at three fixed values of the time.

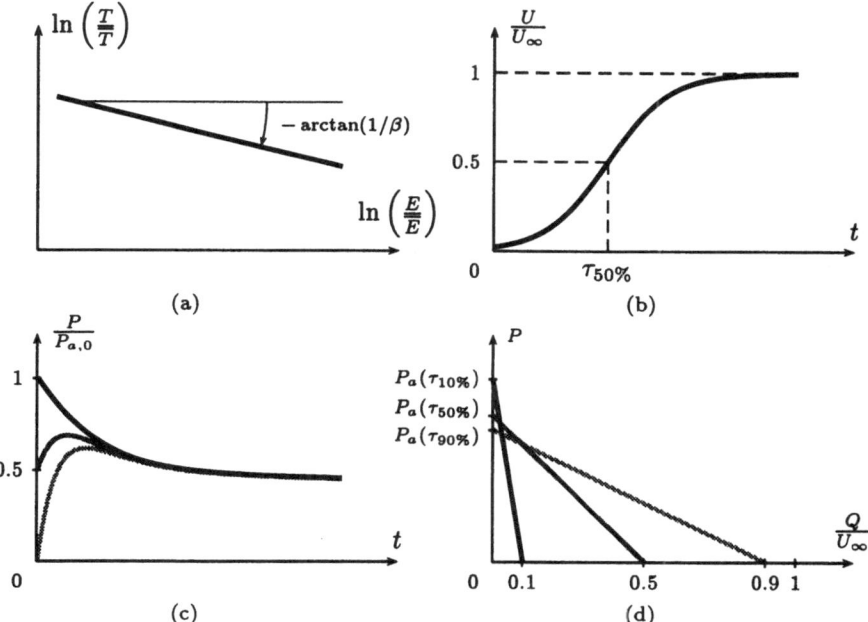

Figure 6.1 (a) Experience curve; (b) Production life cycle (logistic curve); (c) Price as a function of time at three fixed values of the sales rate: $Q = 0$ (black line), $Q = 0.5U_0$ (dark grey line) and $Q = U_0$ (light grey line); (d) Price as a function of the sales rate at three fixed values of the time: $t = \tau_{10\%}$ (black line), $t = \tau_{50\%}$ (dark grey line) and $t = \tau_{90\%}$ (light grey line).

6.2.3   Problem formulation

The complete model of the firm that is studied in this chapter reads as follows:

$$\max_{I(t), D(t), Z} \left\{ J = \int_0^Z e^{-it} D(t) \, dt + e^{-iZ} X(Z) \right\} \tag{6.14a}$$

$$\dot{K}(t) = I(t) - aK(t), \quad K(0) = K_0 \tag{6.14b}$$

$$\dot{X}(t) = (1 - f)\{S(t, Q(t)) - vG(t) - wL(t) - aK(t) -$$

$$rY(t)\} - D(t), \quad X(0) = X_0 \tag{6.14c}$$

$$Q(t) = \overline{Q} \left(\frac{K(t)}{\overline{K}} \right)^{\frac{1}{\pi_K}}, \qquad 0 < \pi_K < 1 \tag{6.14d}$$

$$G(t) = \overline{G} \left(\frac{Q(t)}{\overline{Q}} \right)^{\pi_G}, \qquad 0 < \pi_G < 1 \tag{6.14e}$$

$$L(t) = \overline{L} \left(\frac{Q(t)}{\overline{Q}} \right)^{\pi_L}, \qquad 0 < \pi_L < 1 \tag{6.14f}$$

$$K(t) = X(t) + Y(t) \tag{6.14g}$$

$$Y(t) \geq 0 \tag{6.14h}$$

$$Y(t) \leq bX(t) \tag{6.14i}$$

$$I(t) \geq 0 \tag{6.14j}$$

$$D(t) \geq 0 \tag{6.14k}$$

where: $P(t, Q(t)) = S(t, Q(t))/Q(t)$, as given in the previous subsection. Note that the planning horizon Z is endogenous: an optimal value must be determined. More about this later.

The above optimization problem satisfies the required regularity condition (unchanged with respect to the basic model, see Appendix A) and therefore, Theorem 2.1 for deriving the necessary conditions can be used. For this purpose, the Hamiltonian and Lagrangian, respectively, are defined as follows ($\lambda_0 = 1$, see Observation 2.1):

$$\mathcal{H}(t, K, X, I, D, \lambda_1, \lambda_2) = D + \lambda_1 [I - aK] +$$

$$\lambda_2 \left[(1 - f) \left\{ S \left(t, \overline{Q} \left(\frac{K}{\overline{K}} \right)^{\frac{1}{\pi_K}} \right) - v\overline{G} \left(\frac{K}{\overline{K}} \right)^{\frac{\pi_G}{\pi_K}} - \right. \right.$$

Table 6.1 The eight paths which may appear in an optimal string for the model with increasing returns to scale, an experience curve and a production life cycle. The final column contains the conditions, if any, that must apply.

	μ_1	μ_2	ν_1	ν_2	
path 2	0	+	+	0	
path 3	+	0	+	0	only when $i < (1-f)r$
path 4	0	0	+	0	only when $i < (1-f)r$
path 6	0	+	0	+	
path 7	+	0	0	+	only when $i > (1-f)r$
path 8	0	0	0	+	only when $i > (1-f)r$
path 9	+	+	0	0	
path 10	0	+	0	0	

$$w\bar{L}\left(\frac{K}{\overline{\overline{K}}}\right)^{\frac{\pi_L}{\pi_K}} - aK - r(K-X)\bigg\} - D\bigg]$$ (6.15)

and:

$$\mathcal{L}(t, K, X, I, D, \lambda_1, \lambda_2, \mu_1, \mu_2, \nu_1, \nu_2) = \mathcal{H}(t, K, X, I, D, \lambda_1, \lambda_2) +$$

$$\mu_1 I + \mu_2 D + \nu_1[K-X] + \nu_2[(1+b)X - K]$$ (6.16)

where:

$\lambda_1(t)$: costate variable of capital assets

$\lambda_2(t)$: costate variable of equity

$\mu_1(t)$: Lagrange multiplier for lower bound of investment rate (6.14j)

$\mu_2(t)$: Lagrange multiplier for lower bound of dividend rate (6.14k)

$\nu_1(t)$: Lagrange multiplier for lower bound of debt (6.14h)

$\nu_2(t)$: Lagrange multiplier for upper bound of debt (6.14i)

The set of necessary conditions resulting from application of Theorem 2.1 is given in Appendix D. The paths are the same as for the basic model. For completeness, the eight paths which may appear in an optimal string are presented in Table 6.1.

Now, the following extra equation must be added to the necessary conditions obtained via Theorem 2.1, on account of the freely adjustable planning horizon Z:

$$\frac{\partial J}{\partial Z} = D(Z)e^{-iZ} + \dot{X}(Z)e^{-iZ} - iX(Z)e^{-iZ} = 0$$ (6.17)

Making use of equation (6.14c), this condition can easily be rewritten as:

$$(1-f)\frac{B(Z,K(Z))}{K(Z)} + (1-f)\left\{\frac{B(Z,K(Z))}{K(Z)} - r\right\}\frac{Y(Z)}{X(Z)} = i \qquad (6.18)$$

with $B(t, K)$, the operating income, defined as:

$$B(t,K) = S\left(t, \overline{Q}\left(\frac{K}{\overline{K}}\right)^{\frac{1}{\pi_K}}\right) - v\overline{G}\left(\frac{K}{\overline{K}}\right)^{\frac{\pi_G}{\pi_K}} - w\overline{L}\left(\frac{K}{\overline{K}}\right)^{\frac{\pi_L}{\pi_K}} - aK$$

$$(6.19)$$

The lefthand side of (6.18) is the quotient of net profit (W) and equity, i.e. the return on equity. The expression is the well-known leverage formula which describes the connection between the return on equity and the return on total assets, the latter being the quotient of operating income and total assets. Thus, the optimal planning horizon is the instant when the return on equity becomes precisely equal to the cost of equity (and it is falling).

On the other hand, the optimal size of the firm is characterized by the equality of the *marginal* return on equity and the cost of equity, both on path 4, when equity is cheaper than debt, and on path 8, in the reverse case:

$$(1-f)\frac{\partial B}{\partial K}(t, K(t)) + (1-f)\left\{\frac{\partial B}{\partial K}(t, K(t)) - r\right\}\frac{Y(t)}{X(t)} = i \qquad (6.20)$$

with: $Y(t) = 0$ on path 4 and $Y(t)/X(t) = b$ on path 8. This equation can easily be derived from the equality of marginal returns and marginal costs (see Subsection 3.3.3).

Hamiltonian (6.15) is no longer necessarily concave in K everwhere, depending upon the productivity coefficients of the various production factors. In the following section, an example of this is given.

6.3 Case study

Below, the numerical results for the case of expensive equity, $i > (1-f)r$, are presented. The parameter values chosen are characteristic of an average firm in the chemical industry (see Section 3.4 too): $a = 0.1$; $b = 2$; $f = 0.4$; $i = 0.08$; $r = 0.1$; $\overline{K} = 0.5859375$; $\overline{Q} = 0.009375$; $w\overline{L} = 0.1875$; $v\overline{G} = 0.5625$; $\overline{T} = 57.647$; $\overline{U} = 0.0625^3$; $U_0 = 0.0275$; $U_\infty = 1$; $\vartheta_U = 6$; $1/\beta = 0.3$; $\pi_G = 0.99$; $\pi_K = 0.6$; $\pi_L = 0.2$. The firm is assumed to be on path 8 at the start so that $K_0 = (1+b)X_0$ is fixed via equation (6.20) for $t = 0$. ($\Delta t = 0.25$.)

---

[3]Substituting this value for $U(t)$ in equation (6.13) gives $\overline{E}$.

For the previous set of parameter values, at the 'reference point', the firm has a 15% share of the total market sales which, in turn, amounts to 6.25% of the limiting value. It applies further that:

$$\overline{P} = \left(\overline{T} + \frac{v\overline{G}}{\overline{Q}} \right) \left(1 - \frac{\overline{Q}}{\overline{U}} \right) = 100$$

$$\frac{v\overline{G}}{\overline{Q}} = 60$$

$$\frac{w\overline{L}}{\overline{Q}} = 20$$

$$\frac{a\overline{K}}{\overline{Q}} = 6.25$$

A number of financial ratios can be calculated simply from these equations, for example: the total assets turnover (1.6) and the return on total assets (22%). The usual '10-6-2' rule applies to the productivity coefficients for the chemical industry: i.e. 10% more production requires 6% more capital assets and 2% more labour (and 9.9% more raw materials).

In Figure 6.2, the optimal course of I, D, K, W/X, Q/U and P is depicted. Furthermore: $Z = \tau_{99.94\%} = 66.5$, $X(t) = (1 + b)^{-1} K(t)$, $\lambda_1(t) = \mu_1(t) = \mu_2(t) = \nu_1(t) = 0$, $\lambda_2(t) = 1$ and $\nu_2 = (i - (1 - f)r)(1 + b)^{-1}$. In Figure 6.2(b), it can be seen that U_0 has been chosen in such a way that $D(0) = 0$ and $\dot{D}(0) > 0$. The return on equity at that instant is already higher than the cost of equity. For $t < 0$, path 8 is not feasible because it implies a negative dividend rate there.

The two graphs in Figure 6.3 show the development of the firm over time with the help of the most important financial ratios. The gross margin B/S is plotted against the total assets turnover S/K ('productivity of capital') and the wages turnover S/wL ('productivity of labour'), respectively. From both graphs, it appears that the accent in the initial stage of the planning period, when the product is at the start of its production life cycle, lies on increasing the margin. As the product matures, the margin falls. This is acceptable if the productivity rises by an amount so that, the product of these two ratios, the return on total assets and labour respectively, does not fall. From a certain instant, both the margin and productivity (and thus the return too) start to fall. The falling earnings caused by the autonomously decreasing market price per product unit cannot be covered any longer by higher productivity of the production factors via scale increases. Now should be the time for the firm to apply new products which are just at the start of their production life cycle.

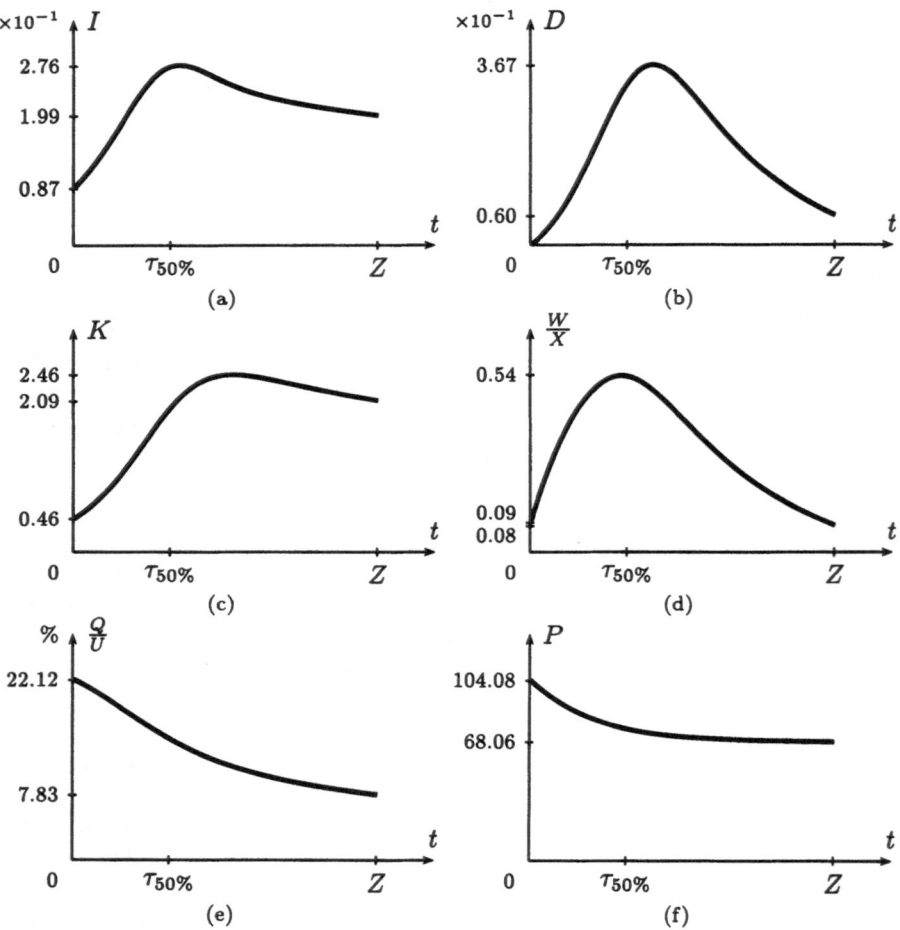

Figure 6.2 Model with increasing returns to scale, experience curve and production life cycle in the case of $i > (1 - f)r$. $Z = \tau_{99.94\%} = 66.5$; optimal string of paths: 8.

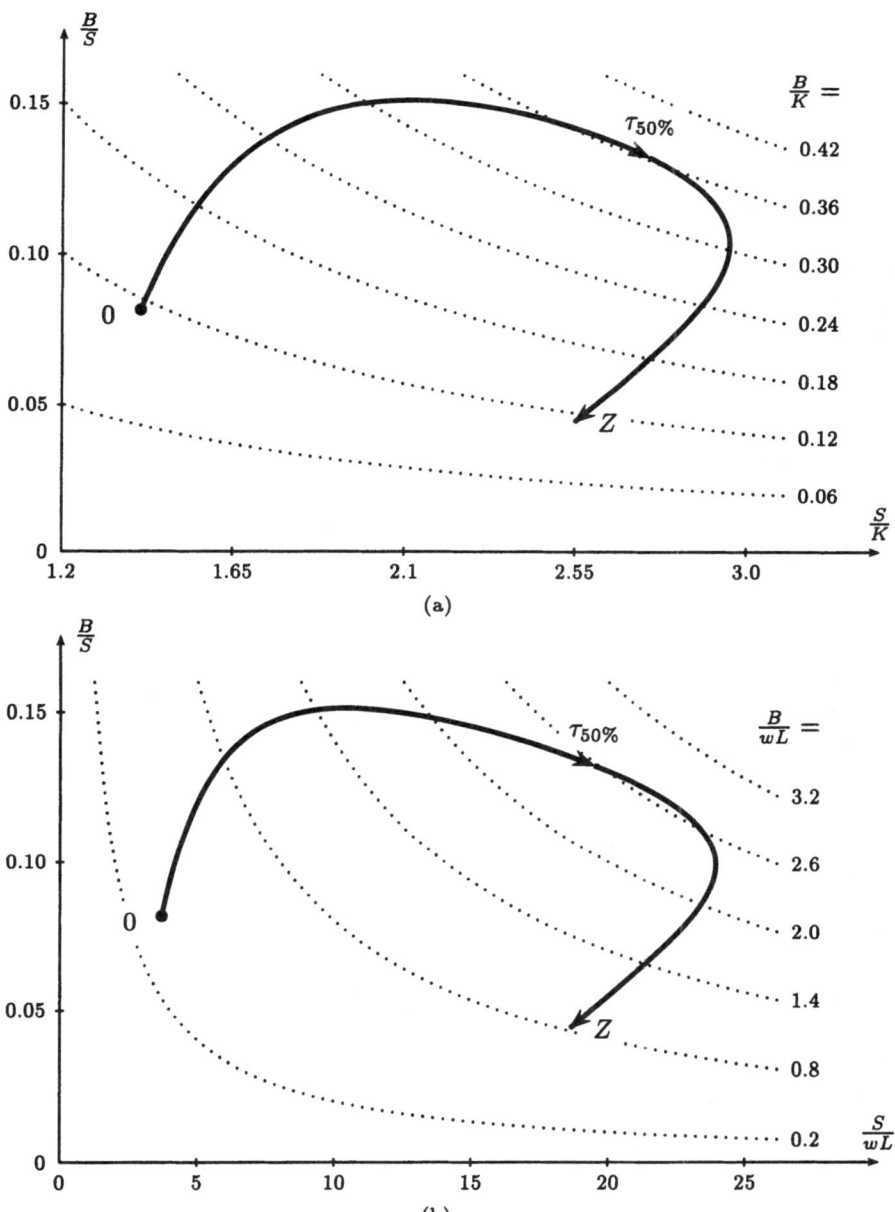

Figure 6.3 Gross margin plotted against: (a) the total assets turnover; (b) the wages turnover.

In Figure 6.4, the operating income is presented as a function of the capital assets stock for three instances in the production life cycle ($\tau_{2.70\%}$, $\tau_{50\%}$ and $\tau_{99.94\%}$), as well as, the financing costs (before tax) $c_8 K$, with

$$c_8 = \frac{b}{1+b}r + \frac{1}{1+b} \cdot \frac{i}{1-f} \tag{6.21}$$

as defined in Chapter 3. From this figure, the size of the capital assets stock on path 8 can be determined graphically for the three instances: this is the horizontal coordinate of the point on the curve for B that lies to the right of the point of inflection and where the slope of the tangent equals c_8 (see equation (6.20)). Another interesting value for the size of the capital assets stock, which can be found simply from Figure 6.4 for the three instances mentioned before, is the one where the return on total assets is maximal, and thus the following applies:

$$\frac{\partial B}{\partial K}(t, K) = \frac{B(t, K)}{K} \tag{6.22}$$

Seen graphically, this is the horizontal coordinate of the point on the curve for B that lies to right of the origin and where the tangent goes through the origin. The return on equity is maximal too at this size of the capital assets stock (assuming equity and debt financing in a fixed ratio).

Figure 6.4 shows that a return on total assets greater than c_8, which is equivalent with a return of equity greater than i, can be achieved only between $\tau_{2.70\%}$ and $\tau_{99.94\%}$ when the size of the capital assets stock lies in an interval with positive upper and lower bounds, where the values vary with the instant in the life cycle (for example, at $\tau_{50\%}$ this interval is: $\langle 0.74; 2.82 \rangle$). Between $\tau_{2.70\%}$ and $\tau_{99.94\%}$, the size of the capital assets stock on path 8 is greater than where the return on equity is maximal; outside this, the reverse is the case.

Finally, Figure 6.5 shows the stock of capital assets related to path 8, and the stock of capital assets for which both the return on equity and the return on total assets are maximal, as a function of time. Furthermore, for each instant between $\tau_{2.70\%}$ and $\tau_{99.94\%}$, the interval is given within which the size of the stock of capital assets must lie so that the return on equity exceeds the time preference rate of the shareholder. This is illustrated by shading. The values for the stock of capital assets that have been determined graphically from Figure 6.4 are shown along the vertical axis.

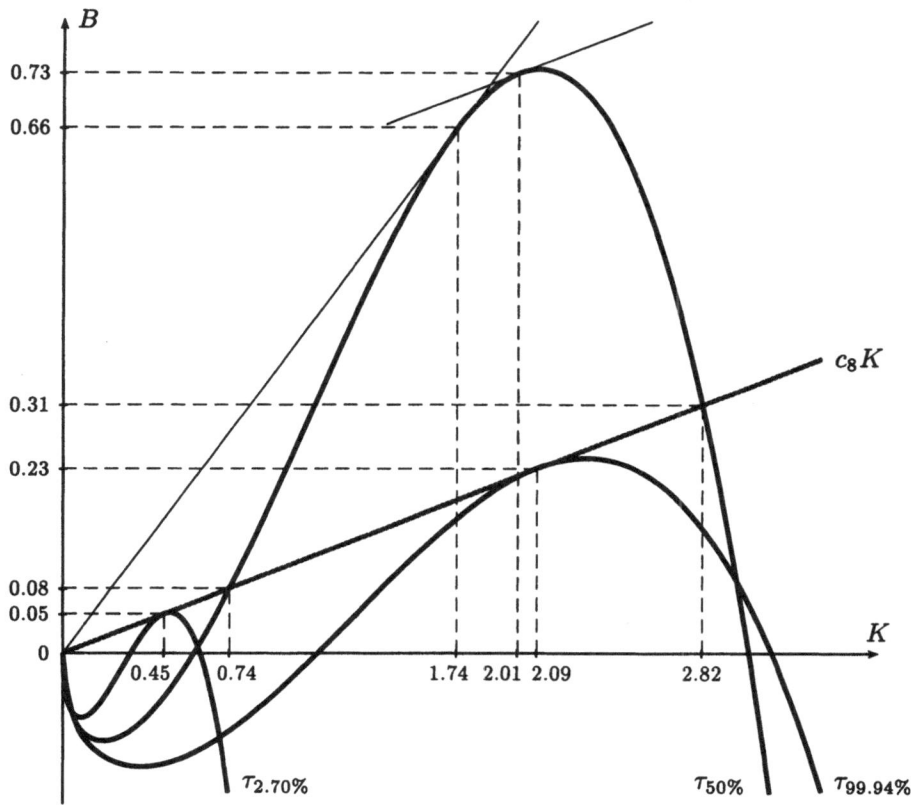

Figure 6.4 Operating income for three different points of time in the production life cycle ($\tau_{2.70\%}$, $\tau_{50\%}$ and $\tau_{99.94\%}$) and financing costs as a function of the stock of capital assets.

6.4   Conclusions

For the model of the firm with increasing returns to scale, experience curve and production life cycle, two instants of time exist, the one early in the life cycle and the other late, before and after which, respectively, a return on equity exceeding the time preference rate of the shareholder (cost of equity) cannot

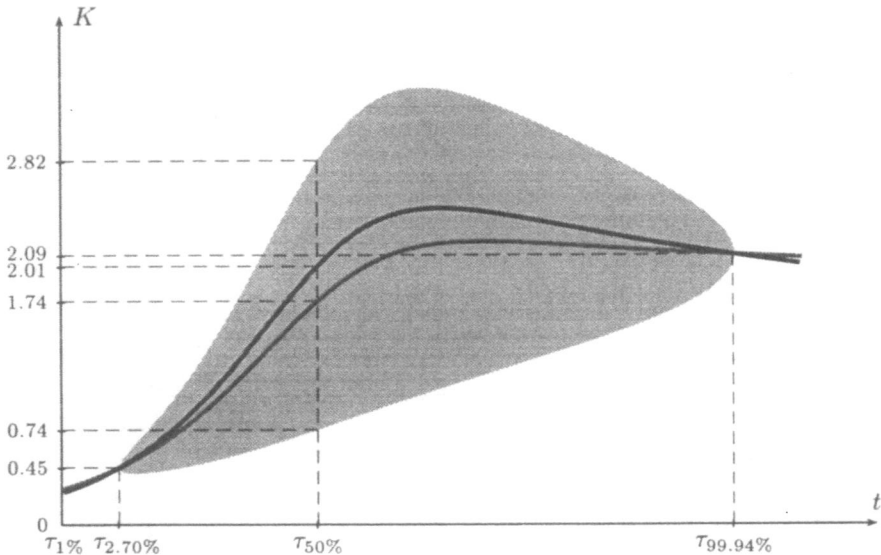

Figure 6.5 As a function of time, the stock of capital assets on path 8 (black line) and the stock of capital assets where both the return on equity and the return on total assets are maximal (grey line), are shown graphically. Within the shaded area: $B/K \geq c_8 \Leftrightarrow W/X \geq i$; outside it: $B/K < c_8 \Leftrightarrow W/X < i$.

be achieved for any size of the stock of capital assets. During the period between these instances, an interval of capital assets stock with positive minimum and maximum bounds exists, on which the return on equity is greater than the time preference rate of the shareholder, whilst it is smaller elsewhere. The stock of capital assets related to path 4 and path 8 is greater than the size for which the return on equity is maximal, but smaller than the maximum size for which the return on equity exactly equals the time preference rate of the shareholder. One thing and the other is in contrast to the basic model where the return on equity is maximal at $K = 0$, irrespective of the instant of time.

Appendices

Appendix A

Mathematical Details for Chapter 3

A.1 Problem formulation

After eliminating the variables Q, L and Y, the dynamic optimization problem that has to be solved can be formulated as follows:

$$\max_{I,D}\left\{J = \int_0^z e^{-it}D(t)\,\mathrm{d}t + e^{-iz}X(z)\right\} \tag{A.1a}$$

$$\dot{K}(t) = I(t) - aK(t), \quad K(0) = K_0 \tag{A.1b}$$

$$\dot{X}(t) = (1-f)\left\{S(k^{-1}K(t)) - wlk^{-1}K(t) - aK(t) - \right.$$

$$\left. r(K(t) - X(t))\right\} - D(t), \quad X(0) = X_0 \tag{A.1c}$$

$$K(t) - X(t) \geq 0 \tag{A.1d}$$

$$(1+b)X(t) - K(t) \geq 0 \tag{A.1e}$$

$$I(t) \geq 0 \tag{A.1f}$$

$$D(t) \geq 0 \tag{A.1g}$$

A.2 Necessary conditions for optimality

The weak constraint qualification for this problem is satisfied if the matrix:

$$\begin{pmatrix} 1 & 0 & I(t) & 0 \\ 0 & 1 & 0 & D(t) \end{pmatrix} \tag{A.2}$$

has full row rank 2. This is always the case.

The Hamiltonian and Lagrangian are defined by ($\lambda_0 = 1$, see Observation 2.1):

$$\mathcal{H}(K, X, I, D, \lambda_1, \lambda_2) = D + \lambda_1 [I - aK] +$$

$$\lambda_2 \left[(1 - f) \left\{ S(k^{-1}K) - wlk^{-1}K - aK - r(K - X) \right\} - D \right] \quad \text{(A.3)}$$

$$\mathcal{L}(K, X, I, D, \lambda_1, \lambda_2, \mu_1, \mu_2, \nu_1, \nu_2) = \mathcal{H}(K, X, I, D, \lambda_1, \lambda_2) +$$

$$\mu_1 I + \mu_2 D + \nu_1 [K - X] + \nu_2 [(1 + b)X - K] \quad \text{(A.4)}$$

Applying Theorem 2.1 results in the following set of necessary conditions:

$$\dot{\lambda}_1(t) - i\lambda_1(t) = a\lambda_1(t) - (1 - f) \left\{ \frac{dS}{dK} \left(k^{-1}K(t) \right) - wlk^{-1} - \right.$$

$$\left. a - r \right\} \lambda_2(t) - \nu_1(t) + \nu_2(t) \quad \text{(A.5)}$$

$$\dot{\lambda}_2(t) - i\lambda_2(t) = -(1 - f)r\lambda_2(t) + \nu_1(t) - (1 + b)\nu_2(t) \quad \text{(A.6)}$$

$$\lambda_1(t) + \mu_1(t) = 0 \quad \text{(A.7)}$$

$$1 - \lambda_2(t) + \mu_2(t) = 0 \quad \text{(A.8)}$$

$$\mu_1(t) \geq 0, \quad \mu_1(t)I(t) = 0 \quad \text{(A.9)}$$

$$\mu_2(t) \geq 0, \quad \mu_2(t)D(t) = 0 \quad \text{(A.10)}$$

$$\nu_1(t) \geq 0, \quad \nu_1(t)\left(K(t) - X(t)\right) = 0 \quad \text{(A.11)}$$

$$\nu_2(t) \geq 0, \quad \nu_2(t)\left((1 + b)X(t) - K(t)\right) = 0 \quad \text{(A.12)}$$

$$\lambda_1(z) = \gamma_1 - \gamma_2 \quad \text{(A.13)}$$

$$\lambda_2(z) = 1 - \gamma_1 + (1 + b)\gamma_2 \quad \text{(A.14)}$$

$$\gamma_1 \geq 0, \quad \gamma_1 \left(K(z) - X(z)\right) = 0 \quad \text{(A.15)}$$

$$\gamma_2 \geq 0, \quad \gamma_2 \left((1 + b)X(z) - K(z)\right) = 0 \quad \text{(A.16)}$$

When (λ_1, λ_2) is discontinuous in τ, then:

$$\lambda_1(\tau^-) = \lambda_1(\tau^+) + \eta_1(\tau) - \eta_2(\tau) \quad \text{(A.17)}$$

$$\lambda_2(\tau^-) = \lambda_2(\tau^+) - \eta_1(\tau) + (1 + b)\eta_2(\tau) \quad \text{(A.18)}$$

$$\eta_1(\tau) \geq 0, \quad \eta_1(\tau)\left(K(\tau) - X(\tau)\right) = 0 \quad \text{(A.19)}$$

$$\eta_2(\tau) \geq 0, \quad \eta_2(\tau)\left((1 + b)X(\tau) - K(\tau)\right) = 0 \quad \text{(A.20)}$$

The Hamiltonian (A.3) is linear and therefore concave in X, I and D, as well as, concave in K, because S as a function of Q is assumed to be concave. The residual term in the objective function and all inequality constraints are linear in K, X, I and D. Hence, the necessary conditions for optimality are sufficient too.

A.3   Elaborating the transversality conditions

The final path in an optimal string must satisfy the transversality conditions (A.13)–(A.16). They take into account the possibility that (λ_1, λ_2) can be discontinuous at instant z. The transversality conditions (A.13) and (A.14) must be read as follows:

$$\lambda_1(z^+) = 0, \quad \lambda_1(z^-) = \gamma_1 - \gamma_2 \tag{A.21}$$

$$\lambda_2(z^+) = 1, \quad \lambda_2(z^-) = 1 - \gamma_1 + (1+b)\gamma_2 \tag{A.22}$$

Then, using equations (A.7) and (A.8) produces:

$$\mu_1(z^-) = -\gamma_1 + \gamma_2 \tag{A.23}$$

$$\mu_2(z^-) = -\gamma_1 + (1+b)\gamma_2 \tag{A.24}$$

From (A.15) and (A.16), it follows that γ_1 and γ_2 cannot both be positive. Furthermore, (A.9) and (A.23) exclude a combination of $\gamma_1 > 0$ and $\gamma_2 = 0$. Consequently, two alternatives still remain:

1. $\gamma_1 = \gamma_2 = 0 \Rightarrow \mu_1(z^-) = \mu_2(z^-) = 0$.
   Here, at instant z, λ_1 and λ_2 are continuous. The paths with this property are not only paths 4 and 8, but possibly also the other paths from Table 3.2. For the fact that $\mu_i(t) > 0$ does not exclude that $\mu_i(z^-) = 0$.

2. $\gamma_1 = 0$, $\gamma_2 > 0 \Rightarrow \mu_1(z^-) > 0$, $\mu_2(z^-) > 0$.
   Here, at instant z, two jumps equal to γ_2 and $-(1+b)\gamma_2$, respectively, appear in λ_1 and λ_2. Only path 9 has the property described above.

A.4   Further examination of some paths

Paths 1 and 5.   These paths can be excluded, because the number of positive Lagrange multipliers ($=3$) is larger than the number of control variables ($=2$).

Paths 11 and 12.   These paths can be excluded, because they imply that $i = (1 - f)r$, which follows directly after substituting $\lambda_2(t) = 1 + \mu_2(t)$ (A.8) in equation (A.6) and putting $\mu_2(t)$, $\nu_1(t)$ and $\nu_2(t)$ equal to zero.

Paths 3 and 4.   These paths may appear in an *optimal* string only when $i < (1 - f)r$; for substituting $\lambda_2(t) = 1 + \mu_2(t)$ (A.8) in equation (A.6) and putting $\mu_2(t)$ and $\nu_2(t)$ equal to zero, gives:

$$i + \nu_1(t) = (1 - f)r \tag{A.25}$$

with $\nu_1(t) > 0$.

Paths 7 and 8. These paths may appear in an *optimal* string only when $i > (1 - f)r$; for substituting $\lambda_2(t) = 1 + \mu_2(t)$ (A.8) in equation (A.6) and putting $\mu_2(t)$ and $\nu_1(t)$ equal to zero, gives:

$$i = (1 - f)r + (1 + b)\nu_2(t) \qquad\qquad (A.26)$$

with $\nu_2(t) > 0$.

Appendix B

Mathematical Details for Chapter 4

B.1 Problem formulation

After eliminating the variables $L(t)$ and $Y(t)$, the dynamic optimization problem that has to be solved can be formulated as follows:

$$\max_{I(t),D(t),\dot{Q}(t)} \left\{ J = \int_0^z e^{-it} D(t)\,\mathrm{d}t + e^{-iz} X(z) \right\} \tag{B.1a}$$

$$\dot{K}(t) = I(t) - aK(t), \quad K(0) = K_0 \tag{B.1b}$$

$$\dot{X}(t) = (1-f)\left\{ S(Q(t)) - wlQ(t) - aK(t) - \right.$$

$$\left. r(K(t) - X(t)) \right\} - D(t), X(0) = X_0 \tag{B.1c}$$

$$Q(0) = Q_0 \tag{B.1d}$$

$$K(t) - X(t) \geq 0 \tag{B.1e}$$

$$bX(t) - K(t) \geq 0 \tag{B.1f}$$

$$k^{-1}K(t) - Q(t) \geq 0 \tag{B.1g}$$

$$k^{-1}K(t) - Q(t) - \vartheta_q \dot{Q}(t) \geq 0 \tag{B.1h}$$

$$I(t) \geq 0 \tag{B.1i}$$

$$D(t) \geq 0 \tag{B.1j}$$

B.2 Necessary conditions for optimality

The weak constraint qualification for this problem is satisfied if the matrix:

$$\begin{pmatrix} 1 & 0 & 0 & I(t) & 0 & 0 \\ 0 & 1 & 0 & 0 & D(t) & 0 \\ 0 & 0 & -\vartheta_Q & 0 & 0 & k^{-1}K(t) - Q(t) - \vartheta_Q \dot{Q}(t) \end{pmatrix} \tag{B.2}$$

has full row rank 3 heeft. For $\vartheta_Q > 0$ this is always the case.

The Hamiltonian and Lagrangian are defined by ($\lambda_0 = 1$, see Observation 2.1):

$$\mathcal{H}(K, X, Q, I, D, \dot{Q}, \lambda_1, \lambda_2, \lambda_3) = D + \lambda_1 \left[I - aK \right] +$$

$$\lambda_2 \left[(1 - f) \left\{ S(Q) - wlQ - aK - r(K - X) \right\} - D \right] + \lambda_3 \dot{Q} \tag{B.3}$$

$$\mathcal{L}(K, X, Q, I, D, \dot{Q}, \lambda_1, \lambda_2, \lambda_3, \mu_1, \mu_2, \mu_3, \nu_1, \nu_2, \nu_3) =$$

$$\mathcal{H}(K, X, Q, I, D, \dot{Q}, \lambda_1, \lambda_2, \lambda_3) + \mu_1 I + \mu_2 D +$$

$$\mu_3 [k^{-1} K - Q - \vartheta_Q \dot{Q}] + \nu_1 [K - X] +$$

$$\nu_2 [(1 + b)X - K] + \nu_3 [k^{-1} K - Q] \tag{B.4}$$

Applying Theorem 2.1 results in the following set of necessary conditions:

$$\dot{\lambda}_1(t) - i\lambda_1(t) = a\lambda_1(t) + (1 - f)(a + r)\lambda_2(t) - \nu_1(t) + \nu_2(t) -$$

$$k^{-1} \big(\mu_3(t) + \nu_3(t) \big) \tag{B.5}$$

$$\dot{\lambda}_2(t) - i\lambda_2(t) = -(1 - f)r\lambda_2(t) + \nu_1(t) - (1 + b)\nu_2(t) \tag{B.6}$$

$$\dot{\lambda}_3(t) - i\lambda_3(t) = -(1 - f) \left\{ S'(Q(t)) - wl \right\} \lambda_2(t) + \mu_3(t) + \nu_3(t) \tag{B.7}$$

$$\lambda_1(t) + \mu_1(t) = 0 \tag{B.8}$$

$$1 - \lambda_2(t) + \mu_2(t) = 0 \tag{B.9}$$

$$\lambda_3(t) - \vartheta_Q \mu_3(t) = 0 \tag{B.10}$$

$$\mu_1(t) \geq 0, \quad \mu_1(t)I(t) = 0 \tag{B.11}$$

$$\mu_2(t) \geq 0, \quad \mu_2(t)D(t) = 0 \tag{B.12}$$

$$\mu_3(t) \geq 0, \quad \mu_3(t) \big(k^{-1}K(t) - Q(t) - \vartheta_Q \dot{Q}(t) \big) = 0 \tag{B.13}$$

$$\nu_1(t) \geq 0, \quad \nu_1(t) \big(K(t) - X(t) \big) = 0 \tag{B.14}$$

$$\nu_2(t) \geq 0, \quad \nu_2(t) \big((1 + b)X(t) - K(t) \big) = 0 \tag{B.15}$$

$$\nu_3(t) \geq 0, \quad \nu_3(t)\big(k^{-1}K(t) - Q(t)\big) = 0 \tag{B.16}$$

$$\lambda_1(z) = \gamma_1 - \gamma_2 + k^{-1}\gamma_3 \tag{B.17}$$

$$\lambda_2(z) = 1 - \gamma_1 + (1+b)\gamma_2 \tag{B.18}$$

$$\lambda_3(z) = -\gamma_3 \tag{B.19}$$

$$\gamma_1 \geq 0, \quad \gamma_1\big(K(z) - X(z)\big) = 0 \tag{B.20}$$

$$\gamma_2 \geq 0, \quad \gamma_2\big((1+b)X(z) - K(z)\big) = 0 \tag{B.21}$$

$$\gamma_3 \geq 0, \quad \gamma_3\big(k^{-1}K(z) - Q(z)\big) = 0 \tag{B.22}$$

When $(\lambda_1, \lambda_2, \lambda_3)$ is discontinuous in τ, then

$$\lambda_1(\tau^-) = \lambda_1(\tau^+) + \eta_1(\tau) - \eta_2(\tau) + k^{-1}\eta_3(\tau) \tag{B.23}$$

$$\lambda_2(\tau^-) = \lambda_2(\tau^+) - \eta_1(\tau) + (1+b)\eta_2(\tau) \tag{B.24}$$

$$\lambda_3(\tau^-) = \lambda_3(\tau^+) - \eta_3(\tau) \tag{B.25}$$

$$\eta_1(\tau) \geq 0, \quad \eta_1(\tau)\big(K(\tau) - X(\tau)\big) = 0 \tag{B.26}$$

$$\eta_2(\tau) \geq 0, \quad \eta_2(\tau)\big((1+b)X(\tau) - K(\tau)\big) = 0 \tag{B.27}$$

$$\eta_3(\tau) \geq 0, \quad \eta_3(\tau)\big(k^{-1}K(\tau) - Q(\tau)\big) = 0 \tag{B.28}$$

The Hamiltonian (B.3) is linear and therefore concave in K, X, I, D and $\dot{Q}$, as well as, concave in Q, because S as a function of Q is assumed to be concave. The residual term in the objective function and all inequality constraints are linear in K, X, Q, I, D and $\dot{Q}$. Hence, the necessary conditions for optimality are sufficient too.

B.3   Elaborating the transversality conditions

The final path in an optimal string must satisfy the transversality conditions (B.17)–(B.22). They take into account the possibility that $(\lambda_1, \lambda_2, \lambda_3)$ can be discontinuous at instant z. The transversality conditions (B.17)–(B.19) must be read as follows:

$$\lambda_1(z^+) = 0, \quad \lambda_1(z^-) = \gamma_1 - \gamma_2 + k^{-1}\gamma_3 \tag{B.29}$$

$$\lambda_2(z^+) = 1, \quad \lambda_2(z^-) = 1 - \gamma_1 + (1+b)\gamma_2 \tag{B.30}$$

$$\lambda_3(z^+) = 0, \quad \lambda_3(z^-) = -\gamma_3 \tag{B.31}$$

Then, using equations (B.8)-(B.10) produces:

$$\mu_1(z^-) = -\gamma_1 + \gamma_2 - k^{-1}\gamma_3 \tag{B.32}$$

$$\mu_2(z^-) = -\gamma_1 + (1+b)\gamma_2 \tag{B.33}$$

$$\mu_3(z^-) = -\gamma_3/\vartheta_Q \tag{B.34}$$

From (B.20) and (B.21), it follows that γ_1 and γ_2 cannot both be positive. Furthermore, (B.12) and (B.33) exclude a combination of $\gamma_1 > 0$ and $\gamma_2 = 0$, and (B.13) and (B.34) imply that $\gamma_3 = 0$. Consequently, two alternatives must be examined still:

1. $\gamma_1 = \gamma_2 = \gamma_3 = 0 \Rightarrow \mu_1(z^-) = \mu_2(z^-) = \mu_3(z^-) = 0$.
   Here, at instant z, λ_1, λ_2 and λ_3 are continuous. The paths with this property may possibly be all the paths form Table 4.1, with the exception of paths 2b and 6b (see below).

2. $\gamma_1 = 0$, $\gamma_2 > 0$, $\gamma_3 = 0 \Rightarrow \mu_1(z^-) > 0$, $\mu_2(z^-) > 0$, $\mu_3(z^-) = 0$.
   Here, at instant z, two jumps equal to γ_2 and $-(1+b)\gamma_2$, respectively, appear in λ_1 and λ_2. All paths with $\mu_1 = 0$ and/or $\mu_2 = 0$ can be excluded in this case so that paths 9a and 9b remain.

B.4   Further examination of some paths

Paths 1a, 1b, 2c, 5a, 5b and 6c.   Since here the number of positive Lagrange multipliers (=4) is larger than the number of control variables (=3), these paths can be excluded.

Paths 11a, 11b, 12a, 12b and 12c.   These paths imply $i = (1-f)r$ which follows directly after substitution of $\lambda_2(t) = 1 + \mu_2(t)$ (B.9) in equation (B.6) and putting $\mu_2(t)$, $\nu_1(t)$ and $\nu_2(t)$ equal to zero, and therefore can be excluded from taking part in an optimal string.

Path 2a.   On this path, $k^{-1}K(t) = Q(t)$ and $\dot{Q}(t) \le 0$ apply, which implies that $\dot{K}(t) = I(t) - aK(t) \le 0$. Since $D(t) = \dot{Y}(t) = 0$, this means a non-positive net profit, which in the absence of debt, can only point to an overcapacity. Maximum investment then is not optimal (with a price function that is not explicitly time-dependent) and path 2a can be excluded.

Path 2b.   Substituting $\lambda_1(t) = -\mu_1(t)$ (B.8) and $\lambda_2(t) = 1 + \mu_2(t)$ (B.9) into equation (B.5), after putting $\mu_1(t)$, $\nu_2(t)$ and $\nu_3(t)$ equal to zero, gives:

$$\nu_1(t) = (1-f)(a+r)\big(1 + \mu_2(t)\big) - k^{-1}\mu_3(t) \tag{B.35}$$

Substituting this outcome into equation (B.6) after using (B.9) and putting $\nu_2(t)$ equal to zero produces:

$$\dot{\mu}_2(t) = \left(i + (1 - f)a\right)\left(1 + \mu_2(t)\right) - k^{-1}\mu_3(t) \tag{B.36}$$

Path 2b does not satisfy the transversality conditions in the case of $\gamma_1 = \gamma_2 = \gamma_3 = 0$, since $\mu_2(z^-) = \mu_3(z^-) = 0$ implies that $\dot{\mu}_2(z-) > 0$, and thus, $\mu_2(t) < 0$ for $t < z$ (μ_2 continuous in z).

Path 6a. Here, $\mu_1(t) = \mu_3(t) = 0$ applies. Then, it follows from equations (B.8) and (B.10) that $\lambda_1(t) = \lambda_3(t) = 0$. In addition, $\nu_1(t) = 0$. Inserting these data into equation (B.7) gives:

$$\nu_3(t) = (1 - f)\left(S'(Q(t)) - wl\right)\lambda_2(t) \tag{B.37}$$

Substituting this outcome with other data into equation (B.5) leads to:

$$\nu_2(t) = (1 - f)\left(S'(Q(t)) - wl - (a + r)k\right)k^{-1}\lambda_2(t) \tag{B.38}$$

Given that $\lambda_2(t) = 1 + \mu_2(t) > 1$ (B.9) and $\nu_2(t) > 0$, it holds that:

$$S'(Q(t)) > wl + (a + r)k \tag{B.39}$$

Since S is strictly concave and also increasing on the relevant interval for Q with $S(0) = 0$ and further, $k\dot{Q}(t) = \dot{K}(t) = (1 + b)\dot{X}(t) = (1 + b)W(t) \leq 0$ on path 6a, it must hold that:

$$S'(Q(t)) < \frac{S(Q(t))}{Q(t)} \leq wl + \left(a + \frac{b}{1+b}r\right)k \tag{B.40}$$

That is in conflict with inequality (B.39), therefore, path 6a can be excluded from participating in an optimal string.

Path 6b. Substituting $\lambda_1(t) = -\mu_1(t)$ (B.8) and $\lambda_2(t) = 1 + \mu_2(t)$ (B.9) into equation (B.5), after putting $\mu_1(t)$, $\nu_1(t)$ and $\nu_3(t)$ equal to zero, gives:

$$\nu_2(t) = -(1 - f)(a + r)\left(1 + \mu_2(t)\right) + k^{-1}\mu_3(t) \tag{B.41}$$

Substituting this outcome into equation (B.6), after using (B.9) and putting $\nu_1(t)$ equal to zero, produces:

$$\dot{\mu}_2(t) = \left(i + (1 - f)(a(1 + b) + br)\right)\left(1 + \mu_2(t)\right) - (1 + b)k^{-1}\mu_3(t) \tag{B.42}$$

Path 6b does not satisfy the transversality conditions in the case of $\gamma_1 = \gamma_2 = \gamma_3 = 0$, since $\mu_2(z^-) = \mu_3(z^-) = 0$ implies that $\dot{\mu}_2(z-) > 0$, and thus $\mu_2(t) < 0$ for $t < z$ (μ_2 continuous in z).

Paths 4a, 4b and 4c. Here, $\mu_1(t) = \mu_2(t) = 0$ applies. Then, from equations (B.8) and (B.9) it follows that $\lambda_1(t) = 0$ and $\lambda_2(t) = 1$. In addition, $\nu_2(t) = 0$. Inserting these data into equation (B.6) gives:

$$\nu_1(t) = (1 - f)r - i \tag{B.43}$$

Since $\nu_1(t) > 0$, thus, $i < (1 - f)r$ must apply. Substituting (B.43) with the other data into equation (B.5) gives:

$$\mu_3(t) + \nu_3(t) = (1 - f)\left(a + \frac{i}{1-f}\right)k \tag{B.44}$$

So that via equation (B.7), finally, it is found that:

$$\dot{\mu}_3(t) - i\mu_3(t) = -(1 - f)\left\{S'(Q(t)) - wl - \left(a + \frac{i}{1-f}\right)k\right\}\vartheta_Q^{-1} \tag{B.45}$$

On path 4a, $\mu_3(t) = 0$. Equation (B.44) then leads to:

$$\nu_3(t) = (1 - f)\left(a + \frac{i}{1-f}\right)k \tag{B.46}$$

and equation (B.45) to:

$$S'(Q(t)) = wl + \left(a + \frac{i}{1-f}\right)k \tag{B.47}$$

so that path 4a is stationary i.e. $\dot{K}(t) = \dot{X}(t) = k\dot{Q}(t) = 0$. Path 4a satisfies the transversality conditions in the case of $\gamma_1 = \gamma_2 = \gamma_3 = 0$.

On path 4b, $\nu_3(t) = 0$. Equation (B.44) then leads to:

$$\mu_3(t) = (1 - f)\left(a + \frac{i}{1-f}\right)k \tag{B.48}$$

and equation (B.45) to:

$$S'(Q(t)) = wl + \left(a + \frac{i}{1-f}\right)(1 + i\vartheta_Q)k \tag{B.49}$$

so that path 4b is stationary. Path 4b does not satisfy the transversality conditions in the case of $\gamma_1 = \gamma_2 = \gamma_3 = 0$, because $\lim_{t\uparrow z} \mu_3(t) \neq 0$. Nor does Path 4b satisfy those conditions in the case of $\gamma_1 = 0$, $\gamma_2 > 0$, $\gamma_3 = 0$, because $\lim_{t\uparrow z} \mu_1(t) = \lim_{t\uparrow z} \mu_2(t) = 0$. Seeing that a stationary path in an optimal string for an autonomous problem must always be the final path, path 4b can be excluded.

Path 4c, by definition, is stationary. In order for path 4c to satisfy the transversality conditions in the case of $\gamma_1 = \gamma_2 = \gamma_3 = 0$, it is necessary that $\lim_{t\uparrow z} \mu_3(t) = 0$ applies. Then, solving differential equation (B.45) gives:

$$\mu_3(t) = (1 - f)\left\{S'(Q_{4c}) - wl - \left(a + \frac{i}{1-f}\right)k\right\}\frac{1 - e^{-i(z-t)}}{i\vartheta_Q} \tag{B.50}$$

Path 8a, 8b and 8c. Here, $\mu_1(t) = \mu_2(t) = 0$ applies. Then, from equation (B.8) and (B.9) it follows that $\lambda_1(t) = 0$ and $\lambda_2(t) = 1$. In addition, $\nu_1(t) = 0$. Inserting this data into equation (B.6) gives:

$$\nu_2(t) = \frac{i - (1 - f)r}{1 + b} \tag{B.51}$$

Since $\nu_2(t) > 0$, thus, $i > (1 - f)r$ must apply. Substituting (B.51) with the other data in equation (B.5) produces:

$$\mu_3(t) + \nu_3(t) = (1 - f)\left(a + \frac{1}{1 + b}\frac{i}{1 - f} + \frac{b}{1 + b}r\right)k \tag{B.52}$$

so that via equation (B.7), finally, it is found that:

$$\dot\mu_3(t) - i\mu_3(t) = -(1 - f)\left\{S'(Q(t)) - wl - \right.$$

$$\left.\left(a + \frac{1}{1 + b}\frac{i}{1 - f} + \frac{b}{1 + b}r\right)k\right\}\vartheta_Q^{-1} \tag{B.53}$$

On path 8a, $\mu_3(t) = 0$. Equation (B.52) then leads to:

$$\nu_3(t) = (1 - f)\left(a + \frac{1}{1 + b}\frac{i}{1 - f} + \frac{b}{1 + b}r\right)k \tag{B.54}$$

and equation (B.53) to:

$$S'(Q(t)) = wl + \left(a + \frac{1}{1 + b}\frac{i}{1 - f} + \frac{b}{1 + b}r\right)k \tag{B.55}$$

so that path 8a is stationary. Path 8a satisfies the transversality conditions only in the case of $\gamma_1 = \gamma_2 = \gamma_3 = 0$.

On path 8b, $\nu_3(t) = 0$. Equation (B.52) then leads to:

$$\mu_3(t) = (1 - f)\left(a + \frac{1}{1 + b}\frac{i}{1 - f} + \frac{b}{1 + b}r\right)k \tag{B.56}$$

and equation (B.53) to:

$$S'(Q(t)) = wl + \left(a + \frac{1}{1 + b}\frac{i}{1 - f} + \frac{b}{1 + b}r\right)(1 + i\vartheta_Q)k \tag{B.57}$$

so that path 8b is stationary. Path 8b does not satisfy the transversality conditions in the case of $\gamma_1 = \gamma_2 = \gamma_3 = 0$, because $\lim_{t\uparrow z}\mu_3(t) \neq 0$. Nor does path 8b satisfy those conditions in the case of $\gamma_1 = 0$, $\gamma_2 > 0$, $\gamma_3 = 0$, because $\lim_{t\uparrow z}\mu_1(t) = \lim_{t\uparrow z}\mu_2(t) = 0$. Seeing that a stationary path in an optimal string for an autonomous problem always must be the final path, path 8b can be excluded.

Path 8c, by definition, is stationary. In order for path 8c to satisfy the transversality conditions in the case of $\gamma_1 = \gamma_2 = \gamma_3 = 0$, it is necessary that $\lim_{t \uparrow z} \mu_3(t) = 0$ applies. Then, solving differential equation (B.53) gives:

$$\mu_3(t) = (1 - f)\left\{ S'(Q_{8c}) - wl - \right.$$

$$\left. \left(a + \frac{1}{1+b}\frac{i}{1-f} + \frac{b}{1+b}r\right)k\right\} \frac{1 - e^{-i(z-t)}}{i\vartheta_Q} \tag{B.58}$$

Paths 10a, 10b and 10c. Here, $\mu_1(t) = 0$ applies. Then, from equation (B.8) it follows that $\lambda_1(t) = 0$. In addition, $\nu_1(t) = \nu_2(t) = 0$. Inserting this data into equation (B.5) and (B.6) respectively, gives

$$\mu_3(t) + \nu_3(t) = (1 - f)(a + r)k\lambda_2 \tag{B.59}$$

$$\dot{\lambda}_2(t) - i\lambda_2(t) = -(1 - f)r\lambda_2(t) \tag{B.60}$$

So that via equation (B.7), finally, it is found that:

$$\dot{\mu}_3(t) - i\mu_3(t) = -(1 - f)\left\{ S'(Q(t)) - wl - (a + r)k\right\}\vartheta_Q^{-1}\lambda_2 \tag{B.61}$$

On path 10a, $\mu_3(t) = 0$. Equation (B.59) then leads to:

$$\nu_3(t) = (1 - f)(a + r)k\lambda_2(t) \tag{B.62}$$

and equation (B.61) to:

$$S'(Q(t)) = wl + (a + r)k \tag{B.63}$$

so that path 10a is 'partially' stationary: $\dot{K}(t) = \dot{Q}(t) = 0$. Path 10a satisfies the transversality conditions only in the case of $\gamma_1 = \gamma_2 = \gamma_3 = 0$.

On path 10b, $\nu_3(t) = 0$. Equation (B.59) then leads to:

$$\mu_3(t) = (1 - f)(a + r)k\lambda_2(t) \tag{B.64}$$

and equation (B.61) to:

$$S'(Q(t)) = wl + (a + r)(1 + (1 - f)r\vartheta_Q)k \tag{B.65}$$

so that path 10b is 'partially' stationary. Path 10b does not satisfy the transversality conditions in the case of $\gamma_1 = \gamma_2 = \gamma_3 = 0$, because $\lim_{t \uparrow z} \mu_3(t) \neq 0$. Nor does path 10b satisfy those conditions in the case of $\gamma_1 = 0$, $\gamma_2 > 0$, $\gamma_3 = 0$, because $\lim_{t \uparrow z} \mu_1(t) = 0$. Without proof, although it can be demonstrated 'experimentally' quite simply[1], it is posed that path 10b will not appear in an

---

[1] In numerical examples for the case of $i < (1 - f)r$ starting with $K(0) = (1 + b)X(0) = kQ(0) = K_{10b}$, not path 10b was observed, but path 10c preceded by the string 6bo9b, for a planning horizon sufficiently distant.

optimal string for this autonomous problem.

Path 10c, by definition, is 'partially' stationary. In order for path 10c to satisfy the transversality conditions in the case of $\gamma_1 = \gamma_2 = \gamma_3 = 0$, it is necessary that $\lim_{t \uparrow \uparrow z} \lambda_2(t) = 1$ and $\lim_{t \uparrow \uparrow z} \mu_3(t) = 0$ apply. Then, solving differential equations (B.60) and (B.61) respectively, gives:

$$\lambda_2(t) = e^{((1-f)r-i)(z-t)} \tag{B.66}$$

$$\mu_3(t) = (1-f)\left\{S'(Q_{10c}) - wl - (a+r)k\right\} \frac{1 - e^{-i(z-t)}}{(1-f)r\vartheta_Q} \tag{B.67}$$

The production rate on path 10c can either be smaller or larger than the production rate on path 10a.

Appendix C

Mathematical Details for Chapter 5

C.1 The basic model

C.1.1 Determining the coupling points for Subsection 5.2.2

For the optimal course of the capital assets stock, the following applies:

$$K(t) = \begin{cases} K_0 e^{gt} & \text{if } 0 \leq t \leq \tau_1; \\ K_0 e^{(a+g)\tau_1} e^{-at} & \text{if } \tau_1 \leq t \leq \tau_5; \\ K_0 e^{-(a+g)(\tau_5 - \tau_1)} e^{gt} & \text{if } \tau_5 \leq t \leq z. \end{cases} \tag{C.1}$$

with: K_0 given by (5.5).

The four equations below fix the coupling points τ_1, τ_2, τ_4 and τ_5; τ_3 being the instant where $\dot{Y}(\tau_3) = bX(\tau_3)$ is not a coupling point because $Y(\tau_3) < bX(\tau_3)$.

The first equation gives the length of period in which nothing is invested (for derivation, see Subsection C.1.2):

$$\tau_5 - \tau_1 = \frac{m}{a+g}(\tau_d - \tau_u) \tag{C.2}$$

The second equation is simply:

$$O_{vi}(\tau_2, K(\tau_2)) = 0 \tag{C.3}$$

The third equation follows from equations (3.6) and (5.8) with the knowledge that $I(t) = D(t) = 0$ for $t \in \langle \tau_2, \tau_4 \rangle$ and $Y(\tau_2) = Y(\tau_4) = 0$:

$$\int_{\tau_2}^{\tau_4} O_{vi}(s, K(s)) e^{(1-f)r(\tau_4 - s)} ds = 0 \tag{C.4}$$

The fourth equation is $\lambda_1(\tau_1) = 0$ with relationship (5.14) for $\lambda_1(\tau_1)$:

$$-1 + \int_{\tau_1}^{\tau_2} \frac{\partial O_{vi}}{\partial K}(s, K(s)) e^{-(a+i)(s-\tau_1)} ds +$$

$$e^{-i(\tau_4-\tau_1)} \int_{\tau_2}^{\tau_4} \frac{\partial O_{vi}}{\partial K}\left(s, K(s)\right) e^{-a(s-\tau_1)} e^{(1-f)r(\tau_4-s)} \mathrm{d}s +$$

$$\int_{\tau_4}^{\tau_5} \frac{\partial O_{vi}}{\partial K}\left(s, K(s)\right) e^{-(a+i)(s-\tau_1)} \mathrm{d}s + e^{-(a+i)(\tau_5-\tau_1)} = 0 \qquad \text{(C.5)}$$

This set of equations cannot be completely solved analytically, so that an iterative method has to be used.

C.1.2   Determining the coupling points for Subsection 5.2.3

The optimal course of the capital assets stock is again given by (C.1). On path 4 is:

$$\frac{\partial S}{\partial K}\left(t, k^{-1}K(t)\right) = wlk^{-1} + a + \frac{i}{1-f} \qquad \text{(C.6)}$$

Since $\frac{\partial S}{\partial K}$ is continuous, this equality applies both for τ_1 and τ_5. Put in another way:

$$\int_{\tau_1}^{\tau_5} \frac{\mathrm{d}}{\mathrm{d}t} \frac{\partial S}{\partial K}\left(s, k^{-1}K(s)\right) \mathrm{d}s = 0 \qquad \text{(C.7)}$$

Working out this integral leads to the following explicit expression for τ_5 in τ_1 and the model parameters:

$$\tau_5 = \tau_1 + \frac{m}{a+g}(\tau_d - \tau_u) \qquad \text{(C.8)}$$

On path 9, $I(t) = D(t) = 0$ applies so that:

$$\dot{Y}(t) - (1-f)rY(t) = -O_{vi}\left(t, K(t)\right) \qquad \text{(C.9)}$$

where:

$$Y(\tau_2) = 0 \qquad \text{(C.10)}$$

$$\dot{Y}(\tau_2) = 0 \qquad \text{(C.11)}$$

$$Y(\tau_3) = \frac{b}{1+b}K(\tau_3) \qquad \text{(C.12)}$$

$$\dot{Y}(\tau_3) = -\frac{ab}{1+b}K(\tau_3) \qquad \text{(C.13)}$$

$$Y(\tau_4) = 0 \qquad \text{(C.14)}$$

Via substituting $t = \tau_2$ in (C.9) and making use of (C.10) and (C.11), the following explicit expression for τ_2 in τ_1 and the model parameters is obtained:

$$\tau_2 = -\frac{a+g}{m-g-a}\tau_1 + \frac{m}{m-g-a}\tau_u + \frac{\varepsilon}{m-g-a}\ln\Gamma \qquad \text{(C.15)}$$

where:

$$\Gamma = \frac{wlk^{-1} + a + \frac{i}{1-f}}{(1 - \varepsilon^{-1})(wlk^{-1} - \frac{af}{1-f})} > 1 \tag{C.16}$$

Via substituting $t = \tau_3$ in (C.9) and making use of (C.12) and (C.13), the following explicit expression for τ_3 in τ_1 and the model parameters is obtained:

$$\tau_3 = \tau_1 + \frac{m}{a+g}(\tau_d - \tau_u) - \frac{\varepsilon}{a+g}\ln\Lambda \tag{C.17}$$

where:

$$\Lambda = \frac{wlk^{-1} + a + \frac{i}{1-f}}{(1 - \varepsilon^{-1})(wlk^{-1} - \frac{af}{1-f} + \frac{b}{1+b}(\frac{a}{1-f} + r))} > 1 \tag{C.18}$$

Integrating (C.9) and making use of (C.10) gives:

$$Y(t) = -\int_{\tau_2}^{t} O_{vi}(s, K(s))e^{(1-f)r(t-s)}ds \tag{C.19}$$

Substituting $t = \tau_3$ in (C.19) and making use of (C.12) then gives:

$$-\int_{\tau_2}^{\tau_3} O_{vi}(s, K(s))e^{(1-f)r(\tau_3-s)}ds = \frac{b}{1+b}K(\tau_3) \tag{C.20}$$

Substituting (C.15) and (C.17) in (C.20) gives an equation with τ_1 and the model parameters which cannot be transformed into an explicit expression for τ_1 in the model parameters. It is only possible to determine τ_1 iteratively after inserting numerical values for the parameters. Via (C.15), (C.17) and (C.8), then the values of τ_2, τ_3 and τ_5, respectively, follow directly.

Substituting $t = \tau_4$ in (C.19) and making use of (C.14) then gives:

$$-\int_{\tau_2}^{\tau_4} O_{vi}(s, K(s))e^{(1-f)r(\tau_4-s)}ds = 0 \tag{C.21}$$

Substituting (C.15) in (C.21) gives an equation with τ_4, τ_1 and the model parameters which cannot be transformed into an explicit expression for τ_4 in τ_1 and the model parameters. This means that τ_4 can be determined only iteratively after inserting numerical values for τ_1 and the model parameters.

And so, the values of the coupling points for the parameter set used are found to be (all figures being significant):

$$\tau_1 = 15.276$$
$$\tau_2 = 32.790$$
$$\tau_3 = 39.915$$
$$\tau_4 = 43.984$$
$$\tau_5 = 50.376$$

These values agree well with the values obtained via numerical optimization which are much less accurate however ($\Delta t = 0.25$).

C.1.3   Deriving relationships (5.22) and (5.27)

The development of an infinitesimally small change in debt between τ and τ_4, with $\tau \in (\tau_2, \tau_3)$, following the extra investment ∂K_{τ_1} at τ_1 and the equity injection ∂X_τ at τ, is described by the following differential equation (first order estimation):

$$\partial \dot{Y}(t) - (1 - f)r\partial Y(t) = -\frac{\partial O_{vi}}{\partial K}(t, K(t))\partial K_{\tau_1}e^{-a(t-\tau_1)} \qquad (C.22)$$

where[1]:

$$\partial Y(\tau) = -\partial X_\tau - \int_{\tau_2}^{\tau} \frac{\partial O_{vi}}{\partial K}(s, K(s))\partial K_{\tau_1}e^{-a(s-\tau_1)}e^{(1-f)r(\tau-s)}ds \qquad (C.23)$$

From the requirement that at τ_3:

$$\partial Y(\tau_3) = \frac{b}{1+b}\partial K_{\tau_1}e^{-a(\tau_3-\tau_1)} \qquad (C.24)$$

applies, a relationship between ∂K_{τ_1} and ∂X_τ can be derived. Integrating (C.22) produces:

$$\partial Y(t) = -\partial X_\tau e^{(1-f)r(t-\tau)} -$$

$$\int_{\tau_2}^{t} \frac{\partial O_{vi}}{\partial K}(s, K(s))\partial K_{\tau_1}e^{-a(s-\tau_1)}e^{(1-f)r(t-s)}ds \qquad (C.25)$$

Then, after substituting $t = \tau_3$ and making use of (C.24) relationship (5.22) is obtained.

The development of an infinitesimally small change in debt between τ and τ_4, with $\tau \in (\tau_2, \tau_3)$, following the compulsory acquisition of capital assets ∂K_τ at τ and the implied investment reduction by ∂K_{τ_1} at τ_1, is described by the following differential equation (first order estimation):

$$\partial \dot{Y}(t) - (1 - f)r\partial Y(t) = -\frac{\partial O_{vi}}{\partial K}(t, K(t))\left[\partial K_\tau e^{-a(t-\tau)} -\right.$$

$$\left.\partial K_{\tau_1}e^{-a(t-\tau_1)}\right] \qquad (C.26)$$

where:

$$\partial Y(\tau) = \partial K_\tau + \int_{\tau_2}^{\tau} \frac{\partial O_{vi}}{\partial K}(s, K(s))\partial K_{\tau_1}e^{-a(s-\tau_1)}e^{(1-f)r(\tau-s)}ds \qquad (C.27)$$

From the requirement that at τ_3:

$$\partial Y(\tau_3) = \frac{b}{1+b}\left[\partial K_\tau e^{-a(\tau_3-\tau)} - \partial K_{\tau_1}e^{-a(\tau_3-\tau_1)}\right] \qquad (C.28)$$

---

[1]By first order estimation, the extra investment ∂K_{τ_1} at τ_1 causes no change in debt at τ_2, because $Y(\tau_2 + \partial\tau_2) = \dot{Y}(\tau_2 + \partial\tau_2) = 0$.

applies, a relationship between ∂K_{τ_1} and ∂K_τ can be derived. Integrating (C.26) produces:

$$\partial Y(t) = \partial K_\tau e^{(1-f)r(t-\tau)} -$$

$$\int_\tau^t \frac{\partial O_{vi}}{\partial K}(s, K(s)) \partial K_\tau e^{-a(s-\tau)} e^{(1-f)r(t-s)} ds +$$

$$\int_{\tau_2}^t \frac{\partial O_{vi}}{\partial K}(s, K(s)) \partial K_{\tau_1} e^{-a(s-\tau_1)} e^{(1-f)r(t-s)} ds \qquad (C.29)$$

Then, after substituting $t = \tau_3$ and making use of (C.28) relationship (5.27) is obtained.

C.1.4 Determining the coupling points for Subsection 5.2.4

For the optimal course of the capital assets stock, again (C.1) applies, however now, with K_0 given by (5.6). The four equations below fix the coupling points τ_1, τ_2, τ_4 and τ_5; τ_3, the instant where $\dot Y(\tau_3) = 0$, is not a coupling point because $Y(\tau_3) > 0$.

The first equation gives the length of period in which nothing is invested (for derivation, see Subsection C.1.5):

$$\tau_5 - \tau_1 = \frac{m}{a+g}(\tau_d - \tau_u) \qquad (C.30)$$

The second and third equations follow from (3.6) and (5.8) with the knowledge that $I(t) = D(t) = 0$ for $t \in \langle \tau_2, \tau_4 \rangle$, $Y(\tau_2) = \frac{b}{1+b}K(\tau_2)$, $Y(\tau_4) = \frac{b}{1+b}K(\tau_4)$ and $\dot Y(\tau_4) = \frac{b}{1+b}\dot K(\tau_4)$:

$$\int_{\tau_2}^{\tau_4} O_{vi}(s, K(s)) e^{(1-f)r(\tau_4-s)} ds = \frac{b}{1+b}\left[K(\tau_2)e^{(1-f)r(\tau_4-\tau_2)} - K(\tau_4)\right]$$

$$(C.31)$$

$$O_{vi}(\tau_4, K(\tau_4)) = yK(\tau_4) \qquad (C.32)$$

The fourth equation is $\lambda_1(\tau_1) = 0$ with relationship (5.37) for $\lambda_1(\tau_1)$:

$$\frac{-1}{1+b} + \int_{\tau_1}^{\tau_2}\left\{\frac{\partial O_{vi}}{\partial K}(s, K(s)) - y\right\}e^{-(a+i)(s-\tau_1)} ds -$$

$$e^{-i(\tau_2-\tau_1)}\left[\frac{b}{1+b}e^{-a(\tau_2-\tau_1)} -\right.$$

$$\int_{\tau_2}^{\tau_4} \frac{\partial O_{vi}}{\partial K}(s, K(s)) e^{-a(s-\tau_1)} e^{-(1-f)r(s-\tau_2)} ds -$$

$$\left. \frac{b}{1+b} e^{-a(\tau_4-\tau_1)} e^{-(1-f)r(\tau_4-\tau_2)} \right] +$$

$$\int_{\tau_4}^{\tau_5} \left\{ \frac{\partial O_{vi}}{\partial K}(s, K(s)) - y \right\} e^{-(a+i)(s-\tau_1)} ds + \frac{e^{-(a+i)(\tau_5-\tau_1)}}{1+b} = 0$$

(C.33)

This set of equations cannot completely solved analytically, so that an iterative method has to be used.

C.1.5 Determining the coupling points for Subsection 5.2.5

The optimal course of the capital assets stock is again given by (C.1), however now with (5.6) for K_0. On path 8 is:

$$\frac{\partial S}{\partial K}(t, k^{-1}K(t)) = wlk^{-1} + a + \frac{1}{1+b}\frac{i}{1-f} + \frac{b}{1+b}r$$

(C.34)

Since $\frac{\partial S}{\partial K}$ is continuous, this equality applies both for τ_1 and τ_5. Put in another way:

$$\int_{\tau_1}^{\tau_5} \frac{d}{dt}\frac{\partial S}{\partial K}(s, k^{-1}K(s))\, ds = 0$$

(C.35)

Working out this integral leads to the following explicit expression for τ_5 in τ_1 and the model paramteters

$$\tau_5 = \tau_1 + \frac{m}{a+g}(\tau_d - \tau_u)$$

(C.36)

This expression is identical with (C.8). On path 9 is $I(t) = D(t) = 0$, so that again (C.9) applies:

$$\dot{Y}(t) - (1-f)rY(t) = -O_{vi}(t, K(t))$$

(C.37)

where now:

$$Y(\tau_2) = \frac{b}{1+b}K(\tau_2)$$

(C.38)

$$Y(\tau_3) = 0$$

(C.39)

$$\dot{Y}(\tau_3) = 0$$

(C.40)

$$Y(\tau_4) = \frac{b}{1+b}K(\tau_4)$$

(C.41)

$$\dot{Y}(\tau_4) = -\frac{ab}{1+b}K(\tau_4)$$

(C.42)

Via substituting $t = \tau_3$ in (C.37) and making use of (C.39) and (C.40), the following explicit expression for τ_3 in τ_1 and the model parameters is obtained:

$$\tau_3 = -\frac{a+g}{m-g-a}\tau_1 + \frac{m}{m-g-a}\tau_u + \frac{\varepsilon}{m-g-a}\ln\Upsilon \qquad (C.43)$$

where:

$$\Upsilon = \frac{wlk^{-1} + a + \frac{1}{1+b}\frac{i}{1-f} + \frac{b}{1+b}r}{(1-\varepsilon^{-1})(wlk^{-1} - \frac{af}{1-f})} > 1 \qquad (C.44)$$

Via substituting $t = \tau_4$ in (C.37) and making use of (C.41) and (C.42), the following explicit expression for τ_4 in τ_1 and the model parameters is obtained:

$$\tau_4 = \tau_1 + \frac{m}{a+g}(\tau_d - \tau_u) - \frac{\varepsilon}{a+g}\ln\Omega \qquad (C.45)$$

where:

$$\Omega = \frac{wlk^{-1} + a + \frac{1}{1+b}\frac{i}{1-f} + \frac{b}{1+b}r}{(1-\varepsilon^{-1})(wlk^{-1} - \frac{af}{1-f} + \frac{b}{1+b}(\frac{a}{1-f} + r))} > 1 \qquad (C.46)$$

Integrating (C.37) and making use of (C.39) gives:

$$Y(t) = -\int_{\tau_3}^{t} O_{vi}(s, K(s))e^{(1-f)r(t-s)}ds \qquad (C.47)$$

Substituting $t = \tau_4$ in (C.47) and making use of (C.41) then gives:

$$-\int_{\tau_3}^{\tau_4} O_{vi}(s, K(s))e^{(1-f)r(\tau_4-s)}ds = \frac{b}{1+b}K(\tau_4) \qquad (C.48)$$

Substituting (C.43) and (C.45) in (C.48) gives an equation with τ_1 and the model parameters which cannot be transformed into an explicit expression for τ_1 in the model parameters. It is only possible to determine τ_1 iteratively after inserting numerical values for the parameters. Via (C.43), (C.45) and (C.36), the the values of τ_3, τ_4 and τ_5, respectively, follow directly.

Substituting $t = \tau_2$ in (C.47) and making use of (C.38) then gives:

$$\int_{\tau_2}^{\tau_3} O_{vi}(s, K(s))e^{(1-f)r(\tau_2-s)}ds = \frac{b}{1+b}K(\tau_2) \qquad (C.49)$$

Substituting (C.43) in (C.49) gives an equation with τ_2, τ_1 and the model parameters which cannot be transformed into an explicit expression for τ_2 in τ_1 and the model parameters. This means that τ_2 can be determined only iteratively after inserting numerical values for τ_1 and the model parameters.

And so, the values of the coupling points for the parameter set used are found
to be (all figures being significant):

$$\tau_1 = 16.029$$
$$\tau_2 = 28.133$$
$$\tau_3 = 32.762$$
$$\tau_4 = 39.903$$
$$\tau_5 = 50.797$$

These values agree well with the values obtained via numerical optimization
which are much less accurate however ($\Delta t = 0.25$).

C.1.6 Deriving relationships (5.45) and (5.49)

The development of an infinitesimally small change in debt between τ and τ_4,
with $\tau \in (\tau_3, \tau_4)$, following the extra investment ∂K_{τ_1} at τ_1 and the equity
injection ∂X_τ at τ, is described by the following differential equation (first
order estimation):

$$\partial \dot{Y}(t) - (1-f)r\partial Y(t) = -\frac{\partial O_{vi}}{\partial K}(t, K(t))\partial K_{\tau_1} e^{-a(t-\tau_1)} \tag{C.50}$$

where[2]:

$$\partial Y(\tau) = -\partial X_\tau - \int_{\tau_3}^{\tau} \frac{\partial O_{vi}}{\partial K}(s, K(s))\partial K_{\tau_1} e^{-a(s-\tau_1)} e^{(1-f)r(\tau-s)} ds \tag{C.51}$$

From the requirement that at τ_4:

$$\partial Y(\tau_4) = \frac{b}{1+b}\partial K_{\tau_1} e^{-a(\tau_4-\tau_1)} \tag{C.52}$$

applies, a relationship between ∂K_{τ_1} and ∂X_τ can be derived. Integrating
(C.50) produces:

$$\partial Y(t) = -\partial X_\tau e^{(1-f)r(t-\tau)} -$$
$$\int_{\tau_3}^{t} \frac{\partial O_{vi}}{\partial K}(s, K(s))\partial K_{\tau_1} e^{-a(s-\tau_1)} e^{(1-f)r(t-s)} ds \tag{C.53}$$

Then, after substituting $t = \tau_4$ and making use of (C.52) relationship (5.45) is
obtained.

The development of an infinitesimally small change in debt between τ and τ_4,
with $\tau \in (\tau_3, \tau_4)$, following the compulsory acquisition of capital assets ∂K_τ

---

[2]By first order estimation, the extra investment ∂K_{τ_1} at τ_1 causes no change in debt at
τ_3, because $Y(\tau_3 + \partial \tau_3) = \dot{Y}(\tau_3 + \partial \tau_3) = 0$.

at τ and the implied investment reduction by ∂K_{τ_1} at τ_1, is described by the following differential equation (first order estimation):

$$\dot{\partial Y}(t) - (1-f)r\partial Y(t) = -\frac{\partial O_{vi}}{\partial K}(t, K(t))\left[\partial K_\tau e^{-a(t-\tau)} - \right.$$

$$\left. \partial K_{\tau_1} e^{-a(t-\tau_1)}\right] \tag{C.54}$$

where:

$$\partial Y(\tau) = \partial K_\tau + \int_{\tau_3}^{\tau} \frac{\partial O_{vi}}{\partial K}(s, K(s))\partial K_{\tau_1}e^{-a(s-\tau_1)}e^{(1-f)r(\tau-s)}ds \tag{C.55}$$

From the requirement that at τ_4:

$$\partial Y(\tau_4) = \frac{b}{1+b}\left[\partial K_\tau e^{-a(\tau_4-\tau)} - \partial K_{\tau_1}e^{-a(\tau_4-\tau_1)}\right] \tag{C.56}$$

applies, a relationship between ∂K_{τ_1} and ∂K_τ can be derived. Integrating (C.54) produces:

$$\partial Y(t) = \partial K_\tau e^{(1-f)r(t-\tau)} -$$

$$\int_\tau^t \frac{\partial O_{vi}}{\partial K}(s, K(s))\partial K_\tau e^{-a(s-\tau)}e^{(1-f)r(t-s)}ds +$$

$$\int_{\tau_3}^t \frac{\partial O_{vi}}{\partial K}(s, K(s))\partial K_{\tau_1}e^{-a(s-\tau_1)}e^{(1-f)r(t-s)}ds \tag{C.57}$$

Then, after substituting $t = \tau_4$ and making use of (C.56) relationship (5.49) is obtained.

C.2 A model with a variable utilization rate

C.2.1 Necessary conditions for optimality

After eliminating the variables L and Y, the dynamic optimization problem that has to be solved can be formulated as follows:

$$\max_{I(t),D(t),Q(t)} \left\{ J = \int_0^z e^{-it}D(t)\,dt + e^{-iz}X(z)\right\} \tag{C.58a}$$

$$\dot{K}(t) = I(t) - aK(t), \quad K(0) = K_0 \tag{C.58b}$$

$$\dot{X}(t) = (1-f)\left\{S(t,Q(t)) - wlQ(t) - aK(t) - \right.$$

$$\left. r(K(t) - X(t))\right\} - D(t), \quad X(0) = X_0 \tag{C.58c}$$

$$K(t) - X(t) \geq 0 \tag{C.58d}$$

$$(1+b)X(t) - K(t) \geq 0 \qquad\qquad\qquad\qquad\qquad \text{(C.58e)}$$

$$I(t) \geq 0 \qquad\qquad\qquad\qquad\qquad\qquad\qquad\quad \text{(C.58f)}$$

$$D(t) \geq 0 \qquad\qquad\qquad\qquad\qquad\qquad\qquad\quad \text{(C.58g)}$$

$$Q(t) \geq 0 \qquad\qquad\qquad\qquad\qquad\qquad\qquad\quad \text{(C.58h)}$$

$$k^{-1}K(t) - Q(t) \geq 0 \qquad\qquad\qquad\qquad\qquad\quad \text{(C.58i)}$$

The weak constraint qualification for this problem is satisfied if the matrix:

$$\begin{pmatrix} 1 & 0 & 0 & I(t) & 0 & 0 & 0 \\ 0 & 1 & 0 & 0 & D(t) & 0 & 0 \\ 0 & 0 & 1 & 0 & 0 & Q(t) & 0 \\ 0 & 0 & -1 & 0 & 0 & 0 & k^{-1}K(t) - Q(t) \end{pmatrix} \qquad \text{(C.59)}$$

has full row rank 4. This is always the case, because $K(t) \geq K_0 e^{-at} > 0$.

The Hamiltonian and Lagrangian are defined by ($\lambda_0 = 1$, see Observation 2.1):

$$\mathcal{H}(t, K, X, I, D, Q, \lambda_1, \lambda_2) = D + \lambda_1[I - aK] +$$

$$\lambda_2\left[(1-f)\{S(t,Q) - wlQ - aK - r(K-X)\} - D\right] \qquad \text{(C.60)}$$

$$\mathcal{L}(t, K, X, I, D, Q, \lambda_1, \lambda_2, \mu_1, \mu_2, \mu_3, \mu_4, \nu_1, \nu_2) =$$

$$\mathcal{H}(t, K, X, I, D, Q, \lambda_1, \lambda_2) + \mu_1 I + \mu_2 D +$$

$$\mu_3 Q + \mu_4[k^{-1}K - Q] + \nu_1[K - X] + \nu_2[(1+b)X - K] \qquad \text{(C.61)}$$

Applying Theorem 2.1 results in the following set of necessary conditions:

$$\dot{\lambda}_1(t) - i\lambda_1(t) = a\lambda_1(t) + (1-f)(a+r)\lambda_2(t) - k^{-1}\mu_4(t) -$$

$$\nu_1(t) + \nu_2(t) \qquad\qquad\qquad\qquad\qquad\qquad \text{(C.62)}$$

$$\dot{\lambda}_2(t) - i\lambda_2(t) = -(1-f)r\lambda_2(t) + \nu_1(t) - (1+b)\nu_2(t) \qquad \text{(C.63)}$$

$$\lambda_1(t) + \mu_1(t) = 0 \qquad\qquad\qquad\qquad\qquad\qquad \text{(C.64)}$$

$$1 - \lambda_2(t) + \mu_2(t) = 0 \qquad\qquad\qquad\qquad\qquad\quad \text{(C.65)}$$

$$(1-f)\left\{\frac{\partial S}{\partial Q}(t, Q(t)) - wl\right\}\lambda_2(t) + \mu_3(t) - \mu_4(t) = 0 \qquad \text{(C.66)}$$

$$\mu_1(t) \geq 0, \quad \mu_1(t)I(t) = 0 \qquad\qquad\qquad\qquad\quad \text{(C.67)}$$

$$\mu_2(t) \geq 0, \quad \mu_2(t)D(t) = 0 \qquad\qquad\qquad\qquad\quad \text{(C.68)}$$

$$\mu_3(t) \geq 0, \quad \mu_3(t)Q(t) = 0 \tag{C.69}$$

$$\mu_4(t) \geq 0, \quad \mu_4(t)\big(k^{-1}K(t) - Q(t)\big) = 0 \tag{C.70}$$

$$\nu_1(t) \geq 0, \quad \nu_1(t)\big(K(t) - X(t)\big) = 0 \tag{C.71}$$

$$\nu_2(t) \geq 0, \quad \nu_2(t)\big((1 + b)X(t) - K(t)\big) = 0 \tag{C.72}$$

$$\lambda_1(z) = \gamma_1 - \gamma_2 \tag{C.73}$$

$$\lambda_2(z) = 1 - \gamma_1 + (1 + b)\gamma_2 \tag{C.74}$$

$$\gamma_1 \geq 0, \quad \gamma_1\big(K(z) - X(z)\big) = 0 \tag{C.75}$$

$$\gamma_2 \geq 0, \quad \gamma_2\big((1 + b)X(z) - K(z)\big) = 0 \tag{C.76}$$

When (λ_1, λ_2) is discontinuous in τ, then:

$$\lambda_1(\tau^-) = \lambda_1(\tau^+) + \eta_1(\tau) - \eta_2(\tau) \tag{C.77}$$

$$\lambda_2(\tau^-) = \lambda_2(\tau^+) - \eta_1(\tau) + (1 + b)\eta_2(\tau) \tag{C.78}$$

$$\eta_1(\tau) \geq 0, \quad \eta_1(\tau)\big(K(\tau) - X(\tau)\big) = 0 \tag{C.79}$$

$$\eta_2(\tau) \geq 0, \quad \eta_2(\tau)\big((1 + b)X(\tau) - K(\tau)\big) = 0 \tag{C.80}$$

The Hamiltonian (C.60) is linear and therefore concave in K, X, I and D, as well as, concave in Q, because S as a function of Q is assumed to be concave. The residual term in the objective function and all inequality constraints are linear in K, X, I, D and Q. Hence, the necessary conditions for optimality are sufficient too.

The final path in an optimal string must satisfy the transversality conditions (C.73)–(C.76). They take into account the possibility that (λ_1, λ_2) can be discontinuous at instant z. The transversality conditions (C.73)–(C.74) must be read as follows:

$$\lambda_1(z^+) = 0, \quad \lambda_1(z^-) = \gamma_1 - \gamma_2 \tag{C.81}$$

$$\lambda_2(z^+) = 1, \quad \lambda_2(z^-) = 1 - \gamma_1 + (1 + b)\gamma_2 \tag{C.82}$$

Using the equations (C.64)–(C.66) and the knowledge that for the price function used $\mu_3(t) = 0$ everywhere, then gives:

$$\mu_1(z^-) = -\gamma_1 + \gamma_2 \tag{C.83}$$

$$\mu_2(z^-) = -\gamma_1 + (1 + b)\gamma_2 \tag{C.84}$$

$$\mu_4(z^-) = (1 - f)\left\{\frac{\partial S}{\partial Q}(z, Q) - wl\right\}(1 - \gamma_1 + (1 + b)\gamma_2) \tag{C.85}$$

From (C.75) and (C.76), it follows that γ_1 and γ_2 cannot both be positive. Furthermore, (C.67) and (C.83) exclude a combination of $\gamma_1 > 0$ and $\gamma_2 = 0$. Consequently, two alternatives still remain:

1. $\gamma_1 = \gamma_2 = 0 \Rightarrow \mu_1(z^-) = \mu_2(z^-) = \mu_3(z^-) = 0, \mu_4(z^-) \geq 0.$
   Here, at instant z, λ_1 and λ_2 are continuous. The paths with this property
   are not only paths 4a and 8a, but possibly also the other paths from
   Table 5.1.

2. $\gamma_1 = 0, \gamma_2 > 0 \Rightarrow \mu_1(z^-) > 0, \mu_2(z^-) > 0, \mu_3(z^-) = 0, \mu_4(z^-) \geq 0.$
   Here, at instant z, two jumps equal to γ_2 and $-(1+b)\gamma_2$, respectively, appear in λ_1 and λ_2. Only the paths 9a and 9b have the property described
   above.

C.2.2   Further examination of some paths

Below are the paths that can be excluded in advance, just like the paths xc
$(x = 1, \ldots, 12)$, together with the reasons for doing so.

Paths 1a and 5a.   Here the number of positive Lagrange multipliers $(=4)$ is
greater than the number of control variables $(=3)$.

Paths 11a, 11b, 12a and 12b.   These imply $i = (1 - f)r$, which follows
directly after substituting $\lambda_2(t) = 1 + \mu_2(t)$ (C.65) into equation (C.63) and
putting $\mu_2(t)$, $\nu_1(t)$ and $\nu_2(t)$ equal to zero.

Paths 5b, 8b and 10b.   Substituting $\lambda_1(t) = -\mu_1(t)$ (C.64) into equation (C.62), after putting $\mu_1(t)$, $\mu_4(t)$ and ν_1 equal to zero, gives:

$$(1 - f)(a + r)\lambda_2(t) + \nu_2(t) = 0 \qquad (C.86)$$

This is in conflict with $\lambda_2(t) = 1 + \mu_2(t) \geq 1$ (C.65) and $\nu_2(t) \geq 0$.

Path 4b.   Substituting $\lambda_1(t) = -\mu_1(t)$ (C.64) and $\lambda_2(t) = 1 + \mu_2(t)$ (C.65)
into equation (C.62), after putting $\mu_1(t)$, $\mu_2(t)$ and $\mu_4(t)$ equal to zero, gives:

$$\nu_1(t) = (1 - f)(a + r) + \nu_2(t) \qquad (C.87)$$

Substituting $\lambda_2(t) = 1 + \mu_2(t)$ (C.65) into equation (C.63), after putting $\mu_2(t)$
equal to zero, gives:

$$\nu_1(t) = (1 - f)r - i + (1 + b)\nu_2(t) \qquad (C.88)$$

Combining these two results then gives: $b\nu_2(t) = i + (1 - f)a$. This is in conflict
with $\nu_2(t) = 0$.

Path 1b. Putting $\mu_3(t)$ and $\mu_4(t)$ equal to zero in equation (C.66) gives:

$$(1-f)\left\{\frac{\partial S}{\partial Q}\big(t,Q(t)\big) - wl\right\}\lambda_2(t) = 0 \tag{C.89}$$

Given that $\lambda_2(t) = 1 + \mu_2(t) > 1$, this leads to:

$$\frac{\partial S}{\partial Q}\big(t,Q(t)\big) = wl \tag{C.90}$$

Since S is strictly concave and also increasing on the relevant interval for Q with $S(t,0) = 0$, it now applies that:

$$S\big(t,Q(t)\big) > Q(t)\frac{\partial S}{\partial Q}\big(t,Q(t)\big) = wlQ(t) \tag{C.91}$$

A positive value of $\nu_1(t)$ implies that: $K(t) = X(t)$ as well as $\dot{K}(t) = \dot{X}(t)$. Equating the righthand side of (C.58b) with the righthand side of (C.58c), after putting $I(t)$ and $D(t)$ equal to zero (because of positive $\mu_1(t)$ and $\mu_2(t)$ respectively), finally, produces:

$$-afK(t) = (1-f)\big\{S\big(t,Q(t)\big) - wlQ(t)\big\} \tag{C.92}$$

The lefthand side of this equation is negative, so that:

$$S\big(t,Q(t)\big) < wlQ(t) \tag{C.93}$$

This is in conflict with inequality (C.91).

Path 5b. Here, equation (C.90) is valid as well. This equation fixes implicitly the production rate as a function of the time. Solving it gives:

$$Q(t) = \overline{Q}\left[\frac{(\varepsilon-1)\overline{P}}{\varepsilon wl}\right]^{\varepsilon} \times \begin{cases} e^{gt} & \text{if } 0 \leq t \leq \tau_u; \\ e^{m\tau_u}e^{-(m-g)t} & \text{if } \tau_u < t \leq \tau_d; \\ e^{-m(\tau_d-\tau_u)}e^{gt} & \text{if } \tau_d < t \leq z. \end{cases} \tag{C.94}$$

With this, the price received per unit of goods sold becomes time-invariable:

$$P\big(t,Q(t)\big) = \frac{\varepsilon wl}{\varepsilon - 1} \tag{C.95}$$

Since $I(t) = 0$ because of $\mu_1(t) > 0$, (C.58b) implies that:

$$K(t) \propto e^{-at} \tag{C.96}$$

A positive value of $\nu_2(t)$ implies that: $K(t) = (1+b)X(t)$ as well as $\dot{K}(t) = (1+b)\dot{X}(t)$. Equating the righthand side of (C.58b) with the product of $(1+b)$ and the righthand side of (C.58c), after putting $I(t)$ and $D(t)$ equal to zero (because of positive $\mu_1(t)$ and $\mu_2(t)$ respectively) and rearranging terms, leads to:

$$[(1 - f)((1 + b)a + br) - a]K(t) = (1 - f)(P(t, Q(t))Q(t) - wlQ(t))$$
(C.97)

Substituting (C.94), (C.95) and (C.96) into this shows that only during a recession with a contraction rate $m - g = a$, the equation may be not conflicting for longer than one instant at a stretch. However, for moderate and severe recessions, $m > a + g$ applies.

C.2.3 Determining the coupling points for Subsection 5.3.2

For the optimal course of the capital assets stock, the following applies:

$$K(t) = \begin{cases} K_0 e^{gt} & \text{if } 0 \le t \le \tau_1; \\ K_0 e^{(a+g)\tau_1} e^{-at} & \text{if } \tau_1 \le t \le \tau_4; \\ K_0 e^{-(a+g)(\tau_4-\tau_1)} e^{gt} & \text{if } \tau_4 \le t \le z. \end{cases}$$
(C.98)

with: K_0 given by (5.5).

The four equations below fix the coupling points τ_i $(i = 1, \ldots, 4)$.

The first equation gives the length of period in which nothing is invested, which is similar to that for the basic model (see Subsection C.1.2):

$$\tau_4 - \tau_1 = \frac{m}{a + g}(\tau_d - \tau_u)$$
(C.99)

The second and third equations are simply:

$$\frac{\partial S}{\partial Q}(\tau_2, k^{-1}K(\tau_2)) = wl$$
(C.100)

$$\frac{\partial S}{\partial Q}(\tau_3, k^{-1}K(\tau_3)) = wl$$
(C.101)

The fourth equation is $\lambda_1(\tau_1) = 0$ with relationship (5.66) for $\lambda_1(\tau_1)$:

$$-1 + \int_{\tau_1}^{\tau_2} \frac{\partial O_{vi}}{\partial K}(s, K(s)) e^{-(a+i)(s-\tau_1)} ds +$$

$$\int_{\tau_2}^{\tau_3} af e^{-(a+i)(s-\tau_1)} ds +$$

$$\int_{\tau_3}^{\tau_4} \frac{\partial O_{vi}}{\partial K}(s, K(s)) e^{-(a+i)(s-\tau_1)} ds + e^{-(a+i)(\tau_4-\tau_1)} = 0 \qquad \text{(C.102)}$$

This set of equations cannot be completely solved analytically, so that an iterative method has to be used.

C.2.4 Determining the coupling points for Subsection 5.3.3

For the optimal course of the capital assets stock, again (C.98) applies, however now, with K_0 given by (5.6). The four equations below fix the coupling points τ_i $(i = 1, \ldots, 4)$.

The first equation gives the length of period in which nothing is invested, which is similar to that of the basic model (see Subsection C.1.5):

$$\tau_4 - \tau_1 = \frac{m}{a+g}(\tau_d - \tau_u) \tag{C.103}$$

The second and third equations are simply:

$$\frac{\partial S}{\partial Q}(\tau_2, k^{-1}K(\tau_2)) = wl \tag{C.104}$$

$$\frac{\partial S}{\partial Q}(\tau_3, k^{-1}K(\tau_3)) = wl \tag{C.105}$$

The fourth equation is $\lambda_1(\tau_1) = 0$ with relationship (5.69) for $\lambda_1(\tau_1)$:

$$\frac{-1}{1+b} + \int_{\tau_1}^{\tau_2}\left\{\frac{\partial O_{vi}}{\partial K}(s, K(s)) - y\right\}e^{-(a+i)(s-\tau_1)}ds +$$

$$\int_{\tau_2}^{\tau_3}(af - y)e^{-(a+i)(s-\tau_1)}ds +$$

$$\int_{\tau_3}^{\tau_4}\left\{\frac{\partial O_{vi}}{\partial K}(s, K(s)) - y\right\}e^{-(a+i)(s-\tau_1)}ds + \frac{e^{-(a+i)(\tau_4-\tau_1)}}{1+b} = 0 \tag{C.106}$$

This set of equations cannot be completely solved analytically, so that an iterative method has to be used.

C.2.5 Determining the coupling points for Subsection 5.3.4

For the optimal course of the capital assets stock, again (C.98) applies, however now, with K_0 given by (5.6). The six equations below fix the coupling points τ_i $(i = 1, \ldots, 6)$.

The first equation gives the length of period in which nothing is invested, which is similar to that of the basic model (see Subsection C.1.5):

$$\tau_6 - \tau_1 = \frac{m}{a+g}(\tau_d - \tau_u) \tag{C.107}$$

The second equation is simply:

$$\frac{\partial S}{\partial Q}(\tau_2, k^{-1}K(\tau_2)) = wl \tag{C.108}$$

The third and fourth equations follow from the fact that the *net* cash flow always amounts to zero and the knowledge that $I(t) = D(t) = 0$ for $t \in \langle \tau_3, \tau_4 \rangle$, $Y(\tau_3) = \frac{b}{1+b}K(\tau_3)$, $Y(\tau_4) = \frac{b}{1+b}K(\tau_4)$ and $\dot{Y}(\tau_4) = \frac{b}{1+b}\dot{K}(\tau_4)$:

$$\frac{b}{1+b}K(\tau_4) = \frac{b}{1+b}K(\tau_3)e^{(1-f)r(\tau_4-\tau_3)} -$$

$$\int_{\tau_3}^{\tau_4} (1-f)\left\{ S(s,Q(s)) - wlQ(s) + \frac{af}{1-f}K(s) \right\} e^{(1-f)r(\tau_4-s)}ds$$

$$(C.109)$$

$$(1-f)\left\{ S(\tau_4, Q(\tau_4)) - wlQ(\tau_4) + \frac{af}{1-f}K(\tau_4) \right\} = yK(\tau_4) \qquad (C.110)$$

where: $Q(t)$ is given by (5.64).

The fifth equation is simply:

$$\frac{\partial S}{\partial Q}(\tau_5, k^{-1}K(\tau_5)) = wl \qquad (C.111)$$

The sixth equation is $\lambda_1(\tau_1) = 0$ with relationship (5.78) for $\lambda_1(\tau_1)$:

$$\frac{-1}{1+b} + \int_{\tau_1}^{\tau_2} \left\{ \frac{\partial O_{vi}}{\partial K}(s, K(s)) - y \right\} e^{-(a+i)(s-\tau_1)}ds +$$

$$\int_{\tau_2}^{\tau_3} (af - y)e^{-(a+i)(s-\tau_1)}ds -$$

$$e^{-i(\tau_3-\tau_1)}\left[\frac{b}{1+b}e^{-a(\tau_3-\tau_1)} - \int_{\tau_3}^{\tau_4} afe^{-a(s-\tau_1)}e^{-(1-f)r(s-\tau_3)}ds - \right.$$

$$\left. \frac{b}{1+b}e^{-a(\tau_4-\tau_1)}e^{-(1-f)r(\tau_4-\tau_3)} \right] + \int_{\tau_4}^{\tau_5} (af - y)e^{-(a+i)(s-\tau_1)}ds +$$

$$\int_{\tau_5}^{\tau_6} \left\{ \frac{\partial O_{vi}}{\partial K}(s, K(s)) - y \right\} e^{-(a+i)(s-\tau_1)}ds + \frac{e^{-(a+i)(\tau_6-\tau_1)}}{1+b} = 0 (C.112)$$

This set of equations cannot be completely solved analytically, so that an iterative method has to be used.

C.3 A model with a cash balance

C.3.1 Necessary conditions for optimality

After eliminating the variables Q, L and Y, the dynamic optimization problem that has to be solved can be formulated as follows:

$$\max_{I(t),D(t),\dot{M}(t)} \left\{ J = \int_0^z e^{-it} D(t)\, dt + e^{-iz} X(z) \right\} \tag{C.113a}$$

$$\dot{K}(t) = I(t) - aK(t), \quad K(0) = K_0 \tag{C.113b}$$

$$\dot{X}(t) = (1 - f)\left\{ S\big(t, k^{-1}K(t)\big) - wlk^{-1}K(t) - aK(t) - \right.$$

$$\left. r(K(t) + M(t) - X(t)) \right\} - D(t), \quad X(0) = X_0 \tag{C.113c}$$

$$M(0) = M_0 \tag{C.113d}$$

$$K(t) + M(t) - X(t) \geq 0 \tag{C.113e}$$

$$(1 + b)X(t) - K(t) - M(t) \geq 0 \tag{C.113f}$$

$$M(t) \geq 0 \tag{C.113g}$$

$$I(t) \geq 0 \tag{C.113h}$$

$$D(t) \geq 0 \tag{C.113i}$$

The weak constraint qualification for this problem is satisfied if the matrix:

$$\begin{pmatrix} 1 & 0 & 0 & I(t) & 0 \\ 0 & 1 & 0 & 0 & D(t) \end{pmatrix} \tag{C.114}$$

has full row rank 2. This is always the case.

The Hamiltonian and Lagrangian are defined by ($\lambda_0 = 1$, see Observation 2.1):

$$\mathcal{H}(t, K, X, M, I, D, \dot{M}, \lambda_1, \lambda_2, \lambda_3) = D + \lambda_1 \left[I - aK \right] +$$

$$\lambda_2 \left[(1 - f)\left\{ S\big(t, k^{-1}K\big) - wlk^{-1}K - aK - \right. \right.$$

$$\left. \left. r(K + M - X) \right\} - D \right] + \lambda_3 \dot{M} \tag{C.115}$$

$$\mathcal{L}(t, K, X, M, I, D, \dot{M}, \lambda_1, \lambda_2, \lambda_3, \mu_1, \mu_2, \nu_1, \nu_2, \nu_3) =$$

$$\mathcal{H}(t, K, X, M, I, D, \dot{M}, \lambda_1, \lambda_2, \lambda_3) + \mu_1 I + \mu_2 D +$$

$$\nu_1 \left[K + M - X \right] + \nu_2 \left[(1 + b)X - K - M \right] + \nu_3 M \tag{C.116}$$

Applying Theorem 2.1 results in the following set of necessary conditions:

$$\dot{\lambda}_1(t) - i\lambda_1(t) = a\lambda_1(t) - (1-f)\left\{\frac{\partial S}{\partial K}(t, k^{-1}K(t)) - wlk^{-1} - \right.$$

$$\left. a - r\right\}\lambda_2(t) - \nu_1(t) + \nu_2(t) \tag{C.117}$$

$$\dot{\lambda}_2(t) - i\lambda_2(t) = -(1-f)r\lambda_2(t) + \nu_1(t) - (1+b)\nu_2(t) \tag{C.118}$$

$$\dot{\lambda}_3(t) - i\lambda_3(t) = (1-f)r\lambda_2(t) - \nu_1(t) + \nu_2(t) - \nu_3(t) \tag{C.119}$$

$$\lambda_1(t) + \mu_1(t) = 0 \tag{C.120}$$

$$1 - \lambda_2(t) + \mu_2(t) = 0 \tag{C.121}$$

$$\lambda_3(t) = 0 \tag{C.122}$$

$$\mu_1(t) \geq 0, \quad \mu_1(t)I(t) = 0 \tag{C.123}$$

$$\mu_2(t) \geq 0, \quad \mu_2(t)D(t) = 0 \tag{C.124}$$

$$\nu_1(t) \geq 0, \quad \nu_1(t)\big(K(t) + M(t) - X(t)\big) = 0 \tag{C.125}$$

$$\nu_2(t) \geq 0, \quad \nu_2(t)\big((1+b)X(t) - K(t) - M(t)\big) = 0 \tag{C.126}$$

$$\nu_3(t) \geq 0, \quad \nu_3(t)M(t) = 0 \tag{C.127}$$

$$\lambda_1(z) = \gamma_1 - \gamma_2 \tag{C.128}$$

$$\lambda_2(z) = 1 - \gamma_1 + (1+b)\gamma_2 \tag{C.129}$$

$$\lambda_3(z) = \gamma_1 - \gamma_2 + \gamma_3 \tag{C.130}$$

$$\gamma_1 \geq 0, \quad \gamma_1\big(K(z) + M(z) - X(z)\big) = 0 \tag{C.131}$$

$$\gamma_2 \geq 0, \quad \gamma_2\big((1+b)X(z) - K(z) - M(z)\big) = 0 \tag{C.132}$$

$$\gamma_3 \geq 0, \quad \gamma_3 M(z) = 0 \tag{C.133}$$

When $(\lambda_1, \lambda_2, \lambda_3)$ is discontinuous in τ, then:

$$\lambda_1(\tau^-) = \lambda_1(\tau^+) + \eta_1(\tau) - \eta_2(\tau) \tag{C.134}$$

$$\lambda_2(\tau^-) = \lambda_2(\tau^+) - \eta_1(\tau) + (1+b)\eta_2(\tau) \tag{C.135}$$

$$\lambda_3(\tau^-) = \lambda_3(\tau^+) + \eta_1(\tau) - \eta_2(\tau) + \eta_3(\tau) \tag{C.136}$$

$$\eta_1(\tau) \geq 0, \quad \eta_1(\tau)\big(K(\tau) + M(\tau) - X(\tau) = 0 \tag{C.137}$$

$$\eta_2(\tau) \geq 0, \quad \eta_2(\tau)\big((1+b)X(\tau) - K(\tau) - M(\tau)\big) = 0 \tag{C.138}$$

$$\eta_3(\tau) \geq 0, \quad \eta_3(\tau)M(\tau) = 0 \tag{C.139}$$

The Hamiltonian (C.115) is linear and therefore concave in X, M, I, D and $\dot{M}$, as well as, concave in K, because S as a function of Q is assumed to be concave. The residual term in the objective function and all inequality constraints are linear in K, X, M, I, D and $\dot{M}$. Hence, the necessary conditions for optimality are sufficient too.

The final path in an optimal string must satisfy the transversality conditions (C.128)–(C.133). They take into account the possibilty that $(\lambda_1, \lambda_2, \lambda_3)$ can be discontinuous at instant z. The transversality conditions (C.128)–(C.130) must be read as follows:

$$\lambda_1(z^+) = 0, \quad \lambda_1(z^-) = \gamma_1 - \gamma_2 \tag{C.140}$$

$$\lambda_2(z^+) = 1, \quad \lambda_2(z^-) = 1 - \gamma_1 + (1+b)\gamma_2 \tag{C.141}$$

$$\lambda_3(z^+) = 0, \quad \lambda_3(z^-) = \gamma_1 - \gamma_2 + \gamma_3 \tag{C.142}$$

Then, using equations (C.120)–(C.122) produces:

$$\mu_1(z^-) = -\gamma_1 + \gamma_2 \tag{C.143}$$

$$\mu_2(z^-) = -\gamma_1 + (1+b)\gamma_2 \tag{C.144}$$

$$0 = \gamma_1 - \gamma_2 + \gamma_3 \tag{C.145}$$

From (C.131) and (C.132), it follows that γ_1 and γ_2 cannot both be positive. Furthermore, (C.145) excludes a combination of $\gamma_2 = 0$ and positive values for γ_1 and/or γ_3, as well as, the combination $\gamma_1 = \gamma_3 = 0$, $\gamma_2 > 0$. Consequently, two alternatives still remain:

1. $\gamma_1 = \gamma_2 = \gamma_3 = 0 \Rightarrow \mu_1(z^-) = \mu_2(z^-) = 0$.
   Here, at instant z, λ_1, λ_2 and λ_3 are continuous. The paths with this property are not only paths 4a and 8a, but possibly also the other paths from Table 5.2.

2. $\gamma_1 = 0$, $\gamma_2 = \gamma_3 > 0 \Rightarrow \mu_1(z^-) > 0$, $\mu_2(z^-) > 0$.
   Here, at instant z, two jumps equal to γ_2 and $-(1+b)\gamma_2$, respectively, appear in λ_1 and λ_2; λ_3 is continuous in z. Only the paths 1b and 9a have the property described above.

C.3.2 Further examination of some paths

The paths which can be excluded in advance are presented below, together with the reasons for doing so.

Paths 1a and 5a. Here the number of positive Lagrange multipliers ($=4$) is greater than the number of control variables ($=3$).

Paths 11a, 11b, 12a and 12b. These imply $i = (1 - f)r$, which follows directly after substituting $\lambda_2(t) = 1 + \mu_2(t)$ (C.121) in equation (C.118) and putting $\mu_2(t)$, $\nu_1(t)$ and $\nu_2(t)$ equal to zero.

Paths 5b, 6b, 7b, 8b, 9b and 10b. These imply $(1 - f)r\lambda_2(t) + \nu_2(t) = 0$, which follows directly after substituting $\lambda_3(t) = 0$ (C.122) into equation (C.119) and putting $\nu_1(t)$ and $\nu_3(t)$ equal to zero. This is in conflict with $\lambda_2(t) = 1 + \mu_2(t) \geq 1$ (C.121) and $\nu_2(t) \geq 0$.

Paths 3b and 4b. Substituting $\lambda_2(t) = 1 + \mu_2(t)$ (C.121) into equation (C.118), after putting $\mu_2(t)$ equal to zero, gives: $(1 - f)r = i + \nu_1(t) - (1 + b)\nu_2(t)$. Substituting $\lambda_2(t) = 1 + \mu_2(t)$ (C.121) and $\lambda_3(t) = 0$ (C.122) into equation (C.119), after putting $\mu_2(t)$ equal to zero: $(1 - f)r = \nu_1(t) - \nu_2(t) + \nu_3(t)$. Combining these two results then leads to: $b\nu_2(t) + \nu_3(t) = i$. This is in conflict with $\nu_2(t) = \nu_3(t) = 0$.

C.3.3   Determining the coupling points for Subsection 5.4.2

For the optimal course of the capital assets stock, the following applies:

$$K(t) = \begin{cases} K_0 e^{gt} & \text{if } 0 \leq t \leq \tau_1; \\ K_0 e^{(a+g)\tau_1} e^{-at} & \text{if } \tau_1 \leq t \leq \tau_6; \\ K_0 e^{-(a+g)(\tau_6-\tau_1)} e^{gt} & \text{if } \tau_6 \leq t \leq z. \end{cases} \tag{C.146}$$

with: K_0 given by (5.5).

The five equations below fix the coupling points τ_1, τ_2, τ_3, τ_5 and τ_6; τ_4 being the instant where $\dot{Y}(\tau_4) = b\dot{X}(\tau_4)$ is not a coupling point because $Y(\tau_4) < bX(\tau_4)$.

The first equation gives the length of period in which nothing is invested; it is similar to that for the basic model (see Subsection C.1.2):

$$\tau_6 - \tau_1 = \frac{m}{a + g}(\tau_d - \tau_u) \tag{C.147}$$

The second equation follows from (5.86) and (5.8) with the knowledge that $I(t) = D(t) = Y(t) = \dot{Y}(t) = 0$ for $t \in \langle \tau_2, \tau_3 \rangle$:

$$\int_{\tau_2}^{\tau_3} O_{vi}(s, K(s)) ds = 0 \tag{C.148}$$

The third equation follows from equations (5.86) and (5.8) with the knowledge that $I(t) = D(t) = \dot{M}(t) = 0$ for $t \in \langle \tau_3, \tau_5 \rangle$ and $Y(\tau_3) = Y(\tau_5) = 0$:

$$\int_{\tau_3}^{\tau_5} O_{vi}(s, K(s)) e^{(1-f)r(\tau_5-s)} ds = 0 \tag{C.149}$$

The fourth equation is relationship (5.94):

$$i(\tau_3 - \tau_2) = ((1-f)r - i)(\tau_5 - \tau_3) \tag{C.150}$$

The fifth equation is $\lambda_1(\tau_1) = 0$ with relationship (5.98) for $\lambda_1(\tau_1)$:

$$-1 + \int_{\tau_1}^{\tau_2} \frac{\partial O_{vi}}{\partial K}(s, K(s)) e^{-(a+i)(s-\tau_1)} ds +$$

$$e^{-i(\tau_5 - \tau_1)} \left[e^{(1-f)r(\tau_5 - \tau_3)} \int_{\tau_2}^{\tau_3} \frac{\partial O_{vi}}{\partial K}(s, K(s)) e^{-a(s-\tau_1)} ds + \right.$$

$$\left. \int_{\tau_3}^{\tau_5} \frac{\partial O_{vi}}{\partial K}(s, K(s)) e^{-a(s-\tau_1)} e^{(1-f)r(\tau_5 - s)} ds \right] +$$

$$\int_{\tau_5}^{\tau_6} \frac{\partial O_{vi}}{\partial K}(s, K(s)) e^{-(a+i)(s-\tau_1)} ds + e^{-(a+i)(\tau_6 - \tau_1)} = 0 \tag{C.151}$$

This set of equations cannot be completely solved analytically, so that an iterative method has to be used.

C.3.4   Determining the coupling points for Subsection 5.4.3

For the optimal course of the capital assets stock, again (C.146) applies. The six equations below fix the coupling points τ_i $(i = 1, \ldots, 6)$.

The first equation gives the length of period in which nothing is invested, which is similar to that for the basic model (see Subsection C.1.2):

$$\tau_6 - \tau_1 = \frac{m}{a+g}(\tau_d - \tau_u) \tag{C.152}$$

The second equation follows from (5.86) and (5.8) with the knowledge that $I(t) = D(t) = Y(t) = \dot{Y}(t) = 0$ for $t \in \langle \tau_2, \tau_3 \rangle$:

$$\int_{\tau_2}^{\tau_3} O_{vi}(s, K(s)) ds = 0 \tag{C.153}$$

The third, fourth and fifth equations follow from (5.86) and (5.8) with the knowledge that $I(t) = D(t) = \dot{M}(t) = 0$ for $t \in \langle \tau_3, \tau_5 \rangle$, $Y(\tau_3) = Y(\tau_5) = 0$, $Y(\tau_4) = \frac{b}{1+b} K(\tau_4)$ and $\dot{Y}(\tau_4) = \frac{b}{1+b} \dot{K}(\tau_4)$:

$$\int_{\tau_3}^{\tau_5} O_{vi}(s, K(s)) e^{(1-f)r(\tau_5 - s)} ds = 0 \tag{C.154}$$

$$\int_{\tau_3}^{\tau_4} O_{vi}(s, K(s)) e^{(1-f)r(\tau_4 - s)} ds = -\frac{b}{1+b} K(\tau_4) \tag{C.155}$$

$$O_{vi}(\tau_4, K(\tau_4)) = yK(\tau_4) \tag{C.156}$$

The sixth equation is $\lambda_1(\tau_1) = 0$ with relationship (5.103) for $\lambda_1(\tau_1)$:

$$-1 + \int_{\tau_1}^{\tau_2} \frac{\partial O_{vi}}{\partial K}(s, K(s)) e^{-(a+i)(s-\tau_1)} ds +$$

$$e^{-i(\tau_2-\tau_1)} \left[\int_{\tau_2}^{\tau_3} \frac{\partial O_{vi}}{\partial K}(s, K(s)) e^{-a(s-\tau_1)} ds + \right.$$

$$\int_{\tau_3}^{\tau_4} \frac{\partial O_{vi}}{\partial K}(s, K(s)) e^{-a(s-\tau_1)} e^{-(1-f)r(s-\tau_3)} ds +$$

$$\left. \frac{b}{1+b} e^{-a(\tau_4-\tau_1)} e^{-(1-f)r(\tau_4-\tau_3)} \right] -$$

$$e^{-i(\tau_5-\tau_1)} \left[\frac{b}{1+b} e^{-a(\tau_4-\tau_1)} e^{(1-f)r(\tau_5-\tau_4)} - \right.$$

$$\left. \int_{\tau_4}^{\tau_5} \frac{\partial O_{vi}}{\partial K}(s, K(s)) e^{-a(s-\tau_1)} e^{(1-f)r(\tau_5-s)} ds \right] +$$

$$\int_{\tau_5}^{\tau_6} \frac{\partial O_{vi}}{\partial K}(s, K(s)) e^{-(a+i)(s-\tau_1)} ds + e^{-(a+i)(\tau_6-\tau_1)} = 0 \qquad \text{(C.157)}$$

This set of equations cannot be completely solved analytically, so that an iterative method has to be used.

C.3.5   Determining the coupling points for Subsection 5.4.5

For the optimal course of the capital assets stock, again (C.146) applies, however, with K_0 now given by (5.6). The six equations below fix the coupling points τ_i $(i = 1, \ldots, 6)$.

The first equation gives the length of period in which nothing is invested, which is similar to that for the basic model (see Subsection C.1.5):

$$\tau_6 - \tau_1 = \frac{m}{a+g}(\tau_d - \tau_u) \qquad \text{(C.158)}$$

The second equation follows from (5.86) and (5.8) with the knowledge that $I(t) = D(t) = \dot{M}(t) = 0$ for $t \in \langle \tau_2, \tau_3 \rangle$, $Y(\tau_2) = \frac{b}{1+b}K(\tau_2)$ and $Y(\tau_3) = 0$:

$$\int_{\tau_2}^{\tau_3} O_{vi}(s, K(s)) e^{(1-f)r(\tau_2-s)} ds = \frac{b}{1+b}K(\tau_2) \qquad \text{(C.159)}$$

The third equation follows from equations (5.86) and (5.8) with the knowledge that $I(t) = D(t) = Y(t) = \dot{Y}(t) = 0$ for $t \in \langle \tau_3, \tau_4 \rangle$:

$$\int_{\tau_3}^{\tau_4} O_{vi}(s, K(s)) ds = 0 \qquad \text{(C.160)}$$

The fourth and fifth equations follow from (5.86) and (5.8) with the knowledge that $I(t) = D(t) = \dot{M}(t) = 0$ for $t \in \langle \tau_4, \tau_5 \rangle$, $Y(\tau_4) = 0$, $Y(\tau_5) = \frac{b}{1+b} K(\tau_5)$ and $\dot{Y}(\tau_5) = \frac{b}{1+b} \dot{K}(\tau_5)$:

$$\int_{\tau_4}^{\tau_5} O_{vi}\big(s, K(s)\big) e^{(1-f)r(\tau_5 - s)} ds = -\frac{b}{1+b} K(\tau_5) \tag{C.161}$$

$$O_{vi}\big(\tau_5, K(\tau_5)\big) = y K(\tau_5) \tag{C.162}$$

The sixth equation is $\lambda_1(\tau_1) = 0$ with relationship (5.111) for $\lambda_1(\tau_1)$:

$$\frac{-1}{1+b} + \int_{\tau_1}^{\tau_2} \left\{ \frac{\partial O_{vi}}{\partial K}\big(s, K(s)\big) - y \right\} e^{-(a+i)(s-\tau_1)} ds -$$

$$e^{-i(\tau_2 - \tau_1)} \left[\frac{b}{1+b} e^{-a(\tau_2 - \tau_1)} - \right.$$

$$\int_{\tau_2}^{\tau_3} \frac{\partial O_{vi}}{\partial K}\big(s, K(s)\big) e^{-a(s-\tau_1)} e^{-(1-f)r(s-\tau_2)} ds -$$

$$e^{-(1-f)r(\tau_3 - \tau_2)} \int_{\tau_3}^{\tau_4} \frac{\partial O_{vi}}{\partial K}\big(s, K(s)\big) e^{-a(s-\tau_1)} ds -$$

$$e^{-(1-f)r(\tau_3 - \tau_2)} \int_{\tau_4}^{\tau_5} \frac{\partial O_{vi}}{\partial K}\big(s, K(s)\big) e^{-a(s-\tau_1)} e^{-(1-f)r(s-\tau_4)} ds -$$

$$\left. \frac{b}{1+b} e^{-a(\tau_5 - \tau_1)} e^{-(1-f)r((\tau_3 - \tau_2)+(\tau_5 - \tau_4))} \right] +$$

$$\int_{\tau_5}^{\tau_6} \left\{ \frac{\partial O_{vi}}{\partial K}\big(s, K(s)\big) - y \right\} e^{-(a+i)(s-\tau_1)} ds + \frac{e^{-(a+i)(\tau_6 - \tau_1)}}{1+b} = 0 \tag{C.163}$$

This set of equations cannot be completely solved analytically, so that an iterative method has to be used.

C.4   A model with an inventory of finished goods

C.4.1   Necessary conditions for optimality

After eliminating the variables L and Y, the dynamic optimization problem that has to be solved can be formulated as follows:

$$\max_{I(t),D(t),Q(t)} \left\{ J = \int_0^z e^{-it} D(t) \, dt + e^{-iz} X(z) \right\} \tag{C.164a}$$

$$\dot{K}(t) = I(t) - aK(t), \quad K(0) = K_0 \tag{C.164b}$$

$$\dot{X}(t) = (1 - f)\left\{S(t, Q(t)) - wlk^{-1}K(t) - aK(t) - \right.$$

$$\left. r(K(t) - X(t))\right\} - D(t), \quad X(0) = X_0 \tag{C.164c}$$

$$\dot{V}(t) = k^{-1}K(t) - Q(t), \quad V(0) = V_0 \tag{C.164d}$$

$$K(t) - X(t) \geq 0 \tag{C.164e}$$

$$(1 + b)X(t) - K(t) \geq 0 \tag{C.164f}$$

$$V(t) \geq 0 \tag{C.164g}$$

$$I(t) \geq 0 \tag{C.164h}$$

$$D(t) \geq 0 \tag{C.164i}$$

$$Q(t) \geq 0 \tag{C.164j}$$

The weak constraint qualification for this problem is satisfied if the matrix:

$$\begin{pmatrix} 1 & 0 & 0 & I(t) & 0 & 0 \\ 0 & 1 & 0 & 0 & D(t) & 0 \\ 0 & 0 & 1 & 0 & 0 & Q(t) \end{pmatrix} \tag{C.165}$$

has full row rank 4. This is always the case.

The Hamiltonian and Lagrangian are defined by ($\lambda_0 = 1$, see Observation 2.1):

$$\mathcal{H}(t, K, X, V, I, D, Q, \lambda_1, \lambda_2, \lambda_3) = D + \lambda_1[I - aK] +$$

$$\lambda_2\left[(1 - f)\{S(t, Q) - wlk^{-1}K - aK - r(K - X)\} - D\right] +$$

$$\lambda_3\left[k^{-1}K - Q\right] \tag{C.166}$$

$$\mathcal{L}(t, K, X, V, I, D, Q, \lambda_1, \lambda_2, \lambda_3, \mu_1, \mu_2, \mu_3, \nu_1, \nu_2, \nu_3) =$$

$$\mathcal{H}(t, K, X, V, I, D, Q, \lambda_1, \lambda_2, \lambda_3) + \mu_1 I + \mu_2 D +$$

$$\mu_3 Q + \nu_1[K - X] + \nu_2[(1 + b)X - K] + \nu_3 V \tag{C.167}$$

Applying Theorem 2.1 results in the following set of necessary conditions:

$$\dot{\lambda}_1(t) - i\lambda_1(t) = a\lambda_1(t) + (1 - f)(wlk^{-1} + a + r)\lambda_2(t) -$$

$$k^{-1}\lambda_3(t) - \nu_1(t) + \nu_2(t) \tag{C.168}$$

$$\dot{\lambda}_2(t) - i\lambda_2(t) = -(1 - f)r\lambda_2(t) + \nu_1(t) - (1 + b)\nu_2(t) \tag{C.169}$$

$$\dot{\lambda}_3(t) - i\lambda_3(t) = -\nu_3(t) \tag{C.170}$$

$$\lambda_1(t) + \mu_1(t) = 0 \tag{C.171}$$

$$1 - \lambda_2(t) + \mu_2(t) = 0 \tag{C.172}$$

$$(1 - f)\frac{\partial S}{\partial Q}(t, Q(t))\lambda_2(t) - \lambda_3(t) + \mu_3(t) = 0 \tag{C.173}$$

$$\mu_1(t) \geq 0, \quad \mu_1(t)I(t) = 0 \tag{C.174}$$

$$\mu_2(t) \geq 0, \quad \mu_2(t)D(t) = 0 \tag{C.175}$$

$$\mu_3(t) \geq 0, \quad \mu_3(t)Q(t) = 0 \tag{C.176}$$

$$\nu_1(t) \geq 0, \quad \nu_1(t)\big(K(t) - X(t)\big) = 0 \tag{C.177}$$

$$\nu_2(t) \geq 0, \quad \nu_2(t)\big((1 + b)X(t) - K(t)\big) = 0 \tag{C.178}$$

$$\nu_3(t) \geq 0, \quad \nu_3(t)V(t) = 0 \tag{C.179}$$

$$\lambda_1(z) = \gamma_1 - \gamma_2 \tag{C.180}$$

$$\lambda_2(z) = 1 - \gamma_1 + (1 + b)\gamma_2 \tag{C.181}$$

$$\lambda_3(z) = \gamma_3 \tag{C.182}$$

$$\gamma_1 \geq 0, \quad \gamma_1\big(K(z) - X(z)\big) = 0 \tag{C.183}$$

$$\gamma_2 \geq 0, \quad \gamma_2\big((1 + b)X(z) - K(z)\big) = 0 \tag{C.184}$$

$$\gamma_3 \geq 0, \quad \gamma_3 V(z) = 0 \tag{C.185}$$

When $(\lambda_1, \lambda_2, \lambda_3)$ is discontinuous in τ, then:

$$\lambda_1(\tau^-) = \lambda_1(\tau^+) + \eta_1(\tau) - \eta_2(\tau) \tag{C.186}$$

$$\lambda_2(\tau^-) = \lambda_2(\tau^+) - \eta_1(\tau) + (1 + b)\eta_2(\tau) \tag{C.187}$$

$$\lambda_3(\tau^-) = \lambda_3(\tau^+) + \eta_3(\tau) \tag{C.188}$$

$$\eta_1(\tau) \geq 0, \quad \eta_1(\tau)\big(K(\tau) - X(\tau)\big) = 0 \tag{C.189}$$

$$\eta_2(\tau) \geq 0, \quad \eta_2(\tau)\big((1 + b)X(\tau) - K(\tau)\big) = 0 \tag{C.190}$$

$$\eta_3(\tau) \geq 0, \quad \eta_3(\tau)V(\tau) = 0 \tag{C.191}$$

The Hamiltonian (C.166) is linear and therefore concave in K, X, V, I and D, as well as, concave in Q, because S as function of Q is assumed to be concave. The residual term in the objective function and all inequality constraints are linear in K, X, V, I, D and Q. Hence, the necessary conditions for optimality are sufficient too.

The final path in an optimal string must satisfy the transversality conditions (C.180)–(C.185). They take into account the possibility that $(\lambda_1, \lambda_2, \lambda_3)$ can be discontinuous at instant z. The transversality conditions (C.180)–(C.182) must be read as follows:

$$\lambda_1(z^+) = 0, \quad \lambda_1(z^-) = \gamma_1 - \gamma_2 \tag{C.192}$$

$$\lambda_2(z^+) = 1, \quad \lambda_2(z^-) = 1 - \gamma_1 + (1 + b)\gamma_2 \tag{C.193}$$

$$\lambda_3(z^+) = 0, \quad \lambda_3(z^-) = \gamma_3 \tag{C.194}$$

Using the equations (C.171)–(C.173) and the knowledge that for the price function used $\mu_3(t) = 0$ everywhere, then gives:

$$\mu_1(z^-) = -\gamma_1 + \gamma_2 \tag{C.195}$$

$$\mu_2(z^-) = -\gamma_1 + (1 + b)\gamma_2 \tag{C.196}$$

$$\gamma_3 = (1 - f)\frac{\partial S}{\partial Q}(z, Q(z))(1 - \gamma_1 + (1 + b)\gamma_2) \tag{C.197}$$

From (C.183) and (C.184), it follows that γ_1 and γ_2 cannot both be positive, so that (C.174) and (C.195) imply that $\gamma_1 = 0$. Furthermore, (C.197) and (3.2) exclude a combination with $\gamma_3 = 0$, seeing as: $1 - \gamma_1 + (1 + b)\gamma_2 \geq 1$. Consequently, two alternatives must still be examined:

1. $\gamma_1 = \gamma_2 = 0$, $\gamma_3 > 0 \Rightarrow \mu_1(z^-) = \mu_2(z^-) = \mu_3(z^-) = 0$.
   Here, at instant z, λ_1 and λ_2 are continuous, and a jump equal to $-\gamma_3$ appears in λ_3. The paths with this property are not only paths 4a and 8a, but possibly also the other paths from Table 5.3.

2. $\gamma_1 = 0$, $\gamma_2 > 0$, $\gamma_3 > 0 \Rightarrow \mu_1(z^-) > 0$, $\mu_2(z^-) > 0$, $\mu_3(z^-) = 0$.
   Here, at instant z, three jumps equal to γ_2, $-(1 + b)\gamma_2$ and $-\gamma_3$, respectively, appear in λ_1, λ_2 and λ_3. Only the paths 1b, 5b, 9a and 9b have the property described above.

C.4.2   Further examination of some paths

Paths 1a and 5a. These paths can be excluded, because the number of positive Lagrange multipliers (=4) is larger than the number of control variables (=3).

Paths 11a, 11b, 12a and 12b. These paths can be excluded, because they imply that $i = (1 - f)r$, which follows directly after substituting $\lambda_2(t) = 1 + \mu_2(t)$ (C.172) into equation (C.169) and putting $\mu_2(t)$, $\nu_1(t)$ and $\nu_2(t)$ equal to zero.

Path 4b. Substituting $\lambda_2(t) = 1 + \mu_2(t)$ (C.172) into equation (C.169), after putting $\mu_2(t)$ and $\nu_2(t)$ equal to zero, produces: $\nu_1(t) = (1 - f)r - i$. Substituting this outcome and $\lambda_1(t) = -\mu_1(t)$ (C.171), as well as, $\lambda_2(t) = 1 + \mu_2(t)$ (C.172) into equation (C.168), after putting $\mu_1(t)$, $\mu_2(t)$ and $\nu_2(t)$ equal to zero, produces:

$$\lambda_3(t) = (1 - f) \left(wl + \left(a + \frac{i}{1-f} \right) k \right) \tag{C.198}$$

Equation (C.170) then implies $\nu_3(t) = i\lambda_3(t) > 0$, so that path 4b can be excluded.

Path 8b. Substituting $\lambda_2(t) = 1 + \mu_2(t)$ (C.172) into equation (C.169), after putting $\mu_2(t)$ and $\nu_1(t)$ equal to zero, produces: $\nu_2(t) = (i - (1 - f)r)/(1 + b)$. Substituting this outcome and $\lambda_1(t) = -\mu_1(t)$ (C.171), as well as, $\lambda_2(t) = 1 + \mu_2(t)$ (C.172) into equation (C.168), after putting $\mu_1(t)$, $\mu_2(t)$ and $\nu_1(t)$ equal to zero, produces:

$$\lambda_3(t) = (1 - f) \left(wl + \left(a + \frac{1}{1+b}\frac{i}{1-f} + \frac{b}{1+b}r \right) k \right) \tag{C.199}$$

Equation (C.170) then implies $\nu_3(t) = i\lambda_3(t) > 0$, so that path 8b can be excluded.

Path 10b. After putting $\nu_3(t)$ equal to zero, it follows from equation (C.170) that: $\lambda_3(t) \propto e^{it}$. Substituting this outcome and $\lambda_1(t) = -\mu_1(t)$ (C.171) into equation (C.168), after putting $\mu_1(t)$, $\nu_1(t)$ and $\nu_2(t)$ equal to zero, produces: $\lambda_2(t) \propto e^{it}$. Substituting this outcome into equation (C.169), after putting $\nu_1(t)$ and $\nu_2(t)$ equal to zero, produces: $0 = -(1 - f)r\lambda_2(t)$ which is in conflict with $\lambda_2(t) = 1 + \mu_2(t) \geq 1$ (C.172), so that path 10b can be excluded.

Paths 3a and 7a. Since $\mu_1(t) > 0$ and $\nu_3(t) > 0$, $Q(t) \propto e^{-at}$ applies. Substituting $\lambda_2(t) = 1 + \mu_2(t)$ (C.172) into equation (C.173), after putting $\mu_2(t)$ and $\mu_3(t)$ equal to zero, produces:

$$\lambda_3(t) = (1 - f)\frac{\partial S}{\partial Q}(t, Q(t)) = (1 - f)(1 - \varepsilon^{-1}) P(t, Q(t)) \tag{C.200}$$

Via equation (C.170) and the knowledge that $\nu_3(t) > 0$, it follows that:

$$\dot{P}(t, Q(t)) - iP(t, Q(t)) < 0 \tag{C.201}$$

Making use of the fact that $Q(t) \propto e^{-at}$, this leads to:

$$((a + g)\varepsilon^{-1} - i)P(t, Q(t)) < 0 \qquad \text{if } t \in [0, \tau_u) \cup \langle \tau_d, z] \tag{C.202}$$

$$((a + g - m)\varepsilon^{-1} - i)P(t, Q(t)) < 0 \qquad \text{if } t \in \langle \tau_u, \tau_d \rangle \tag{C.203}$$

Thus, only when $i > (a + g)\varepsilon^{-1}$, the paths 3a and 7a may appear in an optimal string during a rise in the business cycle. With regard to the recession, the assumption $m > a + g$ has already been made.

Path 9a. Since $\mu_1(t) > 0$ and $\nu_3(t) > 0$, $Q(t) \propto e^{-at}$ applies. After putting $\nu_1(t)$ and $\nu_2(t)$ equal to zero, equation (C.169) implies:

$$\lambda_2(t) \propto e^{(i-(1-f)r)t} \tag{C.204}$$

Substituting this into (C.173), using $\mu_3(t) = 0$, then produces:

$$\lambda_3(t) \propto \frac{\partial S}{\partial Q}(t, Q(t)) e^{(i-(1-f)r)t} \propto P(t, Q(t)) e^{(i-(1-f)r)t} \tag{C.205}$$

Via equation (C.170) and the knowledge that $\nu_3(t) > 0$, it follows that:

$$\dot{P}(t, Q(t)) - (1-f)rP(t, Q(t)) < 0 \tag{C.206}$$

Making use of the fact that $Q(t) \propto e^{-at}$, this leads to:

$$((a+g)\varepsilon^{-1} - (1-f)r)P(t, Q(t)) < 0 \qquad \text{if } t \in [0, \tau_u) \cup \langle \tau_d, z] \tag{C.207}$$

$$((a+g-m)\varepsilon^{-1} - (1-f)r)P(t, Q(t)) < 0 \qquad \text{if } t \in \langle \tau_u, \tau_d \rangle \tag{C.208}$$

Thus, only when $(1-f)r > (a+g)\varepsilon^{-1}$, path 10a may appear in an optimal string during a rise in the business cycle. With regard to the recession, the assumption $m > a + g$ has already been made.

Path 1b. Here $I(t) = D(t) = 0$, $K(t) = X(t)$ and $\dot{K}(t) = \dot{X}(t)$ apply. Via equations (C.164b) and (C.164c), this leads to:

$$-aK(t) = (1-f)\left\{ S(t, Q(t)) - wlk^{-1}K(t) - aK(t) \right\} \tag{C.209}$$

When $K(t) \propto e^{-at}$, then it follows for $Q(t)$:

$$Q(t) \propto e^{(m-g-a\varepsilon)(\varepsilon-1)^{-1}t} \qquad \text{if } t \in [\tau_u, \tau_d] \tag{C.210}$$

Path 3b. After putting $\nu_3(t)$ equal to zero, (C.170) implies: $\lambda_3(t) \propto e^{it}$. Substituting $\lambda_2(t) = 1 + \mu_2(t)$ into (C.173), after putting $\mu_2(t)$ and $\mu_3(t)$ equal to zero, then produces:

$$\lambda_3(t) = (1-f)\frac{\partial S}{\partial Q}(t, Q(t)) \propto e^{it} \tag{C.211}$$

From this follows:

$$Q(t) \propto e^{-(m-g+i\varepsilon)t} \qquad \text{if } t \in [\tau_u, \tau_d] \tag{C.212}$$

Path 9b. After putting $\nu_1(t)$ and $\nu_2(t)$ equal to zero, equation (C.169) implies: $\lambda_2(t) \propto e^{(i-(1-f)r)t}$. Substituting this into (C.173), using $\mu_3(t) = 0$, then produces:

$$\lambda_3(t) \propto \frac{\partial S}{\partial Q}(t, Q(t))e^{(i-(1-f)r)t} \tag{C.213}$$

After putting $\nu_3(t)$ equal to zero, (C.170) implies: $\lambda_3(t) \propto e^{it}$. Combining this outcome with (C.213) produces:

$$\frac{\partial S}{\partial Q}(t, Q(t)) \propto e^{(1-f)rt} \tag{C.214}$$

From this follows:

$$Q(t) \propto e^{-(-g+(1-f)r\varepsilon)t} \qquad \text{if } t \in [0, \tau_u] \cup [\tau_d, z] \tag{C.215}$$

$$Q(t) \propto e^{-(m-g+(1-f)r\varepsilon)t} \qquad \text{if } t \in [\tau_u, \tau_d] \tag{C.216}$$

C.4.3 Determining the coupling points for Subsection 5.5.2

$m > m^*$

For the optimal course of the capital assets stock, the following applies:

$$K(t) = \begin{cases} K_0 e^{gt} & \text{if } 0 \le t \le \tau_1; \\ K_0 e^{(a+g)\tau_1}e^{-at} & \text{if } \tau_1 \le t \le \tau_8; \\ K_0 e^{-(a+g)(\tau_8-\tau_1)}e^{gt} & \text{if } \tau_8 \le t \le z. \end{cases} \tag{C.217}$$

with: K_0 given by (5.5).

For the optimal course of the sales rate, the following applies:

$$Q(t) = \begin{cases} k^{-1}K(t) & \text{if } 0 \le t \le \tau_2; \\ Q(\tau_2)e^{-(m-g+i\varepsilon)(t-\tau_2)} & \text{if } \tau_2 \le t \le \tau_3; \\ Q(\tau_3)e^{(m-g-a\varepsilon)(\varepsilon-1)^{-1})(t-\tau_3)} & \text{if } \tau_3 \le t \le \tau_4; \\ Q(\tau_4)e^{-(m-g+(1-f)r\varepsilon)(t-\tau_4)} & \text{if } \tau_4 \le t \le \tau_d; \\ Q(\tau_d)e^{-(-g+(1-f)r\varepsilon)(t-\tau_d)} & \text{if } \tau_d \le t \le \tau_5; \\ k^{-1}K(t) & \text{if } \tau_5 \le t \le z. \end{cases} \tag{C.218}$$

where: $Q(\tau_2) = k^{-1}K(\tau_2)$, $Q(\tau_3) = k^{-1}K(\tau_2)e^{-(m-g+i\varepsilon)(\tau_3-\tau_2)}$, etc.

The eight equations below fix the coupling points τ_i $(i = 1, \ldots, 8)$.

The first equation gives the length of period in which nothing is invested, which is similar with that for the basic model (see Subsection C.1.2):

$$\tau_8 - \tau_1 = \frac{m}{a+g}(\tau_d - \tau_u) \tag{C.219}$$

The second equation concerns the instant at which the operating cash flow becomes zero ($Y(\tau_3) = 0$):

$$(1 - f)\left\{S\big(\tau_3, Q(\tau_3)\big) - wlQ(\tau_3) + \frac{af}{1 - f}K(\tau_3)\right\} = 0 \qquad (C.220)$$

The third, fourth and fifth equations follow from the fact that the *net* cash flow always amounts to zero and the knowledge that $I(t) = D(t) = 0$ for $t \in \langle \tau_3, \tau_7 \rangle$, $Y(\tau_3) = Y(\tau_7) = 0$, $Y(\tau_6) = \frac{b}{1+b}K(\tau_6)$ and $\dot{Y}(\tau_6) = \frac{b}{1+b}\dot{K}(\tau_6)$:

$$\int_{\tau_3}^{\tau_7} (1 - f)\left\{S\big(s, Q(s)\big) - wlQ(s) + \frac{af}{1 - f}K(s)\right\} e^{(1-f)r(\tau_7 - s)}\mathrm{d}s = 0$$
$$(C.221)$$

$$\int_{\tau_3}^{\tau_6} (1 - f)\left\{S\big(s, Q(s)\big) - wlQ(s) + \frac{af}{1 - f}K(s)\right\} e^{(1-f)r(\tau_6 - s)}\mathrm{d}s =$$

$$-\frac{b}{1+b}K(\tau_6) \qquad (C.222)$$

$$(1 - f)\left\{S\big(\tau_6, k^{-1}K(\tau_6)\big) - wlk^{-1}K(\tau_6) + \frac{af}{1 - f}K(\tau_6)\right\} = yK(\tau_6)$$
$$(C.223)$$

The sixth equation follows from the fact that $V(\tau_2) = V(\tau_5) = 0$:

$$\int_{\tau_2}^{\tau_5} \big(k^{-1}K(s) - Q(s)\big)\,\mathrm{d}s = 0 \qquad (C.224)$$

The seventh equation follows from the continuity of Q at τ_5:

$$Q(\tau_d)e^{-(-g+(1-f)r\varepsilon)(\tau_5 - \tau_d)} = k^{-1}K(\tau_5) \qquad (C.225)$$

The final equation is:

$$\lambda_1(\tau_1) = 0 \qquad (C.226)$$

where: an expression for $\lambda_1(\tau_1)$ can be derived directly from the necessary conditions with the aid of the relationships for $\lambda_2(t)$ and $\lambda_3(t)$ which have been given in Subsection 5.5.2.

This set of equations cannot be completely solved analytically, so that an iterative method has to be used.

$m < m^\star$

In comparison with the situation where $m > m^\star$, here, τ_6 is not a coupling point any longer, because the upper bound of debt is not reached. Below, an equation follows which, in combination with relationships (C.219)–(C.221) and (C.224)–(C.226), fixes the seven coupling points for this case.

The equations stems from the continuity of λ_2 at τ_6:

$$\frac{\frac{\partial S}{\partial Q}\big(\tau_3, Q(\tau_3)\big)}{\frac{\partial S}{\partial Q}\big(\tau_4, Q(\tau_4)\big)} e^{-(1-f)r(\tau_6-\tau_4)} e^{i(\tau_6-\tau_3)} = e^{((1-f)r-i)(\tau_7-\tau_6)} \qquad (C.227)$$

where: use is made of (5.126) and (5.128).

C.4.4 Determining the coupling points for Subsection 5.5.3

For the optimal course of the capital assets, again (C.217) applies, however now, with K_0 given by (5.6).

For the optimal course of the sales rate, the following applies:

$$Q(t) = \begin{cases} k^{-1}K(t) & \text{if } 0 \le t \le \tau_3; \\ Q(\tau_3)e^{-(m-g+(1-f)r\varepsilon)(t-\tau_3)} & \text{if } \tau_3 \le t \le \tau_4; \\ Q(\tau_4)e^{(m-g-a\varepsilon)(\varepsilon-1)^{-1})(t-\tau_4)} & \text{if } \tau_4 \le t \le \tau_5; \\ Q(\tau_5)e^{-(m-g+(1-f)r\varepsilon)(t-\tau_5)} & \text{if } \tau_5 \le t \le \tau_d; \\ Q(\tau_d)e^{-(-g+(1-f)r\varepsilon)(t-\tau_d)} & \text{if } \tau_d \le t \le \tau_6; \\ k^{-1}K(t) & \text{if } \tau_6 \le t \le z. \end{cases} \qquad (C.228)$$

where: $Q(\tau_3) = k^{-1}K(\tau_3)$, $Q(\tau_4) = k^{-1}K(\tau_3)e^{-(m-g+(1-f)r\varepsilon)(\tau_4-\tau_3)}$, etc.

The eight equations below fix the coupling points τ_i $(i = 1, \ldots, 8)$.

The first equation gives the length of period in which nothing is invested, which is similar with that for the basic model (see Subsection C.1.5):

$$\tau_8 - \tau_1 = \frac{m}{a+g}(\tau_d - \tau_u) \qquad (C.229)$$

The second equation concerns the instant at which the operating cash cash flow and the amount of debt become zero:

$$(1-f)\left\{S\big(\tau_4, Q(\tau_4)\big) - wlQ(\tau_4) + \frac{af}{1-f}K(\tau_4)\right\} = 0 \qquad (C.230)$$

The third, fourth and fifth equations follow from the fact that the *net* cash flow always amounts to zero and the knowledge that $I(t) = D(t) = 0$ for

$t \in \langle \tau_2, \tau_7 \rangle$, $Y(\tau_2) = \frac{b}{1+b} K(\tau_2)$, $Y(\tau_4) = Y(\tau_5) = 0$, $Y(\tau_7) = \frac{b}{1+b} K(\tau_7)$ and $\dot{Y}(\tau_7) = \frac{b}{1+b} \dot{K}(\tau_7)$:

$$\int_{\tau_2}^{\tau_4} (1-f) \left\{ S(s, Q(s)) - wlQ(s) + \frac{af}{1-f} K(s) \right\} e^{(1-f)r(\tau_2 - s)} ds =$$

$$\frac{b}{1+b} K(\tau_2) \qquad\qquad\qquad\qquad\qquad\qquad (C.231)$$

$$\int_{\tau_5}^{\tau_7} (1-f) \left\{ S(s, Q(s)) - wlQ(s) + \frac{af}{1-f} K(s) \right\} e^{(1-f)r(\tau_7 - s)} ds =$$

$$-\frac{b}{1+b} K(\tau_7) \qquad\qquad\qquad\qquad\qquad (C.232)$$

$$(1-f) \left\{ S(\tau_7, Q(\tau_7)) - wlQ(\tau_7) + \frac{af}{1-f} K(\tau_7) \right\} = yK(\tau_7) \qquad (C.233)$$

The sixth equation follows from the fact that $V(\tau_3) = V(\tau_6) = 0$:

$$\int_{\tau_3}^{\tau_6} \left(k^{-1} K(s) - Q(s) \right) ds = 0 \qquad\qquad\qquad (C.234)$$

The seventh equation follows from the continuity of Q at τ_6:

$$Q(\tau_d) e^{-(-g+(1-f)r\epsilon)(\tau_6 - \tau_d)} = k^{-1} K(\tau_6) \qquad\qquad (C.235)$$

The final equation is:

$$\lambda_1(\tau_1) = 0 \qquad\qquad\qquad\qquad\qquad\qquad (C.236)$$

where an expression for $\lambda_1(\tau_1)$ can be derived directly from the necessary conditions using the relationships for $\lambda_2(t)$ and $\lambda_3(t)$ given in Subsection 5.5.3.

This set of equations cannot be completely solved analytically, so that an iterative method has to be used.

Appendix D

Mathematical Details for Chapter 6

D.1 Necessary conditions for optimality

After eliminating the variables Q, G, L and Y, the dynamic optimization problem that has to be solved can be formulated as follows:

$$\max_{I(t),D(t),Z} \left\{ J = \int_0^Z e^{-it} D(t)\,\mathrm{d}t + e^{-iZ} X(Z) \right\} \tag{D.1a}$$

$$\dot{K}(t) = I(t) - aK(t), \quad K(0) = K_0 \tag{D.1b}$$

$$\dot{X}(t) = (1-f) \left\{ S\left(t, \overline{Q}\left(\frac{K(t)}{\overline{K}}\right)^{\frac{1}{\pi_K}}\right) - v\overline{G}\left(\frac{K(t)}{\overline{K}}\right)^{\frac{\pi_G}{\pi_K}} - \right.$$

$$\left. w\overline{L}\left(\frac{K(t)}{\overline{K}}\right)^{\frac{\pi_L}{\pi_K}} - aK(t) - r\big(K(t) - X(t)\big) \right\} - D(t),$$

$$X(0) = X_0 \tag{D.1c}$$

$$K(t) - X(t) \geq 0 \tag{D.1d}$$

$$(1+b)X(t) - K(t) \geq 0 \tag{D.1e}$$

$$I(t) \geq 0 \tag{D.1f}$$

$$D(t) \geq 0 \tag{D.1g}$$

The weak constraint qualification for this problem is always satisfied (see Appendix A).

The Hamiltonian and Lagrangian are defined by ($\lambda_0 = 1$, see Observation 2.1):

$$\mathcal{H}(t, K, X, I, D, \lambda_1, \lambda_2) = D + \lambda_1 [I - aK] +$$

$$\lambda_2 \left[(1 - f) \left\{ S \left(t, \overline{Q} \left(\frac{K}{\overline{\overline{K}}} \right)^{\frac{1}{\pi_K}} \right) - v\overline{G} \left(\frac{K}{\overline{\overline{K}}} \right)^{\frac{\pi_G}{\pi_K}} - \right. \right.$$

$$\left. \left. w\overline{L} \left(\frac{K}{\overline{\overline{K}}} \right)^{\frac{\pi_L}{\pi_K}} - aK - r(K - X) \right\} - D \right] \tag{D.2}$$

$$\mathcal{L}(t, K, X, I, D, \lambda_1, \lambda_2, \mu_1, \mu_2, \nu_1, \nu_2) = \mathcal{H}(t, K, X, I, D, \lambda_1, \lambda_2) +$$

$$\mu_1 I + \mu_2 D + \nu_1 [K - X] + \nu_2 [(1 + b)X - K] \tag{D.3}$$

Applying Theorem 2.1 results in the following set of necessary conditions:

$$\dot{\lambda}_1(t) - i\lambda_1(t) = a\lambda_1(t) - (1 - f) \left\{ \frac{\partial S}{\partial K} \left(t, \overline{Q} \left(\frac{K(t)}{\overline{K}} \right)^{\frac{1}{\pi_K}} \right) - \right.$$

$$\left. \frac{v\pi_G \overline{G}}{\pi_K K(t)} \left(\frac{K(t)}{\overline{K}} \right)^{\frac{\pi_G}{\pi_K}} - \frac{w\pi_L \overline{L}}{\pi_K K(t)} \left(\frac{K(t)}{\overline{K}} \right)^{\frac{\pi_L}{\pi_K}} - a - r \right\} \lambda_2(t) -$$

$$\nu_1(t) + \nu_2(t) \tag{D.4}$$

$$\dot{\lambda}_2(t) - i\lambda_2(t) = -(1 - f)r\lambda_2(t) + \nu_1(t) - (1 + b)\nu_2(t) \tag{D.5}$$

$$\lambda_1(t) + \mu_1(t) = 0 \tag{D.6}$$

$$1 - \lambda_2(t) + \mu_2(t) = 0 \tag{D.7}$$

$$\mu_1(t) \geq 0, \quad \mu_1(t)I(t) = 0 \tag{D.8}$$

$$\mu_2(t) \geq 0, \quad \mu_2(t)D(t) = 0 \tag{D.9}$$

$$\nu_1(t) \geq 0, \quad \nu_1(t)\big(K(t) - X(t)\big) = 0 \tag{D.10}$$

$$\nu_2(t) \geq 0, \quad \nu_2(t)\big((1 + b)X(t) - K(t)\big) = 0 \tag{D.11}$$

$$\lambda_1(z) = \gamma_1 - \gamma_2 \tag{D.12}$$

$$\lambda_2(z) = 1 - \gamma_1 + (1 + b)\gamma_2 \tag{D.13}$$

$$\gamma_1 \geq 0, \quad \gamma_1 \big(K(z) - X(z)\big) = 0 \tag{D.14}$$

$$\gamma_2 \geq 0, \quad \gamma_2 \big((1 + b)X(z) - K(z)\big) = 0 \tag{D.15}$$

When (λ_1, λ_2) is discontinuous in τ, then:

$$\lambda_1(\tau^-) = \lambda_1(\tau^+) + \eta_1(\tau) - \eta_2(\tau) \tag{D.16}$$

$$\lambda_2(\tau^-) = \lambda_2(\tau^+) - \eta_1(\tau) + (1 + b)\eta_2(\tau) \tag{D.17}$$

$$\eta_1(\tau) \geq 0, \quad \eta_1(\tau)\big(K(\tau) - X(\tau)\big) = 0 \tag{D.18}$$

$$\eta_2(\tau) \geq 0, \quad \eta_2(\tau)\big((1 + b)X(\tau) - K(\tau)\big) = 0 \tag{D.19}$$

Symbols and Notation

General remarks

The variable running time is represented by t, or sometimes by s (for example when used as an integration variable). Special instants of time are denoted by τ, usually, provided with a subscript; characteristic times (time constants) are denoted by ϑ and always provided with a subscript; Δt symbolizes the stepsize for a discrete time model of the firm.

The superscript * after a symbol is normally used in order to indicate explicitly when it refers to an optimal value of a magnitude. A bar above a symbol is used for time-variable magnitudes in order to show that they refer to time-invariable reference values. A dot placed over a symbol stands for the total time derivative of the respective magnitude represented by that symbol. Furthermore, the following notation convention holds:

$$x(\tau^-) = \lim_{t \uparrow \tau} x(t) \qquad \text{en} \qquad x(\tau^+) = \lim_{t \downarrow \tau} x(t)$$

where: x is an arbitrary function of time.

All symbols throughout this book are introduced at their first appearance. Below, an enumeration and explanation of the most important symbols follow; a distinction is made between endogenous variables, model parameters (exogenous) and derived constants (the units between square brackets are only intended to give examples of the dimensions of the various variables and parameters):

Endogenous variables

B	: operating income	[$/year]
D	: dividend rate	[$/year]
G	: raw materials	[ton/year]
I	: investment rate	[$/year]
J	: objective function of the firm	[$]
K	: stock of capital assets,	[–]
	likewise, book value of capital assets	[$]

L	: labour	[man-year/year]
M	: cash balance	[\$]
O_{vi}	: operating cash flow before paying interest	[\$/year]
O_{ni}	: operating cash flow (after paying interest)	[\$/year]
P	: price per unit of goods sold	[\$/ton]
Q	: production rate and/or sales rate	[ton/year]
S	: turnover	[\$/year]
V	: inventory	[ton]
W	: net profit	[\$/year]
X	: equity	[\$]
Y	: debt	[\$]
Z	: free planning horizon	[year]

Exogenous variables

E	: accumulated total market sales	[ton]
P_a	: autonomous price per unit of goods sold	[\$/ton]
T	: value added per unit of goods sold	[\$/ton]
U	: total market sales rate (production life cycle)	[ton/year]

Model parameters

a	: depreciation rate	[1/year]
b	: maximum debt to equity ratio	[–]
f	: corporate profit tax rate	[–]
g	: growth rate	[1/year]
i	: shareholder's time preference rate	[1/year]
k	: capital to production ratio	[year/ton]
l	: labour to production ratio	[man-year/ton]
m	: $m - g$ is the contraction rate	[1/year]
r	: interest rate	[1/year]
v	: price per unit of raw materials	[\$/ton]
w	: wage rate	[\$/man-year]
z	: fixed planning horizon	[year]
β^{-1}	: market experience coefficient (experience/learning curve)	[–]

ε	: price elasticity of demand	[–]
ϑ_Q	: characteristic time of start-up costs	[year]
ϑ_U	: characteristic time of production life cycle	[year]
π_G	: raw materials productivity coefficient	[–]
π_K	: capital productivity coefficient	[–]
π_L	: labour productivity coefficient	[–]
τ_d	: end of recession	[year]
τ_u	: start of recession	[year]
$\tau_{x\%}$	: instant of time when the total market sales rate amounts to $x\%$ of the limit value	[year]

Derived constants

$$c_4 = \frac{i}{1 - f}$$

$$c_8 = \frac{b}{1 + b}r + \frac{1}{1 + b} \cdot \frac{i}{1 - f}$$

$$c_{10} = r$$

$$y = \frac{b}{1 + b}\left(a + (1 - f)r\right)$$

Bibliography

Bekker, P.C.F. [1991]. *A Lifetime Distribution Model of Depreciable and Reproducible Capital Assets*. VU University Press. Amsterdam.

Bensoussan, A., E.G. Hurst jr. & B. Näslund [1974]. *Management Applications of Modern Control Theory*. Vol. 18 of *Studies in Mathematical and Managerial Economics*. North-Holland. Amsterdam.

Bersselaar, H.J.G.M. van den [1992]. Comparing two models of the firm by means of dynamic optimization. Internal report NR-1751 (in Dutch). System and Control Technology Group, Eindhoven University of Technology.

Blok, M.W.J. [1988]. Adaptation of optimal dynamic control strategies for thermal energy systems. Master's thesis (in Dutch). Eindhoven University of Technology.

Boston Consulting Group [1970]. *Perspectives on Experience*. Boston, Massachusetts.

Delft, A.G.E.P. van [1989]. Dynamic optimisation of thermal energy systems. PhD thesis. Eindhoven University of Technology.

Faessen, R.J.W. [1986]. Dynamic optimization applied to models of the firm. Master's thesis (in Dutch). Eindhoven University of Technology.

Feichtinger, G. & R.F. Hartl [1986]. *Optimale Kontrolle ökonomischer Prozesse, Anwendungen des Maximumprinzips in den Wirtschaftswissenschaften*. De Gruyter. Berlin.

Grefte, H.P.M. de [1984]. Dynamic optimization of an ethane cracker. Master's thesis (in Dutch). Eindhoven University of Technology.

Grinten, P.M.E.M. van der [1979]. Managers and planners: degenerated control engineers? Servobode 25 (in Dutch). System and Control Technology Group, Eindhoven University of Technology.

Grinten, P.M.E.M. van der [1984]. Model building and control strategies for a firm. Internal report NR-1104a (in Dutch). System and Control Technology Group, Eindhoven University of Technology.

Hardy, L.F.C.M. [1991]. The optimal dynamic control strategy for a model of the firm. Master's thesis (in Dutch). Eindhoven University of Technology.

Hilten, O. van [1991]. *Optimal Firm Behaviour in the Context of Technological Progress and a Business Cycle*. Vol. 352 of *Lecture Notes in Economics and Mathematical Systems*. Springer-Verlag. Berlin.

Hilten, O. van, P.M. Kort & P.J.J.M. van Loon [1993]. *Dynamic Policies of the Firm. An Optimal Control Approach*. Springer-Verlag. Berlin.

Jong, H.W. de [1985]. *Dynamic Market Theory*. Stenfert Kroese. Leiden. (in Dutch).

Kocken, T.P. [1990]. Game theory approach to a dynamic investment model. Internal report NR-1627 (in Dutch). System and Control Technology Group, Eindhoven University of Technology.

Kort, P.M. [1989]. *Optimal Dynamic Investment Policies of a Value Maximizing Firm*. Vol. 330 of *Lecture Notes in Economics and Mathematical Systems*. Springer-Verlag. Berlin.

Leban, R. & J. Lesourne [1980]. The firm's investment and employment policy through a business cycle. *European Economic Review* 13, 43–80.

Leban, R. & J. Lesourne [1983]. Adaptive strategies of the firm through a business cycle. *Journal of Economic Dynamics and Control* 5, 201–234.

Lesourne, J. [1973]. *Modèles de Croissance des Enterprises*. Dunod. Paris.

Loon, P.J.J.M. van [1983]. *A Dynamic Theory of the Firm: Production, Finance and Investment*. Vol. 218 of *Lecture Notes in Economics and Mathematical Systems*. Springer-Verlag. Berlin.

Machielsen, K.C.P. [1987]. Numerical solution of optimal control problems with state constraints by sequential quadratic programming in function space. PhD thesis. Eindhoven University of Technology.

Martino, J.P. [1972]. *Technological Forecasting for Decision Making*. Elsevier. Amsterdam.

Meiring, F. [1981]. Dynamic optimisation of slowly changing distributed processes; a methanol proces with an aging catalyst. PhD thesis (in Dutch). Eindhoven University of Technology.

Naus, H.H.J.G. [1992]. Optimal dynamic investment, dividend and production policy of a firm experiencing a business cycle. Master's thesis (in Dutch). Eindhoven University of Technology.

Nickell, S.J. [1974]. On the role of expectations in the pure theory of investments. *Review of Economic Studies* **41**, 1–19.

Putten, C.G.M.W. van de [1988]. Optimal dynamic control strategies for a model of the firm. Master's thesis (in Dutch). Eindhoven University of Technology.

Schijndel, G.J.C.Th. van [1988]. *Dynamic Firm and Investor Behaviour under Progressive Personal Taxation.* Vol. 305 of *Lecture Notes in Economics and Mathematical Systems.* Springer-Verlag. Berlin.

Schoor, W.J.C. van de [1989]. Comparing two models of the firm on the basis of optimal dynamic control strategies. Master's thesis (in Dutch). Eindhoven University of Technology.

Varian, H.R. [1984]. *Microeconomic Analysis.* second ed. Norton & Company. New York.

Verheyen, P.A. [1992]. The jump in models with irreversible investments. In: *Dynamic Economic Models and Optimal Control* (G. Feichtinger, Ed.). Elsevier. Amsterdam. pp. 75–89.

Weston, J.F. & T.E. Copeland [1989]. *Managerial Finance.* eighth ed. The Dryden Press. Chicago.

Summary

The research work that is described in this book makes a contribution to the scientific field of optimal control theory applied to dynamic models of the firm. A characteristic of the literature on this subject is an analytical approach to solving dynamic optimization problems; for example, via Pontryagin's Maximum Principle in combination with the path coupling procedure of Van Loon. In this book, dynamic optimization problems are solved numerically with the aid of a powerful computer and specific programs for optimizing non-linear functions of a finite number of variables under non-linear subsidiary constraints. Consequently, the optimal control of more realistic and complex models of the firm can be determined under diverse circumstances. The aim is to achieve a maximum value of the firm by optimal planning of, for example, investments, inventory, liquidity, dividend and capacity utilization in a given period of time.

After the introduction in Chapter 1, a short explanation about analytically solving time-continuous optimal control problems with pure state constraints is given in Chapter 2, and also, how they can be tackled numerically after discretization. Additionally, the general economic interpretation of adjoint variables is discussed, for both continuous and discrete problems.

Chapter 3 deals with the basic model that forms a starting point for the models of the firm which are presented in the successive chapters. It also serves as the base of many models that appear in the literature. In contrast to reports in literature, here, attention is paid to relatively short planning periods in which the stationary state cannot be attained. Given the initial state and subsidiary conditions, the dynamic optimal strategy comes down to attaining the optimal size of capital assets and equity as soon as possible and maintaining it subsequently, provided that the planning horizon is sufficiently distant, or to approximate it as closely as possible when it is not. In this procedure, the planning horizon has no effect on the required policy during the planning period.

In Chapter 4, a model with start-up costs is discussed. The idea behind this is that in real-life, after an expansion of capital assets, often it is impossible to fully utilize them immediately, due to unavoidable start-up problems; a certain time elapses before normal utilization can be reached. This is simulated by replacing the static relationship between the production rate and the size of the capital assets stock in the basic model with a semi-dynamic one. As a consequence of this, the change in the operating income resulting from extra investment shows an inverse response: it is negative at first, but becomes positive later. Since cost comes before benefit, for example, a firm considering to expand its stock of capital assets should ascertain if the remaining period is long enough to recover the extra costs, with future returns discounted against the time preference rate of the shareholder. Depending on the initial state, this can lead to the final value of capital assets stock, equity and production rate, as well as, the maximum value of the objective function, all being substantially lower than for a similar firm without any start-up costs. In addition to the characteristic time to reach normal utilization, the shareholder's time preference rate and the planning horizon play the most important roles in this process.

Chapter 5 contains the studies of four models in which the firm is experiencing an exogenous business cycle. The first model examined is in fact the basic model, on the understanding that a business cycle is simulated by an explicitly time-dependent price function. Depending upon the parameter values used, discontinuities (jumps) now appear in the costate variables for a dynamic optimal strategy. In addition to the jumps reported in literature, extra jumps have been discovered. For the sake of economic interpretation of these jumps, analytical expressions for the costate variables are given each time. The extra jumps occur when the optimal instant of ceasing to invest, that already comes before the start of the recession, becomes a *boundary* optimum, that is to say: continuing to invest for a longer time inevitably leads, some time later, to exceeding one or more of the subsidiary conditions in the model. The second model includes the addition of a variable utilization rate. It is possible for the firm to underutilize its capital assets and to dispense with labour. By reducing the utilization rate, the firm prevents the marginal *variable* costs of production from becoming greater than the marginal returns from production, so that a negative operating cash flow can be avoided. The third model examined is the first model with the addition of a cash balance. Up to now, the maintaining of a cash balance does not appear in literature on deterministic dynamic models of the firm. Building up a cash balance in time allows the firm to continue investing for a longer period and the instant to stop becomes a free optimum. The extra jumps in the costate variables no longer appear. The last model examined in this chapter includes an expansion with an inventory of finished goods. The effects of the possibility to build up a finished goods inventory on the dynamic optimal strategy are, in essence, the same as those of the possibility to build up a cash balance.

Finally, in Chapter 6, a model of the firm is presented that is expanded essentially in two places with respect to the basic model from Chapter 3. The first expansion concerns the production function of the model which forms the relationship between the production rate and the minimum quantity of production factors required; it describes the achievement of increasing returns to scale ('economies of scale'). The other expansion concerns the price function which deals with the returns per unit of goods sold as a function of the sales rate and time; it attributes increasing returns to experience ('experience curve'). Both expansions emphasize the dynamic nature of product-market combinations. In contrast with the basic model, now, a starting point and an end point in time exist, before and after which, respectively, a return on equity exceeding the time preference rate of the shareholder (costs of equity) cannot be achieved for any size of the stock of capital assets. During the period between these instances, an interval of capital assets stock with positive minimum and maximum bounds exists, on which the return on equity is greater than the time preference rate of the shareholder, whilst it is smaller elsewhere.

Lecture Notes in Economics
and Mathematical Systems

For information about Vols. 1–257
please contact your bookseller or Springer-Verlag